DISPOSITIONALISM AND THE METAPHYSICS OF SCIENCE

TRAVIS DUMSDAY

Concordia University of Edmonton

CAMBRIDGE
UNIVERSITY PRESS

University Printing House, Cambridge CB2 8BS, United Kingdom

One Liberty Plaza, 20th Floor, New York, NY 10006, USA

477 Williamstown Road, Port Melbourne, VIC 3207, Australia

314-321, 3rd Floor, Plot 3, Splendor Forum, Jasola District Centre, New Delhi - 110025, India

79 Anson Road, #06-04/06, Singapore 079906

Cambridge University Press is part of the University of Cambridge.

It furthers the University's mission by disseminating knowledge in the pursuit of education, learning and research at the highest international levels of excellence.

www.cambridge.org
Information on this title: www.cambridge.org/9781108727068
DOI: 10.1017/9781108647502

First published 2019
First paperback edition 2021

A catalogue record for this publication is available from the British Library

ISBN 978-1-108-48013-0 Hardback
ISBN 978-1-108-72706-8 Paperback

For Marc Ereshefsky

Contents

Acknowledgements

The bulk of this manuscript was written during the 2016–17 academic year, when I held the Canada Research Chair in Theology and the Philosophy of Science at Concordia University of Edmonton. I am grateful to the government and taxpayers of Canada for the funding associated with the CRC, and to Concordia's senior administration (in particular President Tim Loreman and then-VP of Research Manfred Zeuch) for their support and extension of my teaching release. That generous assistance was instrumental in the timely completion of the project. My thanks as well to my department chair, Inhee Cho Berg, for her helpful advice on the ins and outs of navigating the academic monograph market.

Sincere thanks are also due to Neil Williams, who provided extensive comments on an early version of Chapter 5. The material that would become Chapters 6 and 8 was initially completed during a 2010–11 post-doctoral fellowship at UNC Chapel Hill, which was funded by the Social Sciences and Humanities Research Council (SSHRC) of Canada. I could not have asked for a more collegial and productive postdoc environment, and I am grateful to Marc Lange for acting as my supervisor and providing me a great deal of helpful input. Various portions of the manuscript have also benefitted from comments received over the years from Jeffrey Brower, Troy Cross, Evan Fales, Thomas Holden, John Keck, Noa Latham, John Roberts, Tuomas Tahko, Steven Weinstein, and audiences at the University of Birmingham (UK), the University of Alberta, and the annual conferences of the Canadian Society for the History and Philosophy of Science, the Canadian Philosophical Association, the Eastern Division of the American Philosophical Association, the American Catholic Philosophical Association, and the American Jacques Maritain Association. Many thanks also to my editor at Cambridge University Press, Hilary Gaskin, both for her insightful feedback and for managing the entire review process with such promptness and efficiency. Two anonymous referees likewise read the entire manuscript and provided useful comments, for which I am grateful. Of course any remaining errors are solely my own responsibility. Thanks are due as well to Sophie Taylor for helpfully shepherding me through the final production stages with Cambridge.

I should mention too some of the colleagues whose conversation and/ or correspondence on issues relating to the metaphysics of science have profited this project and my broader reflections in the field (with apologies to others whose contributions are no doubt slipping my mind just at present): William Bauer, Anjan Chakravartty, Christina Conroy, Sam Cowling, Alice Drewery, Crawford Elder, Cody Gilmore, Tyron Goldschmidt, Elizabeth Goodnick, Andrew Jaeger, William Jaworski, Kathrin Koslicki, Joseph LaPorte, Duncan Maclean, Tarun Menon, Matteo Morganti, Timothy Pawl, Makmiller Pedroso, Vladimir Pitchko, Joshua Rasmussen, Jonathan Schaffer, David Snoke, Erin Stackle, Georg Theiner, Elanor Taylor, Patrick Toner, Matthew Tugby, and Jacob Tuttle. Special thanks to Marc Ereshefsky, who supervised my doctoral dissertation at the University of Calgary and from whom I have learned so much about the vocation of scholarship. With much gratitude I dedicate the book to him.

Some chapters incorporate materials that have previously appeared in print, and I wish to thank the following publishers for their permission to reproduce them:

While largely re-written and re-thought, Chapter 2 includes material republished with permission of John Wiley and Sons Inc., from "Laws of Nature Don't *Have* Ceteris Paribus Clauses, They *Are* Ceteris Paribus Clauses", by Travis Dumsday, *Ratio* 26 (2013): 134–147; permission conveyed through Copyright Clearance Center, Inc.

Chapter 4 includes materials from two prior works, both reprinted by permission from Springer Nature: *Philosophia: Philosophical Quarterly of Israel*, "Atoms vs. Extended Simples: Towards a Dispositionalist Reconciliation", 43, pp. 1023–1033, by Travis Dumsday (2015); and *Synthese*, "MaxCon Extended Simples and the Dispositionalist Ontology of Laws", 194, pp. 1627–1641, by Travis Dumsday (2017). Permission conveyed through Copyright Clearance Center, Inc.

Chapter 5 incorporates three paragraphs from Travis Dumsday (2012) "An Argument for Hylomorphism or Theism (But Not Both)", *Proceedings of the American Catholic Philosophical Association*, 86, pp. 245–254. My thanks to PACPA and its publisher, the Philosophy Documentation Center.

Chapter 6 has previously appeared in print (in much the same form as it is found here), and is reprinted by permission from Springer Nature: *Erkenntnis*, "Using Natural-Kind Essentialism to Defend Dispositionalism", 78, pp. 869–880, by Travis Dumsday (2013a). Permission conveyed through Copyright Clearance Center, Inc.

Chapter 8 has previously appeared in print (in much the same form as it is found here). It is republished with permission of John Wiley and Sons Inc., from "Dispositions, Primitive Activities, and Essentially Active Objects", by Travis Dumsday, *Pacific Philosophical Quarterly* 93 (2012a): 43–64; permission conveyed through Copyright Clearance Center, Inc.

CHAPTER I

Introduction

Dispositionalism is the view that there exist irreducible dispositions, also called 'powers' or 'capacities' or 'potencies,' etc. Dispositions are inherently causally significant. For instance, for an object to possess the disposition 'fragility' entails that under certain circumstances the object can be made to break; by contrast, other sorts of property seem not to carry inherent causal relevance. Consider geometrical/structural properties: at least prima facie, the fact that an object is square tells us nothing about what that object can do or have done to it; being square does not entail being flammable or soluble or visible. Properties allegedly lacking intrinsic causal significance are often called 'categorical properties.'[1]

Roughly stated, the identity conditions of a disposition involve at least: (i) a stimulus or set of stimuli; (ii) a manifestation or set of manifestations; (iii) any *ceteris paribus* clauses.[2] Thus the fragility of a vase could be defined at least in part by reference to (i) the sorts of external conditions necessary for triggering (ii) the ways in which the vase would break, taking into account (iii) the factors that could intrude to block or otherwise affect any of those stimulus conditions or manifestations.[3]

---

[1] Note that 'properties' can for now be taken as neutral between tropes and universals. Historically most dispositionalists have been realists (whether moderate or Platonic) about universals. While this remains quite a common combination in the current literature, there are some who self-identify as nominalists (e.g., Heil (2003; 2012)). I will say more about this in Chapter 2. Note too that 'object' can for now be taken as neutral between the various competing substance ontologies (substratum theory versus bundle theory, etc.). We will explore that topic in Chapter 5. And while my practice of taking 'dispositions' as synonymous with 'powers' and other cognate terms is often adopted, some authors draw fine-grained distinctions between them.

[2] Mumford (1998, chs. 3–4) remains an excellent entry point into what is now an extensive literature on how to understand the precise identity conditions of a disposition.

[3] In phrasing this in terms of 'a stimuli or *set* of stimuli' and 'a manifestation or *set* of manifestations' I am trying to remain neutral between those who think that a disposition can have only a single stimulus condition and a single manifestation condition versus those who think that dispositions can be 'multi-track,' characterized in terms of multiple stimulus and/or manifestation conditions. I am also remaining neutral on the question of what category or categories the stimulus and manifestation belong to – whether property or event or process, etc.

While 'fragility' is useful as a commonsensical illustration, in principle other powers should perhaps be referenced here, insofar as 'fragility' is not itself a fundamental property but rather is presumably reducible to other properties that jointly contribute to making an object breakable (in this case the defeasible bonding powers of an object's parts). Plausibly it is *fundamental* powers that ultimately function as truthmakers for true disposition-ascriptions,[4] and unless otherwise stated from now on I will be referring to these when using 'dispositions' or 'powers,' etc.[5]

Advocates of dispositionalism appeal to dispositions to explain the behaviour of objects, and by extension to explain the natural regularities summarized in scientific laws. As such most dispositionalists maintain that what we typically think of as laws of nature are reducible to (or even eliminable in favour of) dispositions. Dispositions are thus thought to be the truthmakers for true law-statements employed in science. Consider the universal law of gravitation: between any two bodies possessing mass there is an attractive force proportional to the product of the two masses divided by the square of the distance between them. Formalized as an equation, we get $F = GMm/d^2$, where 'F' is the force, 'G' the universal gravitational constant (6.670×10^{-11} N-m^2/kg^2), 'M' and 'm' the masses of the first and second bodies, and 'd' the distance between them. The standard dispositionalist account maintains that this equation captures a natural regularity, which regularity is in turn grounded in a power, mass, possessed by individual objects.[6]

Dispositionalism can be contrasted with categoricalism, according to which the only irreducible properties in nature are categorical (i.e., non-dispositional). Categoricalists cannot reference intrinsic powers to explain the behaviour of objects; accordingly, some maintain that the natural regularities summarized in scientific laws are primitive and not subject to further ontological explanation. This strategy is taken up by advocates of the various versions of regularity theory.[7] Other categoricalists argue that

---

[4] For more on this consult again Mumford (1998, pp. 228–234).

[5] That does not automatically imply that macro-level objects lack dispositions of their own. In fact the question of whether any of the powers apparently exhibited by macro-level objects are wholly reducible to the powers of their parts is one way of framing the debate over whether macro-level objects are genuinely *objects* or whether they are merely aggregates reducible to their parts. Relatedly, the topic of emergentism will be examined in Chapter 9.

[6] Significant dispositionalist discussions of laws include Bird (2007), Ellis (2001), and Mumford (2004). Note that it would be controversial to claim mass as a fundamental property (and therefore a genuine disposition); but for purposes of illustration it is at least a good deal closer to being fundamental than is fragility.

[7] See for instance Barker (2013), Beebee (2011), Miller (2015), and Smart (2013).

regularities are grounded in real, irreducible laws of nature; on this sort of view, known as nomological necessitarianism, laws are not merely *descriptive* of natural regularities, but *prescriptive*. They are conceived of as abstract (i.e., non-concrete) entities that somehow play a governing role in nature.[8] Still other categoricalists adopt views that do not fit neatly into either regularity theory or nomological necessitarianism.[9]

I expect most readers will already have some familiarity with dispositionalism, so hopefully the preceding introductory remarks, rough and incomplete though they are, will suffice as a basic characterization. Certainly the topic is one whose importance for those working in analytic metaphysics, philosophy of science, and the hybrid sub-discipline now commonly labeled *metaphysics of science* should be uncontroversial; in fact anyone interested in the foundational question of what, if anything, accounts for the regularities in nature should take an interest in discussions of dispositionalism (pro or con), and the theory occupies a prominent place in the current literature. A clear example of this prominence may be seen in Schrenk's (2017) textbook on the metaphysics of science, structured as it is around the central theme of dispositionalism. More generally, work on the topic regularly appears in leading journals, and general textbooks in analytic metaphysics devote space to it. Koons and Pickavance (2015) for instance have a dedicated chapter on dispositionalism.

Yet a high profile for the view is a relatively new development. Even after the decline of positivism and corresponding revival of interest in traditional metaphysical debates from the 1960s onward, dispositionalism remained a marginal theory within analytic circles for some time; when it was discussed it was more critiqued (e.g., by Mackie (1977) and Quine (1966, pp. 71–74; 1974, pp. 8–15)) than defended. Yet it gradually acquired proponents such as Harré and Madden (1975), Shoemaker (1980), Swoyer (1982), Franklin (1986), Thompson (1988), Cartwright (1989), and Woodward (1992). These works contributed to the renaissance of dispositionalism that got

---

[8] See for instance Armstrong (1983; 1997), Dretske (1977), Fales (1990; 1993), Foster (2004), Latham (2011), Laudisa (2015), Maudlin (2007), Psillos (2006; 2009), and Tooley (1977). The 'somehow' above is meant to highlight the fact that how exactly this works is understood differently on different versions of nomological necessitarianism; Armstrong's account is importantly different from Maudlin's, for example.

[9] I think especially of Lange's (2004; 2009; 2009a) account, according to which laws are rooted in primitive counterfactual truths, and also Whittle's (2009) similar view referencing primitive functional facts.

underway fully in the mid-1990s, and which has continued through to the present.[10]

While dispositionalists are still engaged in the project of defending the theory against rivals like nomological necessitarianism and regularity theory, it now boasts sufficient support that many today concentrate on its internal development; that is, many today work on explicating more precise accounts of the nature of powers, and exploring how they relate to other philosophical debates.[11] Among the questions being discussed: are all properties powers? If so, how exactly are prima facie distinct types of property (e.g., geometrical/structural properties) reducible to or eliminable in favour of powers? And if not, how do powers relate to distinct kinds of properties? Moreover are all dispositions properties, or might the members of other ontological categories (like *relation* or *substance*) be inherently dispositional? Can a comprehensive ontology of causation be provided using dispositionalism? Can a comprehensive ontology of modality be thus provided? Are there multi-track dispositions? Must all dispositions have stimulus conditions, or could there be some that manifest spontaneously?[12] Must all dispositions be intrinsic, or might there be *extrinsic* dispositions as well? If so, how exactly are the latter to be characterized? Are there emergent dispositions, and if so what exactly is their nature and how do they impact debates on reductionism in various philosophical sub-disciplines?

---

[10] Note that in these historical remarks I am focusing on the analytic literature; the situation was different in other philosophical traditions. Within scholasticism, which was largely unaffected by positivist strains, work on dispositionalism continued through the whole span of the twentieth century. Over the last ten years or so, dispositionalism has in fact constituted one of several bridges between analytic philosophy and contemporary scholastic thought, which now interact much more than in the past. Examples of this interaction can be seen in the anthologies of Huntelmann and Hattler (2014), Novak et al. (2013), Novotny and Novak (2014), and Paterson and Pugh (2006). It is also evident in authors like Feser (2014) and Oderberg (2007), whose works draw on both traditions and address dispositionalism in considerable depth. Looking farther afield, within American pragmatism C. S. Peirce was a staunch defender of dispositionalism; later Peirceans followed suit, thus giving dispositionalism another support base in the days when its stock within analytic philosophy was low. For a relevant discussion of Peirce see Legg (1999).

[11] For a clear instance of the confidence of contemporary dispositionalists, see the introductory chapter to the anthology edited by Groff and Greco (2013), where it is claimed that greater time spent on exploring implications (as opposed to defence) is now thoroughly justified.

[12] Vetter (2015) delves into this important question in considerable depth, developing a novel view according to which stimulus conditions play no part in the essence of a power qua power; on her account, the traditional formulation of dispositionalism in terms of properties having both stimulus and manifestation conditions is false. So far as I can tell, the arguments I develop in this book would remain sound on either Vetter's account or on the more traditional sort of formulation I provided above.

This book can be seen as falling mostly within this 'internal develop-ment' approach. My main goal is to explore the connections between dis-positionalism and a variety of debates in metaphysics, with a focus on those debates that have also been areas of discussion for philosophers of science: for instance those involving laws, structural realism, fundamental material composition, etc.[13] In other words, my chief aim is not to show that dispositionalism is true, or even more likely to be true than its rivals. Rather, I want to ask: *if* dispositionalism *were* true, what would that mean for some of these other debates? Likewise, if we were to adopt one or another specific position in some of these debates, what implications would *that* have for dispositionalism? Such conditionals ought to be of interest to dispositionalists, categoricalists, and participants in these various other debates, insofar as understanding the implications of a phi-losophical position will inevitably assist in providing an assessment of it (whether pro or con).

In the course of drawing out such implications, novel arguments for or against dispositionalism will indeed arise in the chapters that follow; I say 'for or against' since, depending on one's background assumptions, some of these implications will be more or less welcome. I generally find the implications welcome, and so I see the project as pro-dispositionalist on the whole. In that sense I like to think that the project might contri-bute to the broader case in favour of dispositionalism; still, that is not the primary goal, but at best a welcome side-effect.

The remainder of the book can be outlined briefly as follows: Chapter 2 I delve more fully into the proper understanding of laws. As noted above, the tendency among dispositionalists has been to adopt either reductionism or eliminativism with respect to laws. I believe this tendency is mistaken, and argue in this chapter that not only is disposi-tionalism compatible with a robust realism about laws, it actually entails such realism.

Chapter 3 begins with a summary of some of the literature concerning ontic structural realism, laying out a taxonomy of current versions of OSR. On some of these, objects are viewed as reducible to (or eliminable in favour of) relations; this sort of position is sometimes called

---

[13] Dispositionalism arguably has significance for areas outside the metaphysics of science; Mumford, Anjum and Lie (2013) for instance argue that it has important implications for ethics, as do I in my (Dumsday 2016). Considerations both of space and of thematic unity demand that I stick to the metaphysics of science, so I will not delve into these other areas in this book.

'eliminativist OSR' or 'radical OSR.' In others versions, objects and relations are seen as equally fundamental and perhaps symmetrically dependent. This sort of position is sometimes called 'moderate OSR.' Drawing on the law-friendly understanding of dispositionalism developed in Chapter 2 (labeled for convenience 'nomic dispositionalism'), I argue that dispositionalism entails a novel version of moderate OSR that sidesteps some important objections facing existing versions.

In the literature on fundamental material composition the four main competing views are atomism (in two main versions), the theory of gunk, and the theory of extended simples. In Chapter 4 I make the case that atomism version 1 supports dispositionalism and that the theory of extended simples entails it. For those who prefer one or another of those accounts of composition, dispositionalism thereby acquires additional confirmation. Correspondingly, categoricalists are given reason to reject those two accounts of composition.

In Chapter 5 I argue that each of the four major substance ontologies (substratum theory, bundle theory, primitive substance theory, and hylomorphism) supports dispositionalism, insofar as each either entails dispositionalism or is most plausibly understood in dispositionalist terms. Besides highlighting a neglected connection between these areas of metaphysics, this also permits the formulation of a novel disjunctive argument for dispositionalism – or at least it does so for anyone who is a realist about substance. For convinced categoricalists, on the other hand, the conclusion opens the way to a new argument for the rejection of substance as a fundamental category (perhaps by reference to eliminativist OSR or an analogous position).

In Chapter 6 I make the case that dispositionalism ought to be paired with a particularly robust version of natural-kind essentialism, one according to which a kind-essence is something over and above its associated defining properties. Doing so allows dispositionalism to sidestep an important objection levelled against it by Lange (2004; 2009; 2009a) and by Whittle (2009). For dispositionalists the result is a new argument for robust natural-kind essentialism, while for resolute opponents of the latter a new argument against dispositionalism arises.

In Chapter 7 I look at how dispositionalism relates to three debates concerning the metaphysics of spacetime: that between substantivalists versus relationists; that over the possibility of time travel; and the debate over the nature of persistence.

Dispositionalism is supposed to answer some of our deepest questions about the activities of objects, providing us explanations of what lies behind those activities. But might there be room within dispositionalism for a recognition of activities that are not rooted in powers? Chapter 8 explores the possibility of activities grounded not in the powers of an object (or grounded in any of its properties), but directly by the kind-essence of the object. In other words, while robust natural-kind essentialism may be necessary for the defence of dispositionalism (as advocated in Chapter 6), it also opens the door to the idea that not all of an object's activities need be explained in terms of its dispositions. Yet this idea should not be seen as conflicting with dispositionalism, and in a roundabout way supports it.

Finally in Chapter 9 I take up the connection between dispositionalism and emergentism. The latter topic is of course a vast one, and I mostly limit my attention to a recent account that situates emergentism within an explicitly dispositionalist framework: the novel hylomorphic theory of minds and of organisms propounded by Jaworski (2016). After summarizing that account and the specific version of dispositionalism it is tied to (namely *identity theory*, according to which every intrinsic property has both categorical and dispositional identity conditions), I discuss some of the existing critiques of that version of dispositionalism and suggest an alternative framework that Jaworski might employ. That alternative has the advantage of avoiding the criticisms facing identity theory, but it does involve the controversial claim that relations (in this case structural relations) can themselves be dispositional.

Before getting started, a few quick procedural points: first, since each chapter deals with the relationship between dispositionalism and an area of metaphysical debate, and since many readers may be unfamiliar with at least some of these areas, it has been necessary to include in each a concise refresher. This should have the advantage of making each chapter more accessible, and I hope that it will not prompt impatience in cases where the reader is already familiar with the recent literature on the topic. (Don't we all benefit from an occasional refresher?) Second, I recognize that some readers will be specially interested in the impact of dispositionalism on a particular area of debate, and may wish to dip into the book primarily for a certain chapter; similarly, it might transpire that an instructor teaching a course focused on, say, structural realism might wish to assign Chapter 3 to her students, but not the whole work. As such, although the book is cumulative, with some of the later chapters relying explicitly on the findings of the earlier, where that is the case I have included in those later chapters very brief recaps of the main conclusions of the relevant previous discussions. Each chapter should therefore be readable independently. I trust that those working through the entire book will forgive these periodic repetitions. Third, the reader should be forewarned that I am in the habit of stating core arguments in numbered premise/conclusion form. I hope that most will find this practice helpful, insofar as it can promote clarity and serve to highlight important lines of reasoning.

CHAPTER 2

Dispositionalism and the Laws of Nature

2.1 Introduction

Laws of nature are properly conceived as abstract entities somehow playing a governing role in the physical universe, contributing to the fact that events must take place in certain ways rather than others. In this characterization I am following Mumford (2004, ch. 1), among others. He is entirely correct in holding that it is this notion of laws that has been the focus of philosophical dispute both historically and in a great deal of the contemporary literature; however that is not to say that this notion is universally accepted as *the* proper conception. For instance, Beebee (2000), Bird (2007, pp. 191–194), and Lange (2006) question whether lawhood requires governance. I do not wish to spend time defending a governing conception of the nomic,[1] so I will grant for the sake of argument that there may be alternative conceptions of law that are also legitimate. Thus one can properly view Humean regularity theory as an account of what it is to be a law of nature rather than as a theory explaining why we needn't posit real laws of nature at all. However, the question of whether there exist laws of the sort described here, *governing* laws, is clearly a prominent one and important in its own right. In particular, it is key to the dialectic between dispositionalism and nomological necessitarianism, which latter relies on a governing conception of laws in providing a

---

[1] Though for further defences of the governance view consult for instance Cartwright (2004) and Schneider (2007). For some useful historical background on this consult Jaeger (1999, pp. 187–205), Kedar and Hon (2017), Lehoux (2006), Ruby (1986), and Watkins (2016).

competing explanation of natural regularities. As such it is the notion I will work with in what follows.[2,3]

As noted in Chapter 1, within the metaphysics of science literature dispositionalists typically hold that laws are either reducible to, or eliminable in favour of, the dispositions of objects.[4] Why does an apple fall to the ground when dropped? According to most dispositionalists, it is not *because* of the law of universal gravitation; the abstract equation in no way literally contributes to the actual falling. Rather, the apple falls because it is a massive body, and mass (roughly described) is a dispositional property the possession of which enables an object to accelerate toward another massive object proportional to the product of the masses and the distance between them (taking into account too the value of the gravitational constant), all other things being equal (ceteris paribus). Formalized as an equation we get $F = GMm/d^2$, where 'F' is the force, 'G' the universal gravitational constant ($6.670 \text{ H } 10^{-11} \text{ N-m}^2/\text{kg}^2$), 'M' and 'm' the masses of the first and second bodies, and 'd' the distance between them. The law, qua abstract equation, is for most dispositionalists *descriptive* of what happens in nature, not *prescriptive*. It is

---

[2] Foster (2004, pp. 37–38) displays a similar sort of pluralism about lawhood while still favouring the governing conception adopted by Mumford and employed here:

> The term 'law', as it occurs in the context of a discussion of the natural world, can be used in three distinct, though related, senses. In the first place, it can be used to refer to those claims by which, at various times, scientists have tried to characterize the fundamental ways of working of the natural world ... Taken in this sense, laws are not part of nature, but part of our theorizing about it. They are human artefacts, products of the scientific enterprise. Secondly, the term 'law' can be used to refer, not to these scientific claims, but to the natural regularities – the uniform way of working – which the claims are attempts to record ... Thirdly, the term 'law' can, as in the second case, be used to denote aspects of the natural world, but aspects that consist not in the regularities which characterize the world, but in the forms of natural necessity which (in a certain sense) control it ... So, in this sense, to recognize a law of gravity would not be merely to recognize that there is a uniform manner in which bodies attract one another, but to recognize a principle of necessity underlying this uniformity ... Now it is in the third of these senses that I am using the term 'law' in these lectures.

[3] Consequently I will also refrain from discussing the interesting accounts of Demarest (2017), Vetter (2015, pp. 288–290), and Williams (forthcoming, ch. 10), who suggest ways of combining dispositionalism with a version of regularity theory (specifically, Lewis' best systems account) on which laws are understood as non-governing.

[4] And Mumford (2004, p. 121) argues that in the case of laws and dispositions, reduction amounts to elimination: "Reduction is more than just identity. It is also a claim about an asymmetrical ontological dependence. As laws are reduced to things that are not laws – natural kinds and essential properties – in the essentialist view, laws are thereby dependent on these more fundamental things. But if the reduction is right and successful, then it is the reductive grounding that does all the work ... This is significant because the notion of a law, according to nomological realism, is supposed to be precisely the notion of something that controls, governs, moves or plays at least some role. But you cannot claim credit for compliance with a law if everything already acts that way and is already bound to do so."

disposition-laden objects, powerful objects, which do the work, and the resulting regularities can then be captured in the abstract equations we call laws. As Cartwright (1989, p. 181) puts it, "it is not the laws that are fundamental, but rather the capacities … Whatever associations occur in nature arise as a consequence of the actions of these more fundamental capacities. In a sense, there are no laws of association at all. They are epiphenomena." Or for another example consider Williams (2017, p. 144):

> According to the powers ontology, power properties carry their causal potential inside them. They are not reducible to inert qualities acting in accord with the laws of nature, nor are they mere second-order properties that owe their existence to some other property whose nature is not similarly causal. On this view, powers are genuine first-order properties, and they are the basis of all causation. If there are laws of nature in the powers theorist's world, these laws supervene on either the powers or the ways in which the powers have been exercised.

Again, that is the typical dispositionalist perspective, but it has been challenged to some extent. It has been argued that dispositionalism allows for a form of realism about laws even while not requiring it,[5] and it has even been argued that dispositionalists need to make room for laws since dispositions alone cannot explain certain of the *global* regularities found in our universe – i.e., the regularities exhibited by all physical objects.[6] However, few in the current literature argue that nomic realism is demanded by features internal to dispositionalism itself.[7] That is what I am going to attempt here. I think there are multiple routes to this view, but I am going to argue on the basis of certain facts about ceteris paribus (CP) clauses:

Premise 1 At least some dispositions have CP clauses incorporating uninstantiated universals (which CP clauses help to delimit the range of manifestations of those dispositions).

Premise 2 If at least some dispositions have CP clauses incorporating uninstantiated universals (which CP clauses help to delimit the range of manifestations of those dispositions), then laws of nature exist.

Conclusion Therefore laws of nature exist.

---

[5] See again Bird (2007, pp. 189–198); see also the exchange between Bird and Mumford contained in Bird et al. (2006).

[6] See Hughes and Adams (1992) and Dumsday (2011).

[7] In fact I am aware of only one other person who takes such a position, namely Tugby (2016). Tugby's view is similar to my own, though developed independently and defended in rather a different fashion; in particular, in that article he rightly observes that his argument differs from mine in part by virtue of the prominent role I accord to ceteris paribus clauses, which his does not rely on.

The basic idea is that for the dispositionalist, CP clauses themselves meet the proper criteria for lawhood – or rather, they do so at least when they involve uninstantiated universals. And since dispositionalism needs to posit such CP clauses, dispositionalism implies nomic realism. The resulting view, according to which both dispositions and laws belong in fundamental ontology, I will label as *nomic dispositionalism*.

The notion that CP clauses are themselves laws is liable to seem rather counter-intuitive at first glance – after all, we usually think of laws of nature as *having* CP clauses, not as *being* CP clauses. However, it will become clear that on dispositionalism this shift in understanding is rendered quite natural.

The remainder of this chapter is divided as follows: in the next section I expand on and defend the argument's first premise, then in Section 2.3 I briefly do the same for the second premise. Section 2.4 sees an examination of some potential objections, and Section 2.5 concludes with a brief recap.

A quick proviso before proceeding further: as noted in Chapter 1, some dispositionalists take dispositional properties to be universals and others to be tropes. Those who accept *both* universals and tropes as fundamental ingredients in their ontologies (e.g., Ellis (2001; 2002) and Lowe (2006)) could opt to run with the argument as I've just presented it, or they could opt to replace my reference to uninstantiated universals with a reference to unactualized-but-possible-tropes. Nominalist dispositionalists will have to opt for the latter. However, I expect at least some nominalists will have difficulty countenancing unactualized tropes (and perhaps any comparable sort of unactualized particulars) on grounds that such entities would be abstract rather than concrete. It depends on whether their motivation for adopting nominalism is opposition to abstract entities generally or opposition specifically to universals. (The meaning of 'nominalism' is of course variable in the literature; among those meanings, it sometimes refers to opposition to any sort of abstracta, while at others times it refers to opposition to universals but *not* other sorts of abstracta like sets or non-concrete possible worlds.) Seeing as how relation to abstract entities is arguably an essential part of any formulation of dispositionalism (since non-occurrent/unactualized stimulus and/or manifestation conditions are part of the identity conditions of any disposition, or at least any disposition that is not necessarily constantly manifested), I will assume that nominalist dispositionalists are willing to take on board at least unactualized, purely abstract tropes. They are welcome to refor-mulate the argument accordingly.[8]

2.2 CP Clauses

As dispositionalism is traditionally formulated, the identity conditions of dispositions consist in their stimulus and manifestation conditions, including any CP clauses. To illustrate, let's stick with the example invol-ving mass and gravitational attraction: roughly stated, with respect to a single massive body a relevant stimulus condition would be the presence of any other body possessed of any quantity of mass + the distance rela-tion between the two bodies, and the manifestation would be the parti-cular attraction which would then occur given the product of the two masses and the distance relation. But any number of things could block the attraction from occurring, or from occurring with the precise quan-tity of force one would predict based on the equation. For instance, if the disposition were possessed by an object that also possessed some value of electric charge, it is possible that an electromagnetic attraction or repulsion would trump the gravitational. The complete set of these possible interferences constitutes the set of CP clauses.

Some dispositions (indeed probably all dispositions) have CP clauses that include uninstantiated universals. Take some value of mass, and a second value of mass, specify the distance relation, and a physicist could tell us what the resulting attractive force would be, ceteris paribus. We can then specify that the two masses belong to two objects which have a particular value of positive charge actually instantiated in our world, and a physicist could again calculate what the attraction would be, or whether instead it would be trumped by the repulsive force between the two like charges. Now do so for a value of positive charge that is not and has never been instantiated in our world. Once again, a physicist could calcu-late the results. The uninstantiated value is just as legitimate a part of the set of CP clauses of mass as are the instantiated values. And though the example here is of an uninstantiated value of an instantiated type of uni-versal, physicists could likewise run the numbers on a wholly alien type of property, provided the nature of that property be specified with

---

[8] In my (Dumsday 2014) I experiment with a version of nominalist dispositionalism that does away with objective (non-mental) abstract entities entirely. I also show there that such a theory would be incompatible with metaphysical naturalism, such that it would be widely seen as unworkable. Still, such a judgement would have to rest on a broader background assessment of metaphysical naturalism.

sufficient precision. (By 'alien' here is meant a property never found instantiated in our world but whose instantiation is possible.) Alien properties of this sort also figure in CP clauses.

The preceding will be pretty uncontroversial in the eyes of most dispositionalists. However, its significance has not often been fully grasped in the current literature. Dispositions have an inherent ordering to *uninstantiated universals*, where these uninstantiated universals function as (at least partial) truthmakers for various counterfactuals concerning the manifestations of those dispositions. The uninstantiated universals (pure abstracta)[9] figuring in CP clauses help to delimit the range of possible disposition-manifestations, and so contribute to the fact that events in our world must take place in certain ways rather than others. This point leads easily into a justification for premise two of the overarching argument, so let's briefly turn there.

2.3   CP Clauses As Laws

If laws are indeed properly conceived as abstract entities somehow playing a governing role in the physical universe, contributing to the fact that events must take place in certain ways rather than others, then CP clauses (at least those CP clauses involving uninstantiated universals) fit the bill quite handily. For with them we have abstracta determining that certain events can or cannot take place under particular circumstances. If an uninstantiated value of positive charge were instantiated in entities possessing mass, then where those entities would normally undergo a gravitational attraction of a certain force, they might instead be repelled. Or if an alien universal were instantiated, the 'normal' disposition manifestation might otherwise be disrupted. *Even in their uninstantiated state*, these universals serve as truthmakers for counterfactuals involving actual, instantiated dispositions. This counts as playing a governing role in the physical universe, in the relevant sense, and thus premise two goes

---

[9] The status of *instantiated* universals is a matter of some dispute – i.e., whether to count an instantiated property as abstract or concrete is debated, with some maintaining that a universal is abstract no matter its status qua instantiated, and others that an instantiated universal counts as concrete on account of being bound up with a concrete substance or state of affairs. By contrast, all parties agree that uninstantiated universals (if there are any) properly count as abstract entities. Since a law is properly defined as an abstract entity somehow playing a governing role in physical nature, an attempt to prove that laws exist should focus on finding a governing role for uninstantiated universals, the abstract nature of which is uncontested. (For useful entry points on the disputes surrounding how to understand the abstract vs. concrete distinction, consult Cowling (2017, ch. 2), Hoffman and Rosenkrantz (2003) and Lowe (1995).)

through. As the argument is logically valid, I submit that it is sound, and in consequence that dispositionalism implies nomic realism.

2.4 Objections and Replies

As a first objection, one might argue that CP clauses form part of the very identity conditions of dispositions, and so are existentially dependent on those dispositions. But governance requires independence from what is governed, and hence the CP clauses cannot really be counted as laws. (Something akin to the governance-entails-independence idea forms part of the underlying motivation for worries about top-down causation: if the existence of my chair depends on the existence of its parts, then the chair cannot govern the behaviour its parts.) This falsifies premise 2 of the overarching argument.

I certainly grant that the CP clauses do form part of the identity conditions of dispositions, in some sense of 'part.' However, it is important to specify exactly in what way they form part of their identity conditions. The alien properties that figure in some of the CP clauses of an actual instance of mass[10] are not literally *constituents* of that instance of mass (whether one views that instance of mass as an instantiated universal or as a trope). It would be odd indeed to suppose that they were, that the nature of an instantiated universal (or a trope) could *literally consist* partly of an uninstantiated universal (or unactualized purely abstract trope). If an object is instantiated, then ipso facto all of its constituent parts are instantiated (just as we usually think that if an object exists, then ipso facto all of its constituent parts exist). Rather, to be an instance of mass is to have an *inherent ordering towards* these alien properties. And that is very different. Why should this extrinsic (though necessary) ordering relation rule out either independence or governance on the part of that to which the ordering is directed, to the external relatum (the unintantiated universal) of the necessary relation?

As a counter-reply, it might be observed that on a moderate realist ontology of universals, the independence of the uninstantiated universals figuring in the CP clauses of a disposition would automatically be compromised – whatever sort of reality they had would have to be derivative in some way on the reality of the disposition. (By 'moderate realism'

---

[10] Recall that to run the argument, I do not need to maintain that all CP clauses of dispositions function as governing laws, but more specifically the CP clauses incorporating uninstantiated universals.

I just mean the broadly Aristotelian view that universals are real but only exist insofar as they are instantiated in or as concrete entities.) And insofar as moderate realism is a popular view among contemporary dispositionalists, that is a problem for any defence of nomic dispositionalism.

The simplest response to the counter-reply would be to affirm Platonic realism in place of moderate realism. On Platonic realism the independent status of the uninstantiated universals figuring in CP clauses is unproblematic: uninstantiated universals transcend the spatiotemporal universe, existing independently of whether or not they are instantiated by (or in any way related to) concrete particulars.[11] For the Platonist, an *instantiated* universal, such as an instance of the power 'mass,' can be necessarily related to a *transcendent* universal without further complicating the ontological status of either. Moreover, given the independence of transcendent universals from the concrete realm, there is no barrier to the former playing a governing role in the latter (granting the objector's assumption that governance requires independence). As such, at least prima facie, nomic dispositionalism runs most smoothly on Platonic realism. This may constitute an argument for favouring Platonic realism over moderate realism.[12]

That is not to say that nomic dispositionalism is clearly incompatible with moderate realism. Admittedly though, this is a difficult area of inquiry, difficult because some of the relevant ontology remains largely uncharted. Leave aside the objection for a moment, with its concern about the independence of the CP clauses given moderate realism. There is a larger issue here, which has received relatively little attention in the metaphysics of science literature: namely, few have delved into the

[11] The analogue for a nominalist dispositionalist would be recognition of a realm of unactualized, purely abstract tropes. This could be acceptable for certain sorts of nominalists; again, it depends on whether their objection is to universals or to all abstract entities.
[12] Something like this:

Premise 1 If nomic dispositionalism is true, then it is probably the case that Platonic realism is true.
Premise 2 Nomic dispositionalism is true.
Conclusion Therefore, it is probably the case that Platonic realism is true.

The justification for P1 would be the reasoning we've just seen: for entity A to govern the behaviour of entity B, entity A must be existentially independent from B. So for abstract entities to govern concrete entities, they must be existentially independent from those concrete entities. Platonic realism easily accommodates this independence (specifically, the independence of the uninstantiated universals figuring in the CP clauses of the dispositions of concrete objects). If it turned out that Platonic realism was the *only* way to accommodate this independence, then the argument could be reformulated to reach the stronger conclusion of an entailment between nomic dispositionalism and Platonic realism.

existential status of uninstantiated universals that figure in some way in the identities of instantiated universals – or rather, few have done so from within a moderate realist stance on universals. This despite the fact that many dispositionalists are moderate realists and that dispositionalists in general want to affirm that dispositions can supply truthmakers for a huge range of counterfactuals, including counterfactuals concerning presently uninstantiated kinds of entities. As such it is peculiar that dispositionalists have given little consideration to the existential status of the *uninstantiated* universals bound up with the identity conditions of *instantiated* dispositional properties.

What then can a moderate realist dispositionalist say here? Here are six suggestions:

(1)   It might seem as if these uninstantiated universals have at least a kind of 'thin being' by virtue of being that towards which certain instantiated universals are necessarily related/ordered. This might be thought to grant them a sort of privileged ontological status – anyway a greater status than uninstantiated universals to which *no* instantiated universals bear any necessary relation. Does this point towards a blind spot in traditional ways of looking at universals, according to which a universal is either instantiated or uninstantiated, with no room for a middle ground? Perhaps the moderate realist dispositionalist should seek to develop a three-valued account of instantiation, whereby (1) instantiated universals are real, (2) uninstantiated universals are not, but (3) *quasi-instantiated* universals are in some sense real, where to be quasi-instantiated is to be an uninstantiated universal figuring in some way in the identity conditions of an instantiated universal.

(2)   Or, along similar lines, perhaps one might suggest a distinction between *direct* versus *mediate* instantiation, where an example of the first would be the possession of negative charge by a concrete object like an electron, and an example of the second would be any of the many properties figuring in the ceteris paribus clauses of negative charge that are not possessed by anything in our physical world but which have an indirect tie to our physical world precisely because they so figure.

(3)   Alternatively, moderate realist dispositionalists might adopt some version of the view that there are degrees of being, such that instantiated universals have full being whereas any uninstantiated universals to which they are necessarily related have a lesser being.

The notion that there are degrees of being (and, relatedly, the notion that predications of existence are often made by analogy rather than univocally), has been much-discussed in the history of philosophy and has recently returned to the analytic literature, for instance in McDaniel (2010; 2010a; 2013).

(4) In what is arguably a more radical suggestion, Paoletti (2016, p. 205) mentions the idea that a Meinongean could affirm both dispositionalism and moderate realism without having to admit uninstantiated universals. Rather, seemingly uninstantiated universals are actually instantiated, it's just that they are instantiated by objects that do not exist.

(5) Just as we normally tend to think of 'instantiated' and 'uninstantiated' as mutually exclusive options with no middle ground, we normally think of 'existent' and 'non-existent' in the same way. But of course there has been much debate over the precise existential status of *possibilia*, whether possibly-instantiated-but-presently-uninstantiated properties or possible individuals or possible worlds. In the analytic literature a broadly Quinean notion of existence is often taken for granted, such that possible worlds and/or possible individuals are automatically taken to exist insofar as they are thought to function as the values of bound variables quantified over within our best theories. In that case the philosophically weighty distinction is arguably transferred from 'existent vs. non-existent' to 'actual vs. non-actual' or 'concrete vs. non-concrete.' From within that framework, perhaps the moderate realist dispositionalist can resign herself to affirming the reality (in the minimal, Quinean sense) of uninstantiated universals by claiming that, when reformulated in contemporary terms, the core commitment of moderate realism is to the denial of uninstantiated universals *in our actual world* rather than to the denial of uninstantiated universals located ('located') in *merely possible worlds*. A universal in a merely possible world 'exists' in Quine's sense of 'existence' but is not actual. A downside of this alternative is that some moderate realists, while accepting possible worlds semantics as a useful tool, question whether possible worlds irreducibly exist, either because they want to ground facts about possible worlds in actual entities[13] or because they reject the Quinean criterion of existence to begin with.

---

[13] Such a view of modality is favoured by some dispositionalists (whether moderate realists or not), who suggest that modal facts are made true by dispositions. See Borghini and Williams (2008), Heil (2017), Jacobs (2010), Martin and Heil (1999), Pawl (2017), Pruss (2011), and Vetter (2015).

(6)   A moderate realist dispositionalist could consider adopting
      something akin to *Augustinian* or *scholastic* realism. On this view
      universals only exist when concretely instantiated in the actual
      world (thus preserving much of the underlying motivation behind
      moderate realism), and are concretely instantiated not only in
      physical objects and as concepts within individual human acts of
      cognition but also, necessarily and eternally, as the content of
      divine ideas – as God's concepts. On this view the dispositions of
      physical objects would be oriented towards those ideas, which
      would be existentially independent from those dispositions. Nomic
      dispositionalism + scholastic realism would thus provide an account
      of the existential status of the uninstantiated-in-our-physical-world
      universals figuring in the identity conditions of the dispositions of
      concrete objects, while sidestepping the governance-entails-
      independence concern (since the content of divine ideas are the
      independent paradigms of concrete physical things).[14] However,
      being incompatible with metaphysical naturalism, this option
      would obviously court additional controversy.[15]

Those are at least some of the ways in which a moderate realist dispositionalist might try to explicate the existential status of the uninstantiated (or quasi-instantiated, etc.) universals figuring in the identity
conditions of the dispositions of concrete objects, including their CP
clauses. I doubt that these six exhaust the range of available options, and
again this is an issue that deserves more attention than it has received.
But to bring it back to the problem at hand, options 1–3 seem unable to
help with the governance-entails-independence objection, for whether
those universals are merely quasi-instantiated, mediately instantiated, or
real but possessed of some lesser degree of being, the moderate realist
seems bound to claim that their quasi-instantiation/meagre existence still
depends on the instantiated disposition. The CP clauses (and whatever
universals are incorporated in them) only have any sort of 'being'
(degreed or not) because the concretely instantiated dispositions exist.
No dispositions, no CP clauses. Surely then the CP clauses with their

---

[14] See for instance Peterson (1996) for an explication of this sort of account.
[15] Note that for present purposes I am assuming Platonic realism is compatible with metaphysical
naturalism. This is commonly held but has of course been disputed, and disputed within the literature on laws: Armstrong (1983, p. 82) rejected Platonic realism precisely because he viewed it
as incompatible with metaphysical naturalism. Of course, one person's modus ponens is another's
modus tollens; Moreland (2000) for instance agrees that they are incompatible and attacks metaphysical naturalism on the basis of Platonism.

uninstantiated universals depend on the dispositions. And how can they govern what they depend on? So if dependence rules out governance, then it will still seem as if the moderate realist dispositionalist ought still to reject nomic dispositionalism, if options 1–3 are in play. That leaves options 4–6 as live possibilities for the moderate realist dispositionalist, provided she is willing to entertain either Meinongeanism or a fairly robust ontology of possibilia or theism. Should those appear unpalatable, then abandoning moderate for Platonic realism remains as an alternative for addressing the independence worry.

All of which assumes that the objector is correct in thinking that governance entails independence. But that too can be challenged, in at least two ways: (a) even granting moderate realism, if the CP clauses depend in some way on the dispositions for whatever sort of reality they possess, the dependence appears to be at least symmetrical in the case of dispositions. If indeed the identity conditions of dispositions are tied in with their CP clauses (as the objector concedes), then the dispositions are just as dependent on the CP clauses for *their* reality. No CP clauses, no dispositions.[16] Perhaps instances of symmetrical dependence sidestep the general principle that governance entails independence. Relatedly, (b) even if the laws wouldn't exist without the dispositions, does this really conflict with their lawhood? In other words, is the underlying assumption (that governance entails independence) actually true, or at least true in this context? Compare our everyday notion of laws. If there existed no human communities, there would exist no systems of criminal law, no abstract sets of rules that people would be expected to follow. On the other hand, systems of criminal law are genuinely governing – they genuinely serve to regulate and order peoples' actual behaviour. (Though granted, the civil/criminal law analogy starts to break down when one recognizes that the identity conditions of a community typically aren't tied in to some particular set of laws in the way that (most) dispositionalists would claim that the identity conditions of a disposition are tied in with the CP clauses of that disposition.)

As a very different sort of objection against nomic dispositionalism, it might be pointed out that the 'laws' being put forward as real by the

---

[16] For the Platonist, if there is any asymmetry here it would seem to be on the side of the uninstantiated universals figuring in the CP clauses. After all, one and the same abstractum can play a governing role for *multiple different* dispositions, any one of which can be destroyed while the abstractum continues playing that role for all the others.

theory (namely the CP clauses of powers) are not the same as the laws typically discussed by scientists. The universal law of gravitation would not count as a law on nomic dispositionalism, since it is not an abstract entity that literally plays a governing role in nature. Rather, as on standard dispositionalism, what we think of as the law of gravitation is properly cashed out in terms of certain dispositional properties like 'mass,' the manifestation of which results in natural regularities accurately summarized in the relevant equation. The real laws (i.e., the abstract entities that play an irreducible governing role in nature) are the CP clauses of those dispositional properties (or to be more precise, all those CP clauses incorporating uninstantiated universals). The resulting worry is that the picture of laws being presented here will seem counter-intuitive, insofar as it will seem divorced from standard scientific usage.

In reply it must be granted that most of what gets labeled as 'laws' in science will not count as laws in the relevant metaphysical sense. This is a departure from standard scientific usage and this is indeed a disadvantage. However, in terms of fit with scientific terminology and conceptualizations, nomic dispositionalism at least has a leg up on standard dispositionalism, where it is often argued that laws of nature have no place at all in fundamental ontology. *That* claim seems even more out of step with standard usage. Indeed, given the pride of place accorded laws in a typical student's science education, it is unsurprising that one of the stumbling blocks in trying to communicate the plausibility of dispositionalism to undergraduates (at least those just starting out in philosophy of science) is finding a diplomatic way to break the news that laws of nature don't really exist. By contrast, nomic dispositionalism is not quite so radical a break, insofar as it still accords a place for laws in fundamental ontology – in fact an indispensable place, on the plausible assumption that some or all dispositions have their CP clauses essentially. Law-talk is ubiquitous in all the basic sciences, and so is capacity-talk. It seems that an ontology bestowing some legitimacy on both sides of standard scientific usage may hold at least a mild advantage over an ontology which dismisses law-talk as fundamentally off-base insofar as it fails to line up with any actual fundamental features of reality (the standard dispositionalist view) or which dismisses capacity-talk as fundamentally off-base (many nomological necessitarians). Granting that our metaphysics of science should if possible not stray far from scientific conventions, at the same time without being slavishly beholden to scientific conventions, nomic dispositionalism should not be ruled out.

2.5   Conclusion

To recap: dispositionalists often argue that laws of nature are either reducible to or eliminable in favour of dispositions. I've defended a somewhat contrarian stance according to which dispositionalism is not only compatible with nomic realism, but actually entails it. The strategy I have employed has made use of facts about the CP clauses figuring in the identity conditions of dispositions, but as noted I do not think this is the only route to nomic dispositionalism.[17] The overarching argument ran as follows:

> **Premise 1** At least some dispositions have CP clauses incorporating uninstantiated universals (which CP clauses help to delimit the range of manifestations of those dispositions).
>
> **Premise 2** If at least some dispositions have CP clauses incorporating uninstantiated universals (which CP clauses help to delimit the range of manifestations of those dispositions), then laws of nature exist.
>
> **Conclusion** Therefore laws of nature exist.

Justifications for premises one and two were laid out in Sections 2.2 and 2.3, respectively, and then in Section 2.4 I attempted to address two objections: one according to which the laws on offer here cannot govern events in the physical world because they are not really independent of the physical world, and the other that these laws fail to match up with those referenced in science. In answering the first objection it was suggested that nomic dispositionalism might be run most easily on a Platonic ontology of universals, but I also provided options for carrying the argument through on moderate realism, and said a bit about how the nominalist dispositionalist might re-formulate the overarching argument in terms of unactualized tropes rather than uninstantiated universals. The second objection carries some force, but nomic dispositionalism still comes out looking better on this score than do standard formulations of dispositionalism.

---

[17] Again I refer the reader to Tugby's (2016) alternative approach, which does not rely on CP clauses. It is worth noting that Tugby's argument has the advantage of being applicable even on versions of dispositionalism according to which CP clauses are excluded as factors in the identity conditions of powers; while such exclusion is not commonly defended, Williams (forthcoming, ch. 6) develops an interesting argument for the view that all genuine dispositions (on his view, the fundamental powers of fundamental objects) lack CP clauses.

CHAPTER 3

Dispositionalism and Ontic Structural Realism

3.1 Introduction to OSR

The debate between advocates of scientific realism and advocates of scientific antirealism is among the longest-running in philosophy of science. The former maintain that scientists can properly aim at attaining beliefs that are rationally justified and true (or at least *approximately* true) concerning the natural world, including beliefs about entities belonging to the unobservable realms of nature, e.g., sub-atomic particles. (Read 'entity' as synonymous with 'object' or 'substance,' while remaining neutral between the various competing substance ontologies.) The latter maintain by contrast that the acquisition of justified true beliefs concerning unobservables is not possible for us, and in consequence scientists should moderate their aims: they should seek truth about the observable realm of nature, but concerning the unobservable they should remain agnostic. Scientists should not believe in the reality of unobservable objects like sub-atomic particles; they are welcome instead to adopt weaker epistemic attitudes toward them, such as 'acceptance,' where acceptance involves taking unobservables on board provisionally as working elements in theories (for the sake of making accurate predictions) but does not entail belief.

Scientific realism is motivated by a number of different arguments, but the most widely discussed is probably the 'no-miracles argument.' The basic idea here is that our best theories concerning unobservables allow us to make incredibly precise, accurate predictions, and that it is difficult to imagine how this could plausibly occur unless the unobservable entities referenced in these theories actually existed. If they did not exist, the success of these theories would in fact seem like a bizarre coincidence, or in other words a miracle (in a non-theological sense of 'miracle').

Scientific antirealism has also seen multiple justifications: (i) adherence to an empiricist epistemology, according to which we can only have knowledge of what is observable via the five senses; (ii) the long history of apparent scientific errors concerning the unobservable. This second concern is often framed in terms of the 'pessimistic meta-induction'; this states that because scientists have so often been badly wrong about the nature of supposed unobservable entities (from the caloric theory of heat to phlogiston to the luminiferous ether …), we should be dubious of present claims to knowledge about unobservables, however confidently made; (iii) the 'underdetermination argument,' which proposes that for all we know, different sorts of unobservable entities might fulfill equally well or better the explanatory role assigned them by a scientific theory, such that we cannot confidently affirm the reality of the unobservable entities posited by even our best current theories.

Again, the debate is longstanding and ongoing.[1] I bring it up here simply as a lead-in to discussing the re-emergence of structural realism as a key topic in philosophy of science.[2] For while the literature on structural realism has today proceeded rather far beyond the realism versus antirealism dialectic, the idea was initially put forward as a sort of middle-ground position between the two. Specifically, in an influential paper Worrall (1989) presents structural realism as a view according to which science can attain justified true beliefs concerning *relational facts* about the unobservable realm, but cannot attain justified true beliefs concerning the *intrinsic nature* of any objects occupying that realm. That is, the structural content of scientific theories about the unobservable can be known, but facts about the intrinsic nature of the entities that figure as place-holders in those structures cannot be known. This move from a focus on entities that play a theoretical role (like electrons) to the relations obtaining between those entities (like the mathematical structure of the equations involved in their governing laws) is designed to defuse the pessimistic meta-induction. For Worrall argues that in many case studies of theory change in the history of science, *structural* continuity is evident even amidst dramatic shifts in the kinds of unobservable theoretical *entities* posited. As such, the idea that we can have some knowledge of the unobservable realm (in this case, knowledge about relations obtaining within it) is preserved, and thereby at least an aspect of scientific realism

---

[1] For a concise and accessible introduction see Okasha (2002, ch. 4). Important defences of scientific realism include Chakravartty (2007) and Psillos (1999); important defences of scientific antirealism include Laudan (1981), van Fraassen (1980), and Stanford (2006).

[2] 'Re-emergence' is appropriate because various versions of structural realism were discussed by earlier thinkers such as Henri Poincaré, Arthur Eddington, Grover Maxwell, Rudolf Carnap, Bertrand Russell and others. For an overview of some of this history (and more generally for an introduction to structural realism) see Ladyman (2016).

is preserved. At the same time, structural realism constitutes a move away from traditional scientific realism, insofar as the former remains agnostic about the natures of unobservable *entities*, thereby retaining an important component of the antirealist stance – hence Worrall's claim that structural realism can be seen as the 'best of both worlds.'

To illustrate: the case study Worrall focuses most of his attention on is that of the shift in physics from Fresnel's ether theory of light to Maxwell's electromagnetic theory. "Fresnel's theory was based on the assumption that light consists in periodic disturbances originating in a source and transmitted by an all-pervading, mechanical medium. There can be no doubt that Fresnel himself believed in the 'real existence' of this medium ... There is equally no doubt that Fresnel's theory enjoyed genuine predictive success ..." (1989, p. 115). Despite this predictive success, Fresnel's ether was abandoned in favour of Maxwell's electromagnetic theory of light. The conceptualization of the underlying, unobserved nature of light thus changed substantially from Fresnel's theory to Maxwell's. Worrall emphasizes the dramatic nature of the shift when he writes: "One would be hard pressed to cite two things more different than a displacement current, which is what this electromagnetic view makes light, and an elastic vibration through a medium, which is what Fresnel's theory had made it" (1989, p. 116). Consequently it is easy to see how an antirealist might take this as a paradigm case study in support of the pessimistic meta-induction: affirmation of knowledge concerning the nature of an unobservable entity (on account of its serving to explain important predictive successes) is followed by back-pedalling and abandonment of belief in that entity when the theory is replaced by another with better predictive successes. Yet Worrall (1989, pp. 118–119), building on an analysis by Poincaré (1905), maintains that in fact there is an important and neglected continuity between these two theories:

> [While] Fresnel entirely misidentified the nature of light, his theory accurately described not just light's observable effects but its *structure*. There is no elastic solid ether. There is, however, from the later point of view, a (disembodied) electromagnetic field. The field in no clear sense approximates the ether, but disturbances in it do obey *formally* similar laws to those obeyed by elastic disturbances in a mechanical medium. Although Fresnel was quite wrong about *what* oscillates, he was, from this later point of view, right, not just about the optical phenomena, but right also that these phenomena depend on the oscillations of something or other at right angles to the light. Thus if we restrict ourselves to the level of mathematical equations – *not* notice the phenomenal level – there is in fact complete continuity between Fresnel's and Maxwell's theories.

Thus we can in a meaningful sense have knowledge pertaining to unobservables, it is just that this knowledge is about the structural relations (relations typically expressed mathematically) obtaining between them rather than the intrinsic nature of the entities themselves. Fresnel would have been justified in believing in the truth of the structural aspects of his theory, which components were preserved even in the face of changes in thinking about the nature of the objects referenced in it.

To give a full account of Worrall's structural realism a good deal more would have to be said; but hopefully the preceding at least serves to convey the core idea. Among the important follow-ups to Worrall (1989) was Ladyman (1998), who distinguished more clearly between two possible versions of the idea: epistemological structural realism and metaphysical structural realism. On the first (now more commonly labeled *epistemic structural realism*, hereafter ESR), an agnostic stance is preserved with respect to the natures of unobservable entities, but the possibility of knowing the relations obtaining between those entities is affirmed. Note that I keep speaking of agnosticism about the *natures* of these objects; for the most part advocates of ESR retain a belief in the *existence* of unobservable objects, maintaining that their reality needs to be posited insofar as relations (which we can know) need relata. There are however exceptions, with some propounding an understanding of ESR on which one remains skeptical both about the nature *and* the existence of unobservable objects.[3] That more thoroughly agnostic sort of ESR of course raises interesting questions not just for epistemology but also for metaphysics: does it make sense to remain agnostic about the existence of relata while affirming knowledge of relations? Is it possible that relations could exist independently of individual objects? It seems that in order to affirm this sort of ESR one must at least be open-minded with respect to the idea of ontologically fundamental relations, i.e., relations that are not grounded in or supervenient upon individual objects and/or their properties.

---

[3] Morganti (2004, pp. 82–83) writes:

> What exactly does it mean that that something else existing beyond structures remains hidden? Obviously, an immediate reply (in the spirit of Poincaré's original formulation), is that that 'something' are the individuals exhibiting the relations constituting the structures, and that they exist but are not known and not knowable in principle. I think this is indeed what whoever endorses ESR actually, at least on a first instance, believes to be the case. Still, I also think one is entitled to say something more, namely, that since we have favourable evidence as regards structures as partially preserved through theoretical change, we can be realist about those, without any commitment to what exists beyond them ... In short, I think that in a proper interpretation of ESR we should take it to be 'agnostic' in relation to what exists, if anything, beyond knowable structures.

And that is one way to lead into a discussion of metaphysical structural realism (now more commonly labeled *ontic structural realism*, hereafter OSR).[4]

At least some versions of OSR include the rather striking claim that when it comes to the unobservables theorized about within fundamental physics, *relations exist but objects do not*. This type of OSR, which is eliminativist with respect to objects, is the type apparently advocated in Ladyman (1998). Certainly his view was interpreted in this fashion by others,[5] though as we shall see shortly his subsequent stance has become more nuanced and arguably allows for a sort of truncated realism about objects. At any rate, for those already inclined towards scientific realism, the eliminativist variety of OSR has an apparent advantage over ESR insofar as it affirms more decisively our ability to know the unobservable; while ESR says that a significant aspect of the unobservable realm must forever remain opaque to us (namely, the intrinsic natures of the objects referenced in the relevant scientific theories) and that we must content ourselves with knowledge only of the relations between those unknowns, OSR affirms that our knowledge of the unobservable realm is as thoroughgoing as we could wish: we know only the relations, and that is fine because at that level the relations are all there is.

As noted above though, arguments surrounding structural realism have moved beyond the debate between advocates of scientific realism and scientific antirealism, and a good deal of the more recent literature focuses on the extent to which OSR (in its various versions) draws support from our best current theories in physics. It is argued for instance that traditional conceptions of individuality break down at the quantum level, such that the notion of particles as fundamental individual 'objects' with intrinsic identities should be abandoned in favour of fundamental relations;[6] that the metaphysics of quantum field theory is best interpreted along structuralist lines, insofar as symmetries are best seen there

---

[4] It is worth noting though that Morganti is himself leery of a move towards OSR from considerations pertaining to ESR; see again his (2004), and his later (2011).

[5] For instance, Chakravartty (2003, pp. 867–868) writes:

> ESR places a restriction on scientific knowledge; proponents hold that we can know structural aspects of reality, but nothing about the natures of unobservable things whose relations define structures in the first place. OSR, more radically, does away with objects altogether; proponents hold that, at best, we have knowledge of structural aspects of reality because there is, in fact, nothing else to know. Here we have the denial of any traditional metaphysics of objects.

He then footnotes Ladyman (1998), among other sources.

[6] See French and Redhead (1988), French and Ladyman (2011), Ladyman and Ross (2007, pp. 132–140), and Ladyman (2016a).

as ontologically prior to fields;[7] that the metaphysics of quantum gravity is best interpreted along structuralist lines, since particles are best seen there as deriving their identities from their structural context;[8] that structuralism provides for a superior account of the metaphysics of space-time;[9] and that structuralism allows for a novel way of defusing the traditional debate over whether matter at the fundamental level is continuous or discrete, and, relatedly, provides a plausible way of reconceiving wave-particle duality.[10]

Not all of the authors just cited aim to defend what is often termed *eliminativist OSR* – the authors of the paper on space-time in fact defend a view labeled *moderate OSR* in which objects are retained as basic elements in ontology, while the last-cited piece on wave-particle duality is situated within a broader defence of *informational structural realism* (ISR). So there are today various different versions of OSR, and the recent literature has seen the laying out of a number of partially overlapping taxonomies of the theory, including those of Ainsworth (2010), Chakravartty (2012), Esfeld and Lam (2011), French (2010), Frigg and Votsis (2011), and Ladyman (2016). I believe the following list covers the principal options enumerated in these works:

Eliminativist OSR (also called 'Radical OSR' or 'Strong OSR')[11]

Version #1 At the level of fundamental physics (the unobservable realm), relations exist but objects do not. (By extension, properties, conceived in a traditional manner as intrinsic modes or ways of being of objects, also do not exist. However, properties re-conceived as modes or way of being of *relations* may exist.) Does that mean relations have no relata? Yes. This may seem counter-intuitive, but we should not let our fallible intuitions get in the way of re-framing our metaphysics in line with our best available physics.

---

[7] See Kantorovich (2003; 2009).
[8] See Stachel (2006).
[9] See Esfeld and Lam (2008).
[10] See Floridi (2011, ch. 14).
[11] 'Eliminativist OSR' and 'Radical OSR' are commonly employed as synonyms; however, in their usage Frigg and Votsis (2011, p. 262) label the former as a version of eliminative OSR where the structural relations are interpreted at lower levels of abstraction (e.g., 'larger than' or 'to the left of'), whereas they label the latter as a version of eliminative OSR where structural relations are solely of the extensional sort seen in formal logic (e.g., reflexivity or transitivity). While this is a significant distinction, it has not caught on as a way of drawing a terminological divide between Eliminativist OSR and Radical OSR, which in the wider literature are still more commonly taken to be equivalent. As such I will stick to that standard practice and treat them as synonyms. 'Strong OSR' is French (2010, p. 106) preferred label for the view.

Eliminativist OSR (also called 'Radical OSR' or 'Strong OSR')
  Version #2 At the level of fundamental physics (the unobservable
  realm), relations exist but objects do not. (By extension, properties,
  conceived in a traditional manner as intrinsic modes or ways of being
  of objects, also do not exist. However, properties re-conceived as modes
  or way of being of *relations* may exist.) Does that mean relations have
  no relata? No. It simply means that all of the relata are themselves
  relations. There is an infinite non-vicious regress of relations.

Eliminativist OSR (also called 'Radical OSR' or 'Strong OSR')
  Version #3 At the level of fundamental physics (the unobservable
  realm), relations exist and so do objects. However the latter do not
  have any intrinsic identity – they lack anything like 'individuality'
  as traditionally conceived. They have no intrinsic properties and are
  nothing over and above their place/function in the relation. Their
  being (and a very thin being it is) is exhausted by their status as
  nodes in a structure. They have neither existence nor identity
  independently of the structure, and in consequence the structure is
  properly seen as having ontological priority over them. Any
  properties associated with the relational structure are properties of
  the structure, not the objects/nodes within the structure. (By
  analogy, think of the existential status of numbers in the abstract
  realm. One can argue that the existence and identity of the number
  4, for example, is exhausted by its place/function in the number
  series. It is nothing over and above that place/function, and its
  identity conditions are indefinable considered apart from its place/
  function in that structure.[12])

Moderate OSR Version #1 At the level of fundamental physics (the
  unobservable realm), relations exist and so do objects. However the
  latter do not have any intrinsic identity – they lack anything like
  'individuality' as traditionally conceived. They have no intrinsic
  properties and are nothing over and above their place/function in
  the relation. Their being (and a very thin being it is) is exhausted
  by their status as nodes in a structure. They have neither existence
  nor identity independently of the structure; however, the same can
  be said of the structure. Just as the objects/nodes have no identity
  or existence independent of the structure, the structure has no
  identity or existence independent of its objects/nodes. There is no
  ontological priority obtaining between them; rather they are

---

[12] For structuralism within the philosophy of mathematics, see Reck and Price (2000).

symmetrically dependent both in terms of identity and existence. Still, any properties associated with the relational structure are properties of the structure, not the objects/nodes within the structure.

Moderate OSR Version #2 At the level of fundamental physics (the unobservable realm), relations exist and so do objects. The latter have an intrinsic identity defined partly in terms of the possession of intrinsic properties and partly in terms of their place/function in the structure. As such, their identity is not wholly reducible to their structural role, yet they cannot exist independently of the structure. The structure in its turn has an identity distinct from that of the objects it relates, and can exist independently of any of the relata.[13] As such the structure retains ontological priority over the objects.

Moderate OSR Version #3 At the level of fundamental physics (the unobservable realm), relations exist and so do objects. The latter have an intrinsic identity defined partly in terms of the possession of intrinsic properties and partly in terms of their place/function in the structure. As such, their identity is not wholly reducible to their structural role, yet they cannot exist independently of the structure. The identity of the structure in its turn is defined partly in terms of the particular objects/nodes it relates, such that it cannot exist independently of those objects/nodes. Consequently there is no ontological priority obtaining between the objects and the structural relation; rather they are symmetrically dependent both in terms of identity and existence.

Informational Structural Realism (ISR) At the level of fundamental physics (the unobservable realm), there may or may not exist material objects, but there certainly do exist structures consisting of cohering clusters of data. Information, considered in and of itself, underlies the physical without necessarily being physical.[14]

---

[13] This could mean at least two different things: (a) that the structure could persist in existence even in the absence of any objects/nodes whatever, or (b) that the structure could persist in existence through the replacement of any of its particular relata by other relata. On the latter version, the relation would remain dependent on objects/nodes considered as a general *type*, while independent of the existence of any of the *particular* objects/nodes it happened to contain. I don't believe this distinction has been fully articulated in the OSR literature, so I would not here use it to draw a line between further versions of Moderate OSR. But I still think it a distinction worth flagging.

[14] Floridi (2011, p. 361) writes:

> A significant consequence of ISR is that, as far as we can tell, the ultimate nature of reality is informational, that is, it makes sense to adopt LoAs [levels of abstraction] that commit our theories to a view of reality as mind-independent and constituted by structural objects that are neither substantial nor material (they might well be, but we have no need to suppose them to be so) but informational.

The reader will have observed a sort of progression from Eliminativist OSR Version #1 to Moderate OSR Version #3, a progression of gradual increase in the ontological status accorded to objects. (For more on the idea of a 'degreed' conception of the different versions of OSR see especially Chakravartty (2012).) What keeps all of these views under the 'big tent' of OSR is their shared commitment to reversing what is commonly viewed as a traditional metaphysical privileging of the status of objects over and against relations. (I therefore include Floridi's (2011) ISR as falling under this tent.) As Ladyman (2016, section 4) puts it: "On the broadest construal OSR is any form of structural realism based on an ontological or metaphysical thesis that inflates the ontological priority of structure and relations."[15]

In his own recent work Ladyman favours Eliminativist OSR Version #3. For instance, French and Ladyman (2011, p. 30) write:

> An advocate of OSR can allow that quantum particles and space-time points are individuals in a thin sense, while remaining committed to the abandonment of any notion of individual that entails haecceitism.[16] The core claim of OSR that relational structure is ontologically primary can be retained even if the existence of individuals in the weak sense is endorsed.

There follows a footnote clarifying that Ladyman (but presumably not French) supports thin individuals. Or consider Ladyman and Ross (2007, p. 131): "This is the sense in which our view is eliminative; there are objects in our metaphysics but they have been purged of their intrinsic natures, identity, and individuality, and they are not metaphysically fundamental."[17] By contrast, French (2010) defends Eliminativist

---

[15] This big tent view is reiterated by others in the OSR literature; for instance McKenzie (2014, p. 354) writes that "since structuralists hold that mainstream metaphysics is highly 'object-oriented', they will hold that a position that fell short of imparting a uniquely privileged status to structure, but simply raised it to the status of objects, is as legitimate a form of ontic structuralism as one that held the stronger 'superiority' view."

[16] 'Haecceitism' is, roughly, the view that the core identity of any fundamental individual object consists in a special feature (in the broadest sense of 'feature') utterly unique to that object – an individual essence or 'thisness' not subject to empirical or scientific scrutiny. For more on this in the context of the OSR dialectic see Ladyman and Ross (2007, p. 134).

[17] This is at least my own reading of Ladyman's work; there is actually some disagreement in the literature on how best to characterize his current stance. McKenzie (2014, p. 354) identifies him as a proponent of Radical OSR (of the Version #2 variety), as do Briceno and Mumford (2016, p. 199). By contrast, Lam and Wuthrich (2015, p. 607) consider Ladyman to have transitioned from a radical to a non-eliminative OSR. I take it that these divergent readings may reflect the fact that although Ladyman currently affirms Eliminativist OSR Version #3, he still maintains that Versions #1 and #2 are defensible – on that point see in particular Ladyman and Ross (2007, pp. 155 and 228–229). Ladyman's overall preference for Version #3 comes out clearly in his (2016a).

OSR Version #1, arguing that the other two versions (as well as the view I've labeled Moderate OSR Version #1) ultimately collapse back into Eliminativist OSR Version #1, since the notion of an 'object' wholly lacking intrinsic identity conditions is unworkable, and since the attempt to make it work can only lead to the elimination of objects altogether. Chakravartty (2012), without defending Eliminativist OSR, concurs with French on that implication, as does Jantzen (2011). Lam (2014) and Ladyman (2016a) by contrast reply in favour of the workability of the idea.

A great deal more could of course be said by way of expanding on the various versions of OSR and the arguments for and against them, but hopefully the preceding will have given readers unfamiliar with this literature a decent overview of the present landscape. In the following Section 3.2 we'll proceed to examine two objections levelled against OSR: (a) an objection focused on the alleged inability of the theory to distinguish between abstract versus concrete structures, and (b) an objection focused on the allegedly implausible exclusion by OSR of so-called 'lonely object' possible worlds. Then in Section 3.3 I will argue that these objections can be side-stepped in a particularly convincing manner by a novel version of Moderate OSR, one situated within (and in fact entailed by) the theory of nomic dispositionalism articulated in the previous chapter.

3.2   Two Objections Against OSR

3.2.1   Objection (a)

Objection (a) is a longstanding one, and takes as its starting point the fact that we tend to think of structures in abstract rather than concrete terms. Whether at lower levels of abstraction ('larger than' or 'bonded to' or 'to the left of') or higher ('transitively related'), structure seems at first glance to be something multiply instantiable, and so abstract rather than concrete. 'Bonded to' is a relation apparently shared identically (in the sense of type-identity) between innumerable particulars. Of itself it seems therefore to be a universal rather than a particular. Of course, there is an ongoing debate concerning how best to characterize the abstract versus concrete distinction,[18] but one candidate, commonly suggested as at least

---

[18] Again, helpful entry points may be found in Cowling (2017, ch. 2), Hoffman and Rosenkrantz (2003) and Lowe (1995).

a sufficient condition for something's counting properly as an abstract *universal*,[19] is the possibility of instantiation by or in other things. Universals are instantiable whereas concrete particulars are not, and so structures seem like universals.

Still, one might suppose that even though we tend to think of structures as abstracta, there should be no difficulty distinguishing abstract structures from concrete structures; for instance we can recognize that the identity of most types of atom involves the bonding relations obtaining between sub-atomic components, and thus recognize a universal commonly instantiated between them (say, the generic relational universal 'bonded to'), but we can also say of a particular atom in nature that its identity as *that* atom consists in concrete structure, namely the bonding relations obtaining between those concrete sub-atomic particles. In other words, if we are talking about a *type* or *kind* of atom, then the structural relations figuring in the identity conditions of that type or kind will naturally be understood as abstract. By contrast, if we are talking about *instances* of that type or kind, then the structural relations figuring in the identity conditions of those instances will correspondingly be understood as concrete.

However, if the ability to differentiate between abstract and concrete *structure* (e.g., the bonding relations) is founded upon a prior differentiation between abstract and concrete *objects* (e.g., the sub-atomic particles) then this will be a potential concern to advocates of OSR, or at least to advocates of the three versions of Eliminativist OSR and to advocates of the first version of Moderate OSR. For on these four theories, objects are either eliminated altogether or are rendered so devoid of content as to be wholly identity-dependent on the structure to which they belong. On these views objects thus seem exceptionally poor candidates to serve as concretizers of relations (or anything else) – they are simply too ontologically impoverished for that. So what does concretize them? Chakravartty (2003, pp. 875–876) puts the point as follows:

> Structures are defined by relations, and the metaphysical ambiguities that afflict objects are applicable to relations also. One might wonder whether the relations of SR are universals, or to be understood in terms of nominalism. It is unclear how the resemblance of one instance of structure to another, whether it occurs in the same lab at a different time or in another

---

[19] Recall that there may be other sorts of abstracta besides universals, like sets. But any universal is ipso facto an abstract entity (at least when considered apart from its instantiation – as noted in Chapter 2 the status qua abstract of *instantiated* universals is a matter of dispute).

lab altogether, is to be analyzed, if at all. *What constitutes the individuality of an instance of structure?* There had better be an answer to this question, for instances of structure are no less particular than the objects OSR seeks to replace. [Emphasis in original]

He presents this as a question for OSR (especially Eliminativist OSR) rather than as a knock-down objection,[20] and naturally the defenders of the theory have put forward various answers. I will consider five such answers in a moment; but first it might be worth stating the argument a bit more formally. I suggest then that the following captures the core idea of objection (a):

Premise 1 If the concretization of a relation depends on the ontologically prior concretization of its relata, then a relation is neither ontologically prior to nor symmetrically dependent on its relata.

Premise 2 The concretization of a relation depends on the ontologically prior concretization of its relata.

Conclusion 1/Premise 3 Therefore, a relation is neither ontologically prior to nor symmetrically dependent on its relata.

Premise 4 If a relation is neither ontologically prior to nor symmetrically dependent on its relata, then all existing versions of OSR are false.

Final Conclusion Therefore all existing versions of OSR are false.

As an initial justification for premise 2, one could rely on the claim made above that this is the most intuitive, commonsensical way of looking at concretization. The justification for premise 1 would be that it would make little sense to claim that the *concretization* of a concrete relation could rely on the concretization of its component objects, while at the same time claiming that the *existence* of those objects was utterly reliant on the existence of the relation. After all, we normally think that the status of something (whether object, property, relation, or event) as concrete is a necessary rather than contingent fact about it – that if an object is concrete then it could not be abstract, at least in the minimal sense that nothing in this world could transform it into an abstract entity.

---

[20] Kuhlmann (2012, section 5.6) likewise presents it as a serious concern but not as obviously decisive: "OSR takes the paramount significance of symmetry groups to indicate that symmetry structures as such have an ontological primacy over objects. However, since most OSRists are decidedly against Platonism, it is not entirely clear how symmetry structures could be ontologically prior to objects, if they only exist in concrete realizations, namely in those objects that exhibit these symmetries."

(The keyboard I am typing on could not be transformed into a Platonic form.) Now, if the status of something as concrete is necessary for it (and hence for its existence), then whatever constitutes it as concrete is equally necessary for it (and hence for its existence). As such, if the status of a relation as concrete is constituted by the concrete status of its relata, then that relation cannot exist independently of those relata. Premise 3 follows from the first two by modus ponens; the truth of premise 4 is obvious from a run-down of the versions of OSR enumerated above, and the final conclusion follows from premises 3 and 4 by modus ponens.

How might the defender of OSR reply to objection (a)? First, one could opt to formulate a nominalist version of OSR. The immediate downside of that approach is that Ladyman, French, and most other proponents of OSR tend to favour realism about universals, so would prefer a reply compatible with that realism.[21]

Second, one could go to the opposite extreme and press for a view of nature in which universals are all that is real, and concreta are in some way reducible to them. This inevitably looks like Pythagoreanism reborn, whereby physical objects are somehow reduced to abstract mathematical structures. Dipert (1997) and Tegmark (2007) are generally seen as defending such a view, but it has had few other takers;[22] and see O'Conaill (2014, pp. 297–300) for a concise critique of Pythagoreanism in the context of the OSR debate.

Third, one might argue that advocates of OSR are not obliged to provide an account of what exactly demarcates abstract from concrete structures. Ladyman and Ross (2007, p. 158) ask: "What makes the structure physical and not mathematical? That is a question that we refuse to answer. In our view, there is nothing more to be said about this that doesn't amount to empty words …" They go on to argue (2007, pp. 159–161) that this isn't as worrisome a claim as it might initially seem, since on their view some of the standard methods of distinguishing the concrete from the abstract (namely causal efficacy and spatio-temporality) are unworkable, both for general philosophical reasons and because of specific problems arising from their attempted application to the

---

[21] Esfeld and Lam (2011) and Esfeld and Sachse (2011, ch. 2) are notable exceptions. They advocate a version of Moderate OSR formulated in terms of trope nominalism, whereby tropes are seen as relations instead of properties, and objects are real but do not belong to any distinct fundamental category, being reconceived as bundles of tropes (i.e., bundles of relations).

[22] Based on the short description provided above, one might think Floridi's ISR would tend towards Pythagoreanism, but he resists this (2011, p. 368).

ontology of fundamental physics.[23] They are also unlikely to see in the 'instantiability' criterion mentioned above a source of clarification on this issue.[24] Still, this third option (that of declining to answer the question) has seemed unsatisfying to some (like Morganti (2011, pp. 1174)).

A related fourth option would answer the question by saying that the difference between an abstract structure and its concrete instance is primitive and not subject to further elaboration or explanation. This is certainly one way to go, and in fairness any systematic metaphysics must be allowed some primitives. The issue is how many primitives it requires and how plausibly located those primitives are vis-à-vis competing systems. Ontologies that take objects as fundamental ingredients and that are realist about universals (whether moderate or Platonic) typically tell some further story about how concrete objects instantiate abstract kinds such that the demarcation of an abstract object from its concrete instance is not viewed as primitive.[25] With this in mind, the real worry for the proponent of OSR may be that those already sceptical of taking the *existence* of relations as fundamental (rather than as supervenient on or dependent on objects) will likely be doubly hesitant to take the *concretization* of relations as primitive, such that the work of the OSR advocate in trying to gain converts from traditional substance-based ontologies becomes still more onerous.

A fifth option for an OSRist would be allegiance to Moderate OSR Versions #2 or #3; these versions might allow for the option of explaining the concretization of structure by reference to the concretization of its component objects, since on these versions of OSR the latter have at least some intrinsic identity conditions of their own, which could perhaps include whatever it is that provides for concretization.

So there are certainly ways in which the OSRist can reply to objection (a), though each of these five options will be more or less appealing depending on one's favoured version of OSR and one's larger background metaphysics (like where one stands on the debate over universals).

---

[23] Note though that elsewhere French and Ladyman (2011, p. 75) express openness to the causal efficacy criterion, and Esfeld (2009, p. 188) adopts it explicitly.

[24] While not wholly rejecting talk of instantiation, Ladyman and Ross do write this (2007, p. 155): "We ask the reader to consider whether the main metaphysical idea we propose, of existent structures that are not composed out of more basic entities, is any more obscure or bizarre than the instantiation relation in the theory of universals."

[25] E.g., according to some substratum theorists instantiation occurs when a bare particular enters into the extrinsic instantiation relation/primitive tie with a Platonic abstractum, while according to hylomorphists instantiation occurs when prime matter actualizes its inherent potential for the reception of an immanent substance-universal. We'll see more of these and other substance ontologies (and their related accounts of instantiation) in Chapter 5.

An upshot of the preceding dialectic surrounding objection (a) is that the metaphysics of the abstract/concrete divide has been taken to be of considerable importance for OSR; a further point worth emphasizing is that the three versions of Eliminativist OSR and the three versions of Moderate OSR enumerated above are all designed to flesh out the ontology of fundamental *concrete* relations and (in some cases) fundamental *concrete* objects. This is frequently evident in the literature, but Lam (2014, p. 1157) provides a particularly clear formulation of the point when he writes: "The ontological thesis of OSR can be broadly expressed in the following way: what there is in the world at the fundamental level (or in the cases where OSR is relevant) are physical structures, in the sense of networks of concrete physical relations among concrete physical objects (relata)."[26] There is thus a recognition of a need (or at least an alleged need) to explain how all this ties back to abstract relations and/or objects (insofar as most OSRists are realists about universals), but the focus is on concreta. This is hardly surprising, insofar as OSR is chiefly intended as an ontology for fundamental physics, and the physical is necessarily coextensive with the concrete. By contrast, in the literature on mathematical structuralism the focus is manifestly on abstract structures and how they may relate to abstract objects.[27] All of which should lead us to wonder whether there might be space in the dialectic for a theory that meets Ladyman's (2016, section 4) aforementioned minimal criterion for falling under the OSR tent while focusing not on the relation (eliminative or otherwise) between *concrete structures* and *concrete objects* (as on existing versions of OSR), nor on the relation between *abstract structures* and *abstract objects* (as on structuralisms within the philosophy of mathematics), but rather on the relation between *concrete objects* and *abstract objects and structures.* If one could show that concrete objects are essentially related to abstract objects and structures, such that the identity conditions of concrete objects are partly intrinsic and partly relational (where the corresponding relata are abstract objects and abstract structures), one would be left with a metaphysics that inflated the ontological status of relations and structures – just not *concrete* relations and structures. In the next Section 3.3 I will argue that the nomic dispositionalism laid out in the previous chapter provides us with just such a view, one that is independently motivated (i.e., that is motivated by issues external to the

---

[26] The same can be said for ISR. Floridi (2011, p. 356) writes: "Thus, the structuralism in question here is based on relational entities (understood structurally) that are particular, not on 'patterns' that are abstract and universal …"
[27] See again Reck and Price (2000).

OSR debate) and that handily sidesteps objection (a) at least as well as, if not better than, existing versions of OSR.

Before proceeding to that task though, let's lay out the details of objection (b).

3.2.2   Objection (b)

This objection has not received as much attention in the OSR literature and can be summarized more succinctly: insofar as all three versions of Eliminativist OSR and all three versions of Moderate OSR make the claim that objects (if they exist at all) depend on relations, and relations in their turn presuppose multiple relata (except on Eliminativist OSR Version #1), it follows that there cannot exist a lonely object, "where a lonely object is an object that could exist in a possible world in which there are no other objects" (French & Ladyman, 2011, p. 34).[28] A lonely object would be an object existing independently of any other objects and hence independently of any network of relations, and that kind of independence is ruled out by all the versions of OSR enumerated above. (In light of the discussion of objection (a), it is worth emphasizing that the objects and relations discussed in the present objection are all *concrete* – a lonely object is a concrete object existing independently of any other concrete objects and any concrete relations.) Why is this grounds for an objection? Because at least *prima facie*, it seems as if a lonely object is possible; that is, that there are possible worlds containing only a single concrete object, and no corresponding concrete objects or concrete relations. It seems one can coherently conceive of a universe consisting of nothing but a single electron (or perhaps a single electron + spacetime, with the latter being conceived in a non-substantival fashion). Of course it is a much-disputed question whether conceivability ever entails possibility, or even provides evidence for possibility. But if one maintains that in at least some cases it might, then one might find the apparent conceivability of a lonely object troubling for OSR. To put the objection more formally:

> **Premise 1** If it is possible for a concrete object to exist in the absence of any other concrete objects or concrete relations, then all existing versions of OSR are false.

---

[28] Lam (2014, p. 1158) for instance also makes this quite explicit: "In positive terms, the very existence of the OSR objects is relational (structural, contextual – we use these words interchangeably, as capturing the same idea here), in the sense that their very existence depends on the relations in which they stand (the structures they are part of) and on there being other objects ..."

Premise 2 It is possible for a concrete object to exist in the absence of any other concrete objects or concrete relations.

Conclusion Therefore all existing versions of OSR are false.

The justification for premise 2 is the aforementioned apparent conceivability of such a scenario; the truth of premise 1 is clear from an examination of the versions of OSR enumerated above.

Replying to the concern about lonely objects, French and Ladyman (2011, p. 35) write as follows:

> This leaves the issue of the lonely object: the mere possibility of such a situation may be used by the critic to press the claim that intrinsic properties are not structural (Chakravartty, private correspondence).[29] A quite radical response would be to follow Mach, and Leibniz before him, and insist that such a situation does not constitute 'genuine' physical possibility and hence cannot undermine a metaphysics based on current physics. A more moderate approach would be to allow the invocation of such possible worlds for certain purposes, but to note that they only reveal a certain aspect of the relevant properties and effectively miss out on their structural nature, which is revealed not through metaphysical imaginings but reflection on the relevant theory.

Their first suggested reply is clear: deny the truth of premise 2. They are not impressed by the alleged conceivability of lonely objects, and their reference to Mach and to Leibniz indicates an openness to a more robust rejection of them by way of positive philosophical arguments for their impossibility. (The claim that one should not be impressed by alleged conceivability will seem particularly compelling from within the naturalistic epistemology laid out in detail by Ladyman and Ross (2007, ch. 1). A priori intuitions (including intuitions about conceivability and its link to possibility) are given relatively short shrift, especially in comparison with what our best science apparently reveals. Certainly where the two conflict, the latter ought to win out, on their view; and since they take OSR to be the best metaphysical interpretation of our best current science, to the extent that OSR appears to rule out lonely objects, so much the worse for the latter.) I read their second suggested reply as permitting talk of lonely objects for merely heuristic purposes while rejecting any substantive metaphysical conclusions purportedly drawn from our ability to conceive them.

---

[29] French and Ladyman's discussion of the lonely object problem occurs within the context of their broader treatment of intrinsic properties on OSR, but I think the problem can be considered independently of that larger context.

These replies will persuade some, but for those working within different background epistemologies (in particular epistemologies according
more weight to a priori intuition) and/or those who maintain that conceivability is evidence for possibility (at least with respect to the lonely
object case), objection (b) might call out for further comment.

In the following section I will show how the nomic dispositionalism
discussed in Chapter 2 entails a novel and independently motivated version of Moderate OSR, one which also supplies new approaches to
answering objections (a) and (b).

3.3   Nomic Dispositionalism, a Fourth Version of Moderate OSR, and New Replies to the Two Objections

To recap very briefly the main claims of Chapter 2: most dispositionalists
have tended to regard laws of nature (properly conceived as abstract principles that somehow play a governing role in the physical world) as reducible to or even eliminable in favour of dispositions. However, some
have argued that dispositionalism is compatible with nomic realism.
I tried to take such law-friendly dispositionalism one step further, advocating the stronger claim that dispositionalism actually *entails* the reality
of laws. I labeled the resulting view 'nomic dispositionalism.' I argued for
it by pointing out that at least some dispositions (indeed probably all dispositions) have ceteris paribus clauses, and that in all cases these ceteris
paribus clauses incorporate uninstantiated universals – both uninstantiated determinate values of instantiated determinable universals, and
altogether alien universals (universals wholly lacking instances in our
world). Take for instance the solubility of sugar. Sugar is soluble in
water – that is, sugar has a disposition, 'solubility,'[30] whose stimulus condition is being placed in water, and whose manifestation condition is the
breaking apart of its solid crystalline structure. In common with many
other (probably all other) dispositions, the identity conditions of solubility include not just its stimulus and manifestation conditions, but also
its ceteris paribus clauses – possible circumstances under which the stimulus fails to prompt the manifestation. In the case of the solubility of
sugar, its ceteris paribus clauses might include the possible state of affairs
of the sugar's being coated in a protective gel that blocks its dissolution
in water. A chemist could specify an assortment of real and hypothetical

---

[30] Solubility is plausibly *not* a fundamental power, and so strictly speaking it is not a disposition as I
defined the term in Chapter 1. But for ease of illustration, let's take it as a disposition.

substances that could serve this purpose (i.e., could specify various instantiated and uninstantiated kinds that could figure in these ceteris paribus clauses). The key idea is just that ceteris paribus clauses are part (in a specific sense of 'part') of the identity conditions of some (likely all) dispositions, and that these ceteris paribus clauses incorporate uninstantiated universals. What this means is that some (probably all) dispositions have identity conditions that *orient* them or *relate* them or *direct* them towards uninstantiated universals. And because these ceteris paribus clauses help determine the circumstances under which these dispositions can be manifested, they play a meaningful governing role in the physical world despite *essentially incorporating purely abstract* entities, i.e., uninstantiated universals. (The simplest way to read this is as involving an outright commitment to Platonic realism about universals; however, as we saw in Chapter 2 there are also ways of formulating a moderate realist nomic dispositionalism and even a nominalist nomic dispositionalism, so those leery of Platonism can read 'uninstantiated universal' and 'purely abstract entities' in accordance with one or another of the those alternative formulations. More on this momentarily.) Laws of nature, in other words, are irreducibly real, existing as the ceteris paribus clauses of dispositions. Moreover since these ceteris paribus clauses are part of the very identity conditions of dispositions, it turns out that dispositions are not ontologically prior to laws; rather they are both fundamental ingredients in ontology. Nomic dispositionalism will of course be controversial, running contrary as it does to the majority view on laws within dispositonalism, and it was seen to be potentially vulnerable to several objections. I will not review the specifics of my defence of nomic dispositionalism here; hopefully this short recap will suffice for purposes of the present chapter.

Having recalled to mind the basic idea of nomic dispositionalism, we can now consider the following argument:

Premise 1 If nomic dispositionalism is true, then a novel version of Moderate OSR is true.

Premise 2 Nomic dispositionalism is true.

Conclusion Therefore, a novel version of Moderate OSR is true.

Again, I don't wish to review here my defence of nomic dispositionalism, so let's just take premise 2 on board for the sake of argument and focus instead on premise 1. What I want to point out is that nomic dispositionalism is just the sort of view adverted to at the end of our discussion of objection (a) above, one where concrete objects are essentially related to abstract objects and structures. This gives us a metaphysics that meets Ladyman's minimal criterion for belonging to the OSR camp, inflating as it does the ontological status of relations and structures – just not *concrete* relations and structures, insofar as the relata here do not consist wholly of concreta, but rather are a combination of concrete objects and the abstract objects and structures to which they are essentially related.

Why abstract objects and *structures*? Because in these ceteris paribus clauses at least some of the uninstantiated universals will themselves be dispositional in nature (think again of the solubility of sugar and its relation to the hypothetical sugar-coating gel, which itself has the *power* to prevent dissolution). Consequently they will themselves defined in part by their relations to still other uninstantiated universals, at least some of which will themselves be dispositional in nature … Thereby a massive network or structure of relations between abstracta obtains. That dispositionalism entails such abstract networks is of course not a new idea,[31] though its relevance to OSR has gone largely unremarked, insofar as authors writing on this within the OSR literature have not typically been working within standard dispositionalism (according to which powers are intrinsic properties of *objects*).[32]

Provided that every concrete object must have at least one disposition (a claim most dispositionalists would affirm), and that every disposition has ceteris paribus clauses (the most plausible stance here), then every concrete object is essentially related to abstract entities, namely, the uninstantiated universals incorporated into the ceteris paribus clauses of that object's disposition(s). That concrete object could not exist without figuring in those relations, and as such it is dependent on them. This point by itself elevates considerably the ontological status of relations (at least

---

[31] See for instance Bostock (2003).

[32] Yudell (2011) develops an analogous modal structuralism according to which the identity of a property is fixed by its place within a structure of possibilities; however this is done from within a standpoint that is not expressly dispositionalist (or even realist about causation); moreover Yudell (2011, p. 682) makes a point of sharply distinguishing between this modal structuralism and OSR. Note too Esfeld (2009) who, building on an idea suggested by French (2006), argues that the fundamental structures referenced in OSR are themselves inherently causally relevant, such that dispositional *properties* are eliminated in favour of dispositional *relations*. Esfeld and Lam (2011) and Esfeld and Sachse (2011, ch. 2) defend this idea still further, while also displaying more openness to the reality of intrinsic properties (including, I take it, dispositions), provided they are conceived as properties of relations rather than of objects. French and Ladyman (2011) display an openness to the same idea (though elsewhere Ladyman and Ross (2007, ch. 5) take a stance on causation that is at odds with the thoroughly realist understanding assumed in dispositionalism). And Paoletti (2016a), while not an advocate of OSR, defends the idea that at least some powers are grounded in extrinsic relations.

in comparison with the status accorded them in many substance-based ontologies), and allows for the formulation of another version of Moderate OSR:

> **Moderate OSR Version #4** At the level of fundamental physics (the unobservable realm), relations exist and so do objects. The latter have an intrinsic identity defined partly in terms of the possession of intrinsic properties. These intrinsic properties include one or more dispositions, the identity conditions of which place them in essential relation to a vast structure of uninstantiated abstracta. As such, the identity of objects is not wholly reducible to their structural role, yet they cannot exist independently of structure and their identity is essentially bound up with it.

This gives us a version of OSR in which objects have a place in fundamental ontology and so do structures, but the latter are abstract rather than concrete. Note that this formulation leaves open whether the abstract structure itself depends for its existence on the concrete object and its intrinsic disposition. One could opt to go full-blown Platonist here, and argue that the network of uninstantiated abstracta exists necessarily, and thus independently of any instantiated dispositions with ceteris paribus clauses fixing them in relation to that network of abstracta. This would certainly elevate the ontological status of relations still further, and thus might be seen as a more promising formulation from the perspective of OSR proponents; yet as we saw in Chapter 2, the full-blown Platonist reading of nomic dispositionalism is not the only option, and there are ways of formulating the view in terms of moderate realism or a certain sort of nominalism. I will not review here the pros and cons of these perspectives.

It is worth pointing out that although I have just defended Moderate OSR Version #4 by reference to nomic dispositionalism (which is in turn grounded in an analysis of the ceteris paribus clauses of dispositions), one could argue for it by other routes; in fact any account of dispositionalism according to which instantiated powers are essentially related to a network of physically uninstantiated abstracta – for instance Tugby's (2013) Platonic dispositionalism – will supply the necessary ingredients for a defence of Moderate OSR Version #4.

Still, while it will hopefully be of interest to those in the OSR debate that dispositionalism provides for a new version of OSR, it must also be admitted that there are already a good number of versions of OSR present in the literature; is there any value to tossing another player into the game? I believe so, for at least four reasons.

First, Moderate OSR Version #4 is independently motivated, arising from dispositionalism rather than arising directly from concerns internal to the OSR debate. That will help it avoid charges of being ad hoc.

Second, because Moderate OSR Version #4 is explicitly committed to the irreducible reality of both concrete objects and intrinsic properties, it is liable to seem less counter-intuitive to many working within more traditional substance-friendly metaphysical systems. At the same time, it maintains the core of OSR by hugely elevating the ontological status of relations, such that any concrete object relies for its identity and existence on relations – relations to abstracta, but relations nonetheless.

Third, Moderate OSR Version #4 sidesteps objection (a) entirely, insofar as on its account the concrete status of concrete objects is not reliant on any ontologically prior (or symmetrically dependent) concretization of concrete structure. An advocate of this version of OSR can adopt whatever traditional account of the instantiation of concrete objects seems most plausible, and there will be no special difficulty distinguishing concrete from abstract relations. Indeed, the very existence of concrete structure is contingent, insofar as concrete structures involve multiple concrete relata and this version of OSR does not require that there be multiple concrete relata. Granted, our physical world certainly seems to contain a vast multitude of concrete objects, and Moderate OSR Version #4 is compatible with this actually being the case, including at the level of fundamental physics. Hence the first line of its formulation: "At the level of fundamental physics (the unobservable realm), relations exist and so do objects." But it does not rule out there being possible worlds in which there exists just a single concrete object, one that would of course not stand in any relation to other concrete objects and would thus not feature in any concrete relations. (Unless one were to conceive of the link between the concrete object and its own intrinsic powers as a concrete relation, but that is not the sort of concrete relation of interest to most advocates of OSR.)

Fourth, and related to that last point, Moderate OSR Version #4 likewise sidesteps objection (b), since it is compatible with the possibility of a lonely object. Again, the relation invoked in this version of OSR is a relation between a concrete object's intrinsic property and a vast structure of uninstantiated abstracta. That relation can obtain in a world in which there is no more than one concrete object.

3.4 Conclusion

To sum up: in Section 3.1 we reviewed the background of structural realism, looking at its roots in the realism/antirealism debate within philosophy of science. We then proceeded to the distinction between Epistemic Structural Realism and Ontic Structural Realism and its philosophical motivation, laying out a taxonomy of existing versions of the latter. Section 3.2 saw the treatment of two objections facing existing versions of OSR, while Section 3.3 saw the formulation of a new version of the theory, one entailed by nomic dispositionalism and having no vulnerability to the two objections.

It must be admitted, however, that while Moderate OSR Version #4 plausibly does fall under the 'big tent' of OSR, it may do so just barely. Many advocates of OSR, and in particular those who lean towards one or another of the Eliminativist versions, are liable to find this account's unabashed commitment to fundamental objects possessing intrinsic properties (powers, at the least) unappealing; this is especially the case given that some longstanding physics-based arguments for OSR (cited in Section 3.1) are predicated on a rejection of just this sort of objects-with-properties picture of the physical. Consequently a more thorough defence of Moderate OSR Version #4 would have to critically engage with those arguments, a task which I cannot undertake here.

A final point: while the preceding displays a new connection between dispositionalism and OSR, I do not wish to imply that this is the only such connection. In fact I suspect that other aspects of dispositionalism (aspects over and above its implications for relations between concrete objects and abstract structure) could supply further links to OSR, but in the interests of space further exploration of these areas will have to be left to future research.

CHAPTER 4

Dispositionalism and Material Composition

4.1 Introduction

Let's say we take a rock (for instance) and split it into two. Then we repeat for each of the halves. We keep repeating, over and over again, until we bore down into the level of the molecules and then atoms and then subatomic particles and then … what? If we keep going with the process of division, then what, eventually, will we reach? Will we (A) eventually hit 'rock bottom,' a fundamental layer of objects that cannot be divided further? Or (B) might the process of division be capable of continuing forever?

Start with option (A), such that we are left with a layer of entities that admit of no further division. Call these, for historical reasons, 'atoms.' (Obviously 'atom' in the history of metaphysics no longer lines up with 'atom' in contemporary physics.) What must such indivisible entities be like? Here (A) breaks down into two versions: according to *atomism version 1*, they are material simples, having no actual or potential proper parts. On this first view, atoms cannot be spatially extended, insofar as spatial extension plausibly entails divisibility. If an object is extended, then its right and left halves ought to be separable, at least in principle (i.e., irrespective of whether we actually possess the technical means to perform the separation); the two halves could be split apart, or the object's left half could be annihilated while the right half could persist in existence (and vice versa). The existence of the matter composing the left half of an extended thing seems not to entail the existence of the matter composing the right half or vice versa, so one could persist without the other. Thus if material nature bottoms out at a genuinely indivisible entity, that entity will have to be unextended, a point particle.[1] By contrast, on *atomism*

---

[1] Talking of such an atom as a 'point particle' is of course only an analogy; it makes no more sense to speak of an extensionless object as a point than as a square – at least, that's the case if we're thinking of 'point' in the typical imaginative sense of a circularly shaped tiny entity rather than as a geometrical abstraction.

46

version 2, the entailment relation between extension and divisibility is denied, such that there is a fundamental layer of indivisible but extended particles. Despite being spatially extended, nothing could possibly divide these particles. Consequently, although they are spatially extended, they do not possess actual proper parts in the sense that 'proper part' is typically understood (i.e., as involving smaller objects, which objects could in theory exist on their own apart from the whole). And the claim is not merely that they couldn't be divided by us using current or future technology, nor that their division would be inconsistent with contingent physical laws. The impossibility referenced here is not mere *physical* impossibility. Rather, the claim is that it is *metaphysically* impossible (or *logically* impossible, for those who equate metaphysical and logical impossibility) for them to be divided. There is no possible world in which these entities are in any way divided, either by splitting into two or by destroying one section while leaving the rest intact.

What if we instead go with the latter option, (B), and affirm that the process of division might in principle continue forever? Here we are immediately faced with two further options: we might say that if the process of division could continue forever, that is because every material object has actual proper parts that are themselves smaller material objects, such that division is just a process of spatially separating proper parts. This could go on forever precisely because every material object has an actually infinite number of proper parts. Every single object has multiple proper parts, which are themselves objects with multiple proper parts, which are themselves objects with multiple proper parts, etc. ad infinitum. This is the theory of *gunk*. Alternatively, the process of division might be thought to lack an endpoint because eventually a layer of objects is reached which, while spatially extended and hence divisible, lack actual proper parts. This is the theory of *extended simples*. An extended simple is spatially extended, and so has (for example) conceptually distinguishable right and left halves that are in fact separable. But that separability does not imply that those halves are (right now and prior to actual division) distinct actual objects. Rather, there is one object here, one extended simple, with *potential* parts (e.g., the divisible right and left halves) but no *actual* proper parts, i.e., no real parts that are themselves real objects on their own account. Thus an extended simple can be divided into multiple new objects, objects all composed of the same *stuff* that the first object was composed of – but that first object was, prior to division, mereologically simple.[2] In this way, the theory of extended simples is designed to affirm the theoretical possibility of infinite divisibility of matter without also affirming the reality of actual infinities.

To sum up, we have four main theories concerning fundamental material composition (or the lack thereof):

Atomism version 1, according to which material nature bottoms out at a layer of genuinely fundamental, indivisible-because-unextended point particles.

Atomism version 2, according to which material nature bottoms out at a layer of genuinely fundamental, indivisible-but-extended particles.

The theory of gunk, according to which material nature never bottoms out, because every material object has proper parts that are themselves material objects.

The theory of extended simples, according to which material nature bottoms out in a sense, insofar as there exists a layer of material objects that are divisible but possess merely potential parts, not actual proper parts.

Each of these four theories has a distinguished pedigree – for historical background see especially Holden (2004) and Pasnau (2011, pp. 88–92, 279–299, and 606–632). Regarding the contemporary scene, the landscape exhibits a degree of complexity and ambiguity. One *might* argue that atomism is quite widely held, having the status of something like a default position among many; this seems particularly the case for those who work in philosophy of mind, where, as Schaffer (2003) and Nagasawa (2012) both observe, the claim that nature bottoms out in fundamental material objects is an important background assumption in reductionist ontologies of the mental. More generally, accounts of microphysical property reduction often assume the reality of fundamental objects, such that Khalidi (2011, p. 1156) observes: "Many metaphysicians now hold that the only real properties are the fundamental microphysical ones. Which properties are those? Presumably, the properties possessed by the fundamental constituents of the universe, that is to say, the smallest entities in the universe." However, while it is true that there are many advocates of the idea that there must be a fundamental layer to

---

[2] Hence defenders of extended simples often take this to imply a real and irreducible ontological distinction between *objects* and *stuff*, the former properly referenced by the use of count nouns, the latter by mass nouns. More on this shortly.

the material world, oftentimes authors do not specify whether they think that material fundamentality entails atomism version 1, atomism version 2, or whether a bottom layer of extended simples (divisible but not actually possessed of real lower-level proper parts) would suffice to fulfill the explanatory role they think needs to be played by a 'fundamental' level. Sometimes treatments of fundamentality will openly acknowledge the ambiguity between atoms and extended simples, as for instance in Newman (2013). Authors who *unambiguously* defend a specific version of atomism are in fact relatively few in the recent literature, though atomism version 1 does have unambiguous opponents, like Giberman (2012). By contrast, the theory of gunk has been the subject of a number of sympathetic treatments, including by Forrest (2004), Sider (1993), and Zimmerman (1996; 1996a), in addition to the aforementioned pieces by Schaffer (2003), Khalidi (2011), and Nagasawa (2012). Favourable discussions of extended simples include Braddon-Mitchell and Miller (2006), Markosian (1998; 2004; 2015), McDaniel (2007; 2009), and Toner (2008; 2012).[3]

I will not attempt here to review the many arguments pro and con surrounding these four theories, as my aim is to show that this area of debate has some important connections with dispositionalism. To that end, in Section 4.2 I provide a concise review of the existing case that atomism version 1 supports dispostionalism, and in Section 4.3 argue that the theory of extended simples provides for an even stronger connection, namely that of *entailing* dispositonalism. This places the categoricalist in the position of having to favour either atomism version 2 or the theory of gunk. And since atomism version 2 is likely unworkable, really this leaves just one option remaining for the categoricalist: gunk.

4.2 Atomism Version 1 and Dispositionalism

The connection between atomism version 1 and dispositionalism has already been drawn out in the literature, so I will discuss it only briefly here. Mumford (1998, pp. 229–230; 2006) has developed the argument in detail, and though he does not use the terminology of 'atomism version 1,' this is clearly the theory he has in mind. His basic argument is that contemporary physics provides good empirical evidence for the

---

[3] Simons (2004) is sometimes classed as a defender of extended simples, but it is somewhat unclear whether he takes these to be divisible or not (see especially pages 379 and 381 of that article), such that it is unclear whether he advocates extended simples or instead atomism version 2.

existence of point particles lacking spatial extension or any internal compositional structure. Electrons, quarks, and other such particles seem genuinely fundamental and indivisible, insofar as a great deal of experimental manipulation over several decades has failed to uncover any underlying component parts. Moreover the properties that physicists attribute to these point particles all seem to be causal powers rather than categorical properties – mass, charge, spin, etc., are all defined by way of their potential causal significance.[4] With empirical considerations supporting both the truth of atomism version 1 and the claim that the intrinsic properties of these atoms are exclusively dispositional, there is good reason to take atomism version 1 as supporting dispositionalism. Mumford goes on to observe that a categoricalist could reply by turning his modus ponens into a modus tollens, arguing that since there are no dispositional properties a future completed physics will surely show either that these particles and their intrinsic properties are neither of them really fundamental, and/or that properties like mass and charge are not properly definable in terms of their causal import. However Mumford (2006, pp. 480–481) counter-replies by observing that while this approach cannot be ruled out a priori, the categoricalist faces an uphill battle and is left in the uncomfortable position of having to rely on faith that multiple aspects of our best current physics will be overturned in the future.

One might add to Mumford's argument by pointing out that there seems a dearth of realistic candidates for irreducible categorical properties on atomism version 1. Categoricalists often list geometrical/structural properties like shape and size as their central examples of non-dispositional properties. And on some theories of material composition

---

[4] By way of example Mumford (2006, p. 476) quotes the following definitions from Isaacs (2000):

> **Charge** A property of some elementary particles that gives rise to an interaction between them and consequently to the host of material phenomena described as electrical … Two particles that have similar charges (both negative or both positive) interact by repelling each other. **Mass** A measure of a body's inertia, i.e. its resistance to acceleration … Mass can also be defined in terms of the gravitational force it produces. Thus, according to Newton's law of gravitation, $mg = F\, d^2/MG$, … F is the gravitational force. **Spin** The part of the total angular momentum of a particle, atom, nucleus, etc. that is distinct from its orbital angular momentum.

Actually spin is difficult to conceptualize in dispositional terms, such that Mumford is a bit off here in his characterization of that property. The difficulty is that spin's contribution to the angular momentum of the larger system to which it belongs is not really a causal contribution, but more akin to the simple additive contribution of a particle's mass to the mass of the larger system to which it belongs. This probably explains why Isaac's description of spin does not employ capacity-language, while his characterization of charge and mass both do. (See Schumm (2004, pp. 177–187) for an accessible discussion of the nature of spin.) Importantly though, Mumford's point with reference to mass and charge still holds. (My thanks to Marc Lange for the clarification concerning the nature of spin.)

geometrical/structural properties seem perfectly good examples of irreducible categorical properties. On atomism version 2 the atoms all have the property of spatial extension, and the same can be said for the objects posited by the theory of extended simples. On the theory of gunk the chain of spatial composition arrangements, and thereby shape properties, is unending. But on atomism version 1, the fundamental objects, the atoms, are devoid of extension and hence devoid of size and shape, occupying space not by overlapping an extended spatial region but by occupying a spatial point.[5] What we think of as geometrical/structural properties will then be derivative on the spatial arrangements of the unextended atoms – i.e., what we think of as intrinsic geometrical/structural 'properties' are to be cashed out in terms of extrinsic spatial *relations* by the advocate of atomism version 1. Since the categoricalist cannot list geometrical/structural properties as candidate irreducible properties, given atomism version 1, they need to reference some other sort of categorical property. And the only other sort that seems available is a *qualitative* property – i.e., something analogous to colour or texture, but suitable for possession by a fundamental physical particle. The difficulty in the present context is that there seem no plausible candidates for irreducible physical qualitative properties. *Mental* properties (like perceptual qualia) are obviously inadmissible as candidates. And let's assume that something like *colour primitivism* (according to which colours are real intrinsic qualities of objects) is either false or at least not plausibly applicable to the realm of fundamental physics.[6] Let's assume the same for *quidditism* (the idea that there is a type of categorical property, a *quiddity*, with no intrinsic character over and above self-identity and distinction from other quiddities). Whatever might be said for colour primitivism and quidditism more generally, in the context of atomism version 1 they are difficult to countenance; it is not at all clear that a colour (or any intrinsic quality remotely analogous to colour) could be possessed by something lacking spatial extension; moreover the notion that the nature of an atom could

---

[5] It might be argued that for relationists about space, the location of an atom on atomism version 1 seems like it will have to be taken as a primitive fact, since there are no irreducibly real spatial regions or points for them to occupy and thereby acquire determinate location.

[6] Molnar (2003, p. 178) writes that at

> the quantum level of nature, there are no ... qualitative properties ... [P]hysical qualia are not items in good ontological standing ... First, at the level of the fundamental constituents of matter, we are dealing exclusively with sub-observables. No qualities of the fundamental particles are given to us in experience ... Second, any qualities we might postulate for the particles ... are explanatorily idle. The only intrinsic properties needed to explain the behavior of the electron are its powers.

consist of nothing but quiddities (a set of properties whose *own* natures consist of nothing more than self-identity and distinctness from one other) seems both implausible on its own accord (how could such an 'atom' then even count as a *physical* object?) and thoroughly divorced from empirical science. However, considered outside the context of fundamental material composition these ideas might come across as more workable, and we'll have occasion to revisit both colour primitivism and quidditism in Chapter 5.

To sum up the connection between atomism version 1 and dispositionalism:

Premise 1 If atomism version 1 is true, then dispositionalism is probably true.
Premise 2 Atomism version 1 is true.
Conclusion Therefore, dispositionalism is probably true.

The 'probably' here is needed on account of two facts: (a) the fact that Mumford's argument rests in part on the current majority view in physics, which is of course defeasible and supplies at best a strong probabilistic case;[7] and (b) the fact that while there seem to be no plausible candidates for irreducible physical qualitative properties, this does not rule out altogether their possibility.

4.3   Extended Simples and Dispositionalism

In summarizing the basic idea of the theory of extended simples above, it was observed that advocates of the view sometimes flesh it out in terms of a real and irreducible distinction between *objects* and *stuff*. In other words, among the fundamental ontological categories is to be found not only properties and relations and objects, but also stuff, where that category is inextricably linked with that of objects. The notion of stuff is

---

[7] It's worth noting here that McDaniel (2007, p. 131) points to string theory as possibly providing support for the theory of extended simples, and Braddon-Mitchell and Miller (2006) point to still other work in current physics that points in the same direction. (Though for a critique of these claims see Baker (2016).) Some arguments in favour of the ontological primacy of the wavefunction and/or fields over and against particles might also tell against atomism version 1, though perhaps not in favour of extended simples. See for instance Lewis (2006) and Ney (2010). So the relevant science, and its metaphysical implications, certainly remains contested. Nonetheless Mumford is absolutely correct that the current standard model of particle physics is often taken to support the reality of unextended point particles. Moreover the competition provided by string theory, and other (still controversial) views within theoretical physics, is competition for atomism version 1 but not dispositionalism, insofar as the properties referenced by Mumford (like mass and charge) seem still to be understood as essentially dispositional regardless.

particularly important in the version of the theory defended by Markosian (1998; 2004; 2015): *MaxCon extended simples*. His is arguably the most detailed and thoroughly developed account of extended simples in the present literature, and as such it is the one I will be working with here. Moreover I think a strong case can be made that older versions of the theory relied at least implicitly on this key distinction between objects and stuff, or at least on something closely analogous.[8] The overarching argument I wish to defend runs as follows:

Premise 1 If MaxCon extended simples exist, then there is a real and irreducible distinction between objects and stuff.

Premise 2 If there is a real and irreducible distinction between objects and stuff, then dispositionalism is true.

Conclusion Therefore, if MaxCon extended simples exist, then dispositionalism is true.

To see why premise 1 holds, we first need to look in detail at Markosian's account. Then we'll turn to the defence of premise 2.

Onward then: Markosian aims to answer what he calls 'the simple question': what are the necessary and jointly sufficient conditions for a physical object's being a simple? Or, phrased differently, "Under what circumstances is it true of some object that it has no proper parts?" (1998, p. 214) The answer he comes up with is the 'maximally continuous view of simples,' or MaxCon: necessarily, x is simple if x is a maximally continuous object. And what is a maximally continuous object? "x is a *maximally continuous object* = df x is a spatially continuous object and there is no continuous region of space, R, such that (i) the region occupied by x is a proper subset of R, and (ii) every point in R falls within some object or other" (1998, p. 221). So a physical object is simple if and only if it is completely continuous spatially (having no proper parts that are spatially separate from one another) and the spatial region it occupies does *not* overlap with the region occupied by any other physical object. Markosian's formulation is meant to capture an important intuition about proper parts and how those parts relate to a whole:

> The intuitive idea behind MaxCon is that whenever an object has proper parts, those proper parts are spatially separated from one another.

---

[8] I think especially of the mediaeval scholastics, the large majority of whom accepted extended simples as their theory of fundamental material composition. For many, *prime matter* played explanatory roles similar to those played by Markosian's *stuff*. However the two notions are not wholly equivalent (at least on most scholastic accounts of prime matter). We'll encounter the notion of prime matter again in Chapter 5 when discussing hylomorphism.

> Composite objects, on this view, are all scattered objects (although it is
> consistent with the view that the different parts of a composite object
> tend to be not so widely scattered).[9] But simples, according to MaxCon,
> are utterly unscattered – and it is in virtue of being completely connected,
> as opposed to being scattered, that they have no proper parts. (2004,
> p. 405)

This has the important implication that a physical simple can be spatially
extended – indeed, in principle there could be very large MaxCon simples. This goes very much against the atomist view according to which a
physical simple would have to be wholly unextended, occupying no spatial region. Note that Markosian's concern isn't to show that MaxCon
simples are real; he does want to show that they are possible and that
they are the only sorts of things that could actually count as simples (he
thinks atomism faces serious problems on this score), but he is inclined
to think that gunk is also possible. Markosian is thus something of a
pluralist regarding the ontology of material objects.[10]

Naturally the MaxCon model of simples is subject to various objections. The first Markosian takes up is the old argument that being
extended implies having spatially distinguishable sections, which in turn
implies having distinct actual proper parts. And having proper parts is
inconsistent with being simple. He makes several replies to this objection. One is to point out that if the objection is sound, then the
Doctrine of Arbitrary Undetached Parts (DAUP) holds true. DAUP is
the idea that any sub-region of a region occupied by a material object is
itself occupied by a distinct material object.[11] So the region occupied
by the middle 3 cm of my femur contains a distinct material object
(i.e., distinct from me, and also distinct from my femur, if it too constitutes an object). So does the middle centimetre, the middle centimetre
and 2/10 of a centimetre, etc. ad infinitum. But many see this multipli-
cation of objects as counter-intuitive.

---

[9] Note Markosian's assumption that any actual proper parts of an object must themselves be objects.
[10] McDaniel (2007; 2009) follows Markosian in this pluralism; by contrast, Simons (2004) argues
not merely for the possibility of extended simples but for their reality and indeed necessity, in the
sense that matter is real but atoms and gunk are impossible, leaving extended simples as the only
option. (Though as I noted earlier, whether what Simons calls 'extended simples' refers exclusively
to 'extended simples' as defined here is somewhat unclear – he may instead be advocating for atomism version 2.)
[11] Markosian provides a more formal definition (1998, p. 223), derived from van Inwagen (1981,
p. 123): "For every material object M, if R is the region of space occupied by M at time t, and if
sub-R is any occupiable sub-region of R whatever, there exists a material object that occupies the
region sub-R at t."

As an additional reply, Markosian distinguishes between different kinds of 'part.' *Metaphysical parts* are actual proper parts, objects in their own right which come together to compose a larger object. By contrast, *conceptual parts* may or may not be actual proper parts, as they are just the sub-regions of the region occupied by the real object (plus the matter contained in those sub-regions). A genuinely simple object can have conceptual parts, but not metaphysical parts. And that is the situation with MaxCon simples.

It is in response to a further objection that Markosian introduces the object vs. stuff distinction. MaxCon simples could in theory be any sort of shape or size. So a statue of Tim Tebow[12] could be a MaxCon simple, being continuous and possessed of no spatially disconnected parts. Now imagine that the statue is manipulated such that its right arm moves but the rest stays stationary. Doesn't this entail that the right arm is a distinct proper part vis-à-vis the rest of the statue? After all, it is impossible for a single object to be both stationary and non-stationary (or more generally to accommodate simultaneously any incompatible properties), so it seems the only way to allow for this manipulation of the statue is to admit that it is composed of proper parts that are themselves objects. However, that is too quick; an alternative way of conceptualizing the situation is available, whereby

> talk about the motion of the arm of the statue can be translated into talk about the motion of the matter that fills the arm-shaped sub-region of the region occupied by the statue at any given time relative to the matter that fills the remaining sub-region of the region occupied by the statue at that time, in a way that does not commit us to saying that there are two objects involved in the case, one in motion relative to the other. (1998, p. 224)

For this reply to work, Markosian recognizes that he needs a real and irreducible distinction between objects and the matter, or 'stuff,' that constitutes those objects (irreducible because we are talking about simples here). Without this distinction in place, the arm would have to be regarded as a distinct object, as would any part of the statue that is capable of being moved without the rest of the statue moving along with it. But that would in turn imply the truth of DAUP, with all its counter-intuitive consequences.

What about a situation where two MaxCon simples become conjoined, forming one larger spatially continuous object? In this situation

---

[12] I take the liberty of updating Markosian's statue of Joe Montana.

Markosian says that the two former objects cease to exist, and a new object, a larger MaxCon simple, takes their place. Does this imply a sort of creation out of nothing, with something utterly new popping into existence? Thanks to the real distinction between an object and its constituent stuff, this need not be affirmed. True, a new object comes into existence, but it comes into existence out of the stuff of the previous objects, all of which stuff continues to exist just as it did before. Similarly, if a MaxCon simple is split apart, then what were formerly conceptual parts (spatially distinct stuff-filled sub-regions) become objects. New *objects* come into existence, but the same old *stuff* remains, just occupying two (or more) objects rather than one.[13]

Markosian (1998) provides further arguments for the possibility of MaxCon simples, and replies to further objections, which, in the interests of space, I must pass over here. However I should make some additional points concerning the nature of objects and stuff, which Markosian develops in his (2004). I will focus on what will prove relevant to the link with dispositionalism.

Markosian does not attempt to provide an analysis of 'object' or 'stuff,' or the relation that links them, taking these to be primitives. Still, they are primitives that we are familiar with in our everyday concepts and language (evident in our use of count nouns vs. mass nouns), and their ontology can be clarified. He relays some arguments in favour of the idea that an object and its stuff are not identical, arguments familiar from the 'constitution is not identity' literature. For instance, an object and its stuff can possess different modal properties, including diverse persistence conditions. (This was already made evident in the cases above of stuff surviving the destruction and generation of objects.) He also argues that there cannot be stuff without at least one object existing, and that any maximally continuous amount of stuff constitutes a simple object.

> I.e., if there is any matter at all, then there must also be at least one object. Moreover, if there is some matter, and that matter occupies a continuous region of space, and it is not the case that that region falls within a larger continuous region that is also filled with matter, then the matter in question constitutes a simple. (2004, p. 409)

---

[13] So do MaxCon simples count as divisible? If by 'divisible' one refers to the real possibility that an object might be made to go out of existence by a physical stimulus and be replaced by new objects constituted by the stuff that used to constitute the original object, then yes, MaxCon simples are divisible. But they are *not* divisible in the sense that we often think of composites as being divisible, where composites are divisible because the bonding relations obtaining between their actual proper parts can be eliminated, such that the composite object ceases to exist and all that remains is the objects that formerly composed it.

This latter point amounts to saying that any bounded (i.e., determinately shaped) portion of stuff that is spatially distinct from other such bounded portions constitutes an object. So while objects and stuff are not identical, they are inseparable – Markosian goes so far as to consider them mutually supervenient (2004, p. 414).[14] And an infallible mark of the presence of an object is the presence of stuff, insofar as that stuff is characterized by geometrical/structural categorical properties like determinate spatial extension (and therefore shape/structure/form and other notions entailed by determinate spatial extension) and is set off from other spatially distinct stuff.

The preceding should suffice for the explication and defence of premise 1 of my argument. Proceeding to premise 2, it should first be noted that on at least one version of categoricalism (relatively common in the 1960s and 1970s), the truthmaker for any true disposition-ascription will consist *solely* of a categorical property or set of categorical properties. Quine (1966, pp. 71–72) for example writes as follows:

> Advances in chemistry eventually redeem the solubility idea, but only in terms of a full-blown theory. We come to understand just what there is about the submicroscopic form and composition of a solid that enables water to dissolve it. Thenceforward, solubility can simply be equated to these explanatory traits. When we say of a lump that it would necessarily dissolve if in water, we can be understood as attributing to the lump those supposedly enumerated details of submicroscopic structure – those explanatory traits with which we are imagining solubility to have been newly equated.

This sort of point gains part of its force from the fact that solubility (like fragility and some other common examples of dispositions) is multiply realizable (the solubility of sugar in water is not realized in the same way as the solubility of aluminum in sulphuric acid) and not a fundamental property of anything. Dispositions like mass and charge resist such treatment. Moreover, Quinean-style categoricalism is vulnerable to some

---

[14] That's assuming of course that the stuff we're talking about is spatially continuous. Where stuff is discontinuous, it does not constitute an object/thing. As he puts it recently (2015, pp. 665–666):

> Stuff, as I understand it, is what things are made of. Think for example of a solid, homogenous, sphere. That's a thing. Now think of the region occupied by the sphere. That region is filled with stuff. (The very stuff that the sphere is made of, in fact.) Same with all the various subregions of the region occupied by the sphere: they're all filled with stuff, too. In general, stuff fills various regions of space, and some portions of stuff *constitute* things (like the portion of stuff that currently constitutes me), while others don't (like a random portion consisting of some stuff on the moon and the water in my glass).

classic pro-dispositionalist arguments, such as the Aristotelian standby related by Franklin (1986, pp. 62–63):

> Consider Democritus' attempt to reduce all properties of things to the shapes and movements of atoms. He proposed to explain the hardness of solids, for example, by the fact that the atoms of solids were hooked and so stuck to one another. In order to make the solid hard, however, the atoms must not only be hooked, but must retain their hooked shape when they come into contact with other atoms. That is, the hardness of the solid depends not only on the shape of its atoms but also on their rigidity. But rigidity is a disposition, namely the disposition to preserve shape when acted on in certain ways.

This example revolves around the need for dispositions to account for the stability of categorical properties, but examples could be multiplied showing that explanatory factors beyond mere categorical properties are needed to explain the behaviour of objects.

This point is now generally admitted by categoricalists, or at least by those categoricalists who are realists about causation (so excluding Humean regularity theorists from this generalization). This is why most categoricalists now adopt the view that dispositions are eliminable in favour of categorical properties + laws, which commitment gets us the second principal ontology of laws, *nomological necessitarianism*. Advocates of this ontology deny that the truthmakers for true disposition-ascriptions need include irreducible intrinsic dispositions. So the bonding of the hook-shaped 'atoms' could be accounted for by reference to the relevant shapes and to certain operative external laws of nature, without recourse to intrinsic causal powers.

In the face of this challenge, a number of replies have been pursued by dispositionalists. For instance, there is a good deal of literature that focuses on uncovering internal problems faced by the various versions of nomological necessitarianism.[15] Others focus on the idea that dispositionalism is a better fit with certain empirical findings in physics.[16] Still others defend against any form of categoricalism by arguing that categorical properties can themselves be dispensed with altogether as fundamental features of the world, such that all genuinely fundamental properties are dispositional.[17] Less popular has been the strategy of trying to show

---

[15] See Bird (2005; 2006), Handfield (2005), and Mumford (2004, ch. 6) for some examples of this strategy at work.

[16] See for instance Balashov (2002) and Suarez (2007), and of course the works of Mumford cited in the previous section.

[17] See for instance Bauer (2013), Bird (2007), Bostock (2008), and Coleman (2010).

that external laws cannot do all the work that dispositions do – and not because external laws are impossible,[18] but simply because there are some facts that require explanatory reference to intrinsic dispositions. That is precisely the strategy that becomes available when one reflects on the dispositionalist implications of MaxCon simples.

Let's begin by laying out the argument (an argument aimed at justifying premise 2 of the overarching argument presented at the beginning of this section):

Premise 1 If categoricalism is true (and dispositionalism false), then there are no irreducible intrinsic dispositional properties.

Premise 2 But stuff (as understood in Markosian's theory of MaxCon simples) is possessed of at least one irreducible intrinsic dispositional property: the capacity to take on new shapes.

Conclusion Therefore categoricalism is false (and dispositionalism true).

Premise 1 is a basic commitment of categoricalism, as noted earlier. According to categoricalists, the only real, irreducible sorts of property in existence are categorical; there are no intrinsic, irreducible causal powers. Premise 2 is the controversial premise. To justify it, it is necessary to show that the capacity of stuff to acquire new shape is not a capacity that can be reduced to stuff's categorical properties, nor reduced to its categorical properties + an extrinsic governing law or laws (the standard categoricalist strategies for reducing dispositions), but rather that this capacity is an irreducible intrinsic property possessed by stuff.

To that end: we have already seen Markosian's view that MaxCon simples can take on a variety of shapes and even sizes. Correspondingly, stuff (that from which a MaxCon simple is composed) can take on a variety of shapes. Given this openness to a range of different shapes, clearly no determinate, specific shape (rotundity or triangularity or whatnot) is essential to stuff. Yet though no specific shape is possessed essentially by stuff, for Markosian stuff can only exist qua shaped/bounded in such a way that it constitutes a MaxCon simple (or a continuous portion of a larger MaxCon simple). Stuff and object are inseparable (indeed he goes so far as to say they are mutually supervenient), which entails that stuff must always come shaped. No *particular* shape is essential to stuff, but it is essential that stuff have *some shape or other*. But how is this fact about stuff to be explained by the categoricalist?

---

[18] Given my advocacy of nomic dispositionalism in Chapter 2, *that* is certainly not a strategy I would wish to pursue.

There are two obvious categoricalist explanations:

(A)   *The fact that stuff must come shaped, but has no specific shape essentially, is explained by the application of an extrinsic law or laws to stuff. Laws make stuff essentially shaped.* This clearly won't work. If something is essentially x, then it is not x solely by virtue of external causal intervention (some distinct object acting upon it to grant it x). In other words, if it is part of something's very identity conditions that it be x, then nothing else can give it x; in order for a law (or anything else) to interact with something, that something must first exist, and ipso facto must exist with all its identity conditions in place. Extrinsic laws therefore cannot bestow essential traits. (For example, if an electron possesses negative charge essentially, then nothing distinct from it gives it negative charge.) But for Markosian, stuff's being some shape or other is essential to it. Therefore that feature of stuff cannot be bestowed on it by something else.[19] And indeed, the categoricalist had better hope this is true; after all, imagine a state of affairs in which stuff was not essentially shaped, but rather acquired shape via the application of an external cause governed by a law. That would imply that absent such extrinsic causal intervention, stuff could exist devoid of any shape, and hence devoid of any categorical properties. But the possibility of such a state of affairs would disprove catgoricalism.[20]

(B)   *The fact that stuff must come shaped, but has no specific shape essentially, is explained by the fact that stuff essentially possesses the*

---

[19] Note that this claim needs to be distinguished from a very different proposition: "if something is *necessarily* x, then it is not x solely by virtue of external intervention." There could perhaps be counterexamples to the latter proposition; imagine for instance the case of a necessarily existent, necessarily benevolent Leibnizian deity who in all possible worlds wills that Tim Tebow be a skilled football player. In such a scenario, Tebow would necessarily possess a property, *skill*, but would possess it solely by virtue of an external intervention. (I am borrowing here from Kit Fine's (1994) well-known distinction between essential properties – properties definitive of a thing's or kind's identity – and properties that something possesses by logical necessity but which do not form any part of its identity. The standard example is Socrates and his accompanying singleton set.)

[20] In making that last point I am adopting a few plausible background assumptions: if a fundamental entity lacks all categorical properties it must still possess some *other* sort of property, with the only other game in town being dispositions. This further assumes that no entity can exist wholly devoid of properties, wholly characterless. (This might be thought to conflict with substratum theory, but for the most part that is not the case, insofar as most substratum theorists maintain that substrata can only exist while instantiating some attribute or set of attributes. Moreover, I will argue in Chapter 5 that substratum theory itself either supports or entails dispositionalism.) Also I am assuming that something devoid of shape would lack all other geometrical/structural properties (like size), and, for reasons tying back to the previous Section 4.2, would also lack any other sort of categorical property, like an irreducible physical qualitative property.

irreducible intrinsic determinable categorical property 'shape'. This seems much more promising from the categoricalist's perspective. While the status of determinable properties as genuinely irreducible remains a matter of controversy, with some wishing to reduce determinables to determinates, realism about determinables is plausible and has been ably defended.[21] Moreover recourse to the determinable 'shape' – or something closely analogous like 'spatial form' – has the advantage of seeming to fit the bill perfectly: the essential possession of this determinable by stuff would explain why stuff must always possess some shape or other while yet not having any specific shape essentially. After all, to possess a determinable essentially means that the entity must always possess some determinate falling under that determinable,[22] while leaving open which of those determinates does the job.

I don't claim that (A) and (B) exhaust the categoricalist strategies for accommodating the data Markosian's MaxCon simples present us with, yet it is difficult to see what other strategies could be employed; no specific, determinate categorical property will help (for obvious reasons), and as we just saw in (A), laws won't help either. There isn't much else by way of additional, relevant ontological ingredients in the standard nomological necessitarian toolkit. If *determinate* categorical properties and laws of nature are both ruled out, *determinable* categorical properties seem like a good option, especially since the determinable 'shape' seems tailor-made to account for the relevant facts concerning stuff.

(B) is thus a prima facie reasonable way to go; yet as I will now try to show, (B) has the effect of driving one indirectly towards dispositionalism, insofar as there is a tight but heretofore unappreciated connection between dispositions and a certain class of determinables. To draw out this connection, it will help to begin by refuting two other potential connections one might try to make.

First, one might try to argue that a determinable categorical property *just is* a disposition, more precisely a multi-track disposition (a disposition with multiple manifestation conditions), on the grounds that for anything to have a determinable categorical property like 'shape' is ipso

---

[21] Advocates include Armstrong (1983; 1997), Christensen (2014), Elder (1996), Ellis (2001), Fales (1982; 1990), Franklin (2015), Johansson (2000), Tweedale (1984), and Wilson (2011; 2012).

[22] That is, anything coloured is always some colour or other, anything shaped is always some shape or other, etc. – no real entity in nature is *just* generically 'coloured' or 'shaped.' That at least is the broad consensus view; Wilson (2013) though challenges that consensus.

facto to have an openness, a *capacity*, to possess any of the determinates falling under the range of that determinable (in this case properties like rotundity, triangularity, etc.). On this view, to have the determinable 'shape' is just to have the power to become round or triangular, etc. But this won't work, insofar as it seems there are beings which possess some specific determinate shape essentially. That is, it seems there are entities genuinely possessed of the determinable categorical property 'shape' but which have no resultant capacity to take on other shapes while remaining in existence. Consider for example any number of chemical kinds, a water molecule for instance; these are often thought to have their determinate geometrical structure essentially, such that if the structure were altered the molecule would cease to exist as that kind of molecule. Or consider biological kinds, like a porcupine. A porcupine possesses the determinable categorical 'shape,' but that does not bestow upon it the capacity to acquire any determinate of that determinable while remaining in existence. Bend a porcupine too far out of shape, and it will simply be destroyed. So the attempt to draw a tight connection between the irreducible intrinsic reality of determinable categorical properties and the irreducible intrinsic reality of dispositions by simply *identifying* determinables with a certain sort of disposition will not work.

Second, one might try for a slightly subtler connection by arguing that while a determinable categorical property is not *identical* to a disposition, nevertheless it always *entails the presence of* a disposition. On this view, for something to have a determinable categorical property like 'shape' is ipso facto to have an openness, a *capacity*, to possess any of the determinates falling under the range of that determinable (in this case properties like rotundity, triangularity, etc.), not because the determinable is a power, but because it entails the presence of a power. Thus while the determinable is genuinely distinct from the disposition, the presence of the former necessitates the presence of the latter. However, this second attempt at drawing a connection is flawed for precisely the same reason as the first attempt, insofar as the possession of a determinable will not always entail an openness to the possession of any of a range of determinates: that openness will fail to occur whenever the entity in question possesses one determinate of that determinable essentially. (This is an important point the categoricalist strategy **(B)** above failed to recognize explicitly.) And as we've just seen, some entities possess one determinate shape essentially, such that they cannot change determinate shape while remaining in existence as that same entity.

Having laid aside those first two attempts to draw a connection between determinables and dispositions, we can now look at a third and see why it actually works for present purposes. The goal again is to show that stuff is possessed of at least one irreducible intrinsic dispositional property, thus establishing the truth of premise 2. And to do that, one need only point out that while stuff possesses the irreducible intrinsic determinable categorical property 'shape' essentially (recall again that for Markosian stuff must always exist with some shape or other), *there is no determinate shape that it possesses essentially*. So, although one cannot *universally* equate determinables with dispositions (the first option), nor *universally* claim that determinables entail the presence of a disposition (as in the second), one can properly claim that when a determinable is possessed by something essentially but no specific determinate of that determinable is possessed essentially, that determinable is either *identical with* an irreducible capacity to take on different determinates, or, more plausibly, *entails the presence of* a distinct and irreducible capacity to take on different determinates. And that is precisely the state of affairs obtaining of Markosian's stuff. Stuff is essentially shaped but possesses no determinate shape essentially, such that the relevant determinable 'shape' is either identical with a capacity to take on new shapes, or (much more likely) at least implies the presence of such a capacity. This is a capacity possessed irreducibly and intrinsically by stuff – it cannot be reduced or eliminated by reference to the usual ontological tools of nomological necessitarianism, namely extrinsic laws and other categorical properties. There is in fact no room for extrinsic laws or other factors to come into play here: the mere presence of the essentially possessed determinable + lack of an essential determinate entails the presence of the power, with no room leftover for an extrinsic law to step in to do the modal heavy lifting. In other words, the presence of the entailed power is just as essential as the presence of the determinable doing the entailing, and as we saw in the discussion of (**A**) above, essential intrinsic properties cannot be bestowed by extrinsic laws.

I have indicated that I favour the model of the determinable 'shape' entailing a distinct capacity rather than being identical with that capacity. I prefer the former both because it strikes me as prima facie more plausible (categorical properties and powers seem to be genuinely different sorts of property), but also because there will be content to the entailed capacity that will not flow from the categorical property alone, that must somehow be specified in an alternate manner. That is, the categorical property 'shape,' when possessed essentially but with no accompanying essential determinate, directly entails that the entity possessed of 'shape' must have the power to take on new determinate shapes; however, it does not of itself entail the full associated content of that power, e.g., what sorts of causal stimuli will prompt the change in shape, under what conditions, with what ceteris paribus clauses, etc. An essentially possessed categorical determinable property with no accompanying essential determinate entails a power to take on new determinates, but is best thought of as genuinely distinct from that entailed power, because that power will have to possess additional content not specified by the entailing determinable.[23]

That last passage might sound rather technical, but the basic idea is commonsensical: consider silly putty as an analogue for stuff. Silly putty is analogous to stuff insofar as it must possess some shape or other, but has no determinate shape essentially. That is, silly putty has a categorical determinable property essentially, but no accompanying essential determinate of that determinable. This directly entails that silly putty has the capacity to take on new determinate shapes. But the determinable 'shape,' while directly entailing the presence of that capacity, does not of itself determine the entire content of that capacity – thus 'shape' does not determine the degree of force required to manipulate silly putty effectively, does not determine which environmental conditions impact this manipulability (e.g., extreme cold temperatures), etc. As such, 'shape' is best seen as genuinely distinct from that capacity.

At this point one might ask: why not just run this argument for dispositionalism on silly putty (or some other comparable macro-level stuff), rather than bringing in the whole apparatus of MaxCon simples? Because one can plausibly argue that silly putty (and most other analogous macro-level 'stuffs') are fully reducible to collections of individual particles, such that there is really no entity there to possess (uncontroversially) any property, let alone an intrinsic essential determinable. By contrast, MaxCon simples, and the fundamental stuff out of which they are composed, are not thus reducible, such that stuff can (if real) uncontroversially be the bearer of properties, including intrinsic essential determinables.

[23] And what fills in that additional content? Since it must be another essential intrinsic aspect of the entity, I would argue that the best candidate is the entity's *natural-kind essence*. That natural-kind essence grounds the essential presence of the determinable and likewise fixes the conditions under which the non-essential determinates of that determinable are changed. I would in fact wish to argue that the need to posit an intrinsic ground of these facts constitutes evidence for the reality of an irreducible, overarching natural-kind essence of the sort defended by essentialists like Ellis (2001), Lowe (2006), and Oderberg (2007). We will discuss this sort of essentialism further in Chapters 5 and 6.

As a final point, I should observe that while I have framed this discussion of extended simples mostly in terms of the dialectic between nomological necessitarianism and dispositionalism, I believe the argument should also carry weight for the regularity theorist, or at least for those regularity theorists who admit the reality of irreducible determinable properties.[24] The apparent entailment relation between the determinable 'shape' and the openness to take on determinate shapes seems sufficiently tight and intuitively robust that I would like to think it might weaken Humeans' resolve to maintain their standard denial of necessary connections between properties. Moreover this seems a case where the modal force is so clearly rooted in the nature of the relevant irreducible intrinsic property that getting rid of it by reference to counterpart relations obtaining between possible worlds may be unappealing. Naturally the regularity theorist could avoid all of this by rejecting outright the possibility of extended simples, and thereby the possibility of Markosian's 'stuff' and the powers it appears to entail. But that would not impact the argument, which merely sets out to show the conditional: *if* MaxCon extended simples exist, *then* dispositionalism is true.

4.4   Conclusion

To recap: in the introduction Section 4.1 I introduced the four main competing theories of material composition: atomism version 1, atomism version 2, the theory of gunk, and the theory of extended simples. In Section 4.2 I briefly recounted Mumford's argument for a probabilistic connection between atomism version 1 and dispositionalism, and offered additional support to his argument by reference to worries facing alleged categorical properties falling outside the paradigm examples of geometrical/structural properties. Then in Section 4.3 I put forward an argument to the effect that the theory of extended simples (in the form of its most thoroughly developed recent version, Markosian's MaxCon account) entails dispositionalism.

If the preceding is plausible, it follows that the committed categoricalist should be leery of atomism version 1, and must reject the theory of

---

[24] Insofar as many regularity theorists are nominalists, one might suppose that for them at least no such admission would be feasible. That however depends on whether determinable properties must be conceived of as universals, or whether they might instead be understood as tropes (or in some other manner consistent with nominalism). While most of the literature on irreducible determinables (pro or con) does frame them in terms of universals, there are some who discuss them from explicitly nominalist perspectives, including Denby (1999) and Funkhouser (2006; 2014).

extended simples. This leaves atomism version 2 and the theory of gunk as the remaining options. And I would suggest that between those two options, atomism version 2 should probably be dropped out of contention. I cannot argue for this in detail here, so I will just draw attention to what has historically been widely seen as the theory's achilles' heel, a core objection that was already adverted to in the course of laying out the theories in Section 4.1: it seems intuitively obvious that an extended object is subject to division, either by way of splitting into smaller entities or by way of annihilating one portion of the object (the left half, say) while leaving the other in existence. The notion that an extended object could be absolutely immune to such operations, such that not even an omnipotent God could perform one or the other, seems exceedingly counter-intuitive. Granted, the extent to which we should trust our intuitions in such matters (especially our modal intuitions) is controversial. But if we give them any weight at all, then I would suggest that for most, the intuitive pull against atomism version 2 will be strong. As such, the best option for the categoricalist will be to adopt the theory of gunk. For categoricalists already inclined towards that theory, this chapter can be seen as having the virtue of lending it novel support. For those who find the notion of gunk problematic, on the other hand, the upshot of the chapter will be a novel disjunctive argument against categoricalism (i.e., of the four major theories of material composition only two are potentially workable, and they either support or entail dispositionalism).

CHAPTER 5

Dispositionalism and Substance Ontology

5.1 Introduction

A question of core interest within both physics and metaphysics can be formulated as follows: fundamentally, why do objects behave the way they do? Or, phrased differently: what most fundamentally accounts for why things act and react in the ways they do? Seeing as how this question pertains both to substances ('objects' or 'things') and to the explanations for their behaviour, which science typically frames in terms of laws, it follows that providing a complete answer to it will involve addressing two closely related questions: (A) What is the correct account of laws? (B) What is the correct account of physical substance? Consequently these two questions are central areas of focus within the metaphysics of science. Previous chapters have already touched on them, with Chapter 2 presenting an account of laws, Chapter 3 touching on the ontology of objects (by way of the debate over whether they can be eliminated from fundamental ontology) and Chapter 4 doing likewise (by way of the debate over whether objects are infinitely divisible). In the present chapter I will be drawing out some additional, largely neglected connections between the metaphysics of laws and of objects, with the aim of showing that each of the four major competing substance ontologies – substratum theory, bundle theory, primitive substance theory, and hylomorphism – supports dispositionalism.

As a necessary preliminary I'll need to summarize briefly the major competing accounts of law and of substance. In the former case I will focus on four versions of dispositionalism, versions arising out of the different ways of thinking about the relationship between dispositional and categorical properties (something we have not looked at so far in this book). In the latter case I will lay out the four major substance ontologies.

To begin with laws: as we have seen already, aside from dispositionalism the major competitors here are regularity theory and nomological
necessitarianism. On regularity theory the only irreducible intrinsic properties possessed by physical objects are categorical in nature, laws are
purely descriptive of natural regularities, and those regularities have no
further ontological explanation or grounding. (Recall that categorical
properties are typically thought of as *non-dispositional*, and include such
paradigm cases as shape, size, spatial extension, spatial boundaries, and
perhaps qualitative properties like colour (for anyone who takes colour to
be an irreducible feature of reality). Those who maintain that the only
irreducible intrinsic properties possessed by physical objects are categorical in nature are known as *categoricalists*.) For defences of regularity
theory see for instance Barker (2013), Beebee (2011), Miller (2015), and
Smart (2013).

On nomological necessitarianism the only irreducible intrinsic properties possessed by physical objects are categorical in nature, but laws are
robustly real and prescriptive of natural regularities rather than merely
descriptive of them. While their precise formulations differ, proponents
of this approach include Armstrong (1983; 1997), Dretske (1977), Fales
(1990; 1993), Foster (2004), Laudisa (2015), Latham (2011), Maudlin
(2007), Psillos (2006; 2009), and Tooley (1977). I should also draw
attention to the important accounts of Lange (2004; 2009; 2009a) and
Whittle (2009), according to which laws are reducible to primitive
counterfactual truths or primitive functional facts, respectively. Their
accounts clearly do not fit neatly within nomological necessitarianism,
yet they seem closer to that theory than to either regularity theory or
dispositionalism.

Dispositionalism is of course the theory that some or all of the intrinsic properties possessed by objects are dispositional in nature. Note the
'some or all' – one of the prominent debates amongst dispositionalists
concerns whether categorical properties are irreducibly real, and if so
how they relate to dispositions. That debate has given rise to four distinct
versions of dispositionalism, varying according to how this relationship
between dispositional and categorical properties is understood:

–   On the **mixed view** dispositions cannot be reduced to categorical
    properties, nor can they be eliminated in favour of them. And the
    reverse holds as well: categorical properties are neither reducible to
    nor eliminable in favour of powers. Rather, dispositional and
    categorical properties are both included in the inventory of

irreducible kinds of natural property. Advocates of this view include for instance Cross (2005), Ellis (2001; 2002; 2009), Molnar (2003), and Oderberg (2007).

- On *pan-dispositionalism* (also called *dispositional monism*), dispositions are the only irreducible kind of natural property. What we think of as 'categorical properties' either don't really exist, are reducible to dispositional properties, or are actually dispositions themselves (contrary to initial impressions). See for instance Bauer (2013), Bird (2007), Bostock (2008), Coleman (2010), Mumford and Anjum (2011), and Shoemaker (1980).

- For advocates of the *identity theory*, no property is *just* dispositional or *just* categorical; rather, every property is essentially both. In other words, every sort of irreducible natural property has both dispositional and categorical identity conditions. Advocates of versions of this view include Heil (2003; 2005; 2012), Martin (1997), Martin and Heil (1999), Ingthorsson (2013), Jacobs (2011), Schroer (2010), and Strawson (2008).

- Finally, *neutral monism* is the view that our conceptual distinction between dispositional versus categorical properties does not actually map onto a real, objective division in nature. In fact the genuinely irreducible natural properties are, in and of themselves, neither dispositional nor categorical; they are a distinct sort of property, the essence of which is conveyed by us using both dispositional and categorical *concepts*. See Bartels (2013) and Mumford (1998, ch. 8).[1]

So far the arguments of this book have been neutral between those four versions of dispositionalism. However the necessity of laying out these different versions will become apparent below, insofar as one of the substance ontologies under discussion not only supports dispositionalism, but one of those four specific versions.

Moving on then to substance ontology, in the current literature there are four principal views concerning the nature of substance:

- *Substratum theory* is the idea that a substance is a combination of properties (whether conceived as universals or tropes) and a substratum (or 'bare particular,' or 'thin particular'). The properties

---

[1] One is tempted to cite Lowe (2001; 2006) as another neutral monist, but his version of dispositionalism is so unique that to classify it as falling within any of these four would be contentious. See Dumsday (2016a) for discussion of the difficulties involved in classifying's Lowe's account.

inhere[2] in the substratum and are thereby held together, resulting in a whole substance that is both a unified entity and possessed of distinct intrinsic features.[3] Besides functioning as the subject of or ground for properties (thereby unifying them as components of a single substance), the substratum is also what preserves the continuity of a thing through radical change. A substance can exchange some or even all of its properties for others because the substratum is there to function as a source of continuity. Finally, for at least some of those substratum theorists who take properties to be universals, the substratum is that by which a substance is individuated and/or concretized (i.e., the substratum guarantees that the substance as a whole, with its various universals, is a concrete rather than abstract entity and/or is differentiated from every other concrete substance, even those instantiating the same universals). Most maintain that the substratum cannot exist on its own, but must always be paired with one or more properties. Advocates of substratum theory include Armstrong (1997), Connolly (2015), LaBossiere (1994), Martin (1980), Moreland (1998; 2001; 2013), Pickavance (2009; 2014), Vallicella (2000), and Wildman (2015).[4]

— *Bundle theory* is the idea that the intrinsic nature of a substance (or, perhaps, what we *think* of as a substance) consists wholly of properties (whether universals or tropes) that are somehow robustly/reliably grouped together (whether by compresence or co-instantiation or mereological fusion, etc.). Properties do not need to inhere in anything else, like a substratum, but can in principle exist freestanding. (Though whether there can ever be a *single* freestanding property or whether they must always come in combinations is a

---

[2] In place of 'by that *inherence in* one and the same substratum' some would say instead 'by being *borne by* one and the same substratum' or 'by being *instantiated in* one and the same substratum' or 'by being *exemplified by* one and the same substratum.' For now let's take these common turns of phrase as synonymous. In Section (5.3) we will cover two importantly distinct understandings of instantiation in the context of substratum theory.

[3] While occasionally substratum theorists will refer to the substratum as itself the substance or object, it is more common to think of the substratum as a metaphysical *component* of a substance. An individual electron for instance would be seen as a substance constructed out of its substratum and the set of properties – mass, charge, etc. – inhering in it. Note too that some substratum theorists (notably Armstrong (1997)) prefer to speak of 'states of affairs' rather than 'substances' as the products of substrata + properties.

[4] Note that while it is more common for advocates of substrata to assign them the multiple explanatory roles I have just listed, some restrict their functions more narrowly. For instance on Martin's nominalist substratum theory the substratum's central role is to be the subject for properties (tropes) and naturally it plays no role in individuation. By contrast, for Moreland its sole function is individuation.

matter of debate within bundle theory.) See Campbell (1990), Denkel (1996; 1997), Ellis (2009), Giberman (2014), Keinänen (2011), O'Leary-Hawthorne and Cover (1998), Paul (2002), Robb (2005), Shiver (2014), and Simons (1994). Note that while I am here identifying bundle theory as a substance ontology, bundle theorists differ amongst themselves as to whether they are giving an account of the true nature of substance, or instead are eliminating substance altogether (at least when taken as a fundamental category).[5]

– Advocates of ***primitive substance theory*** maintain that a substance is *not* made up out of more foundational metaphysical ingredients. Neither substrata nor properties exist as more foundational constituents of a concrete thing; rather, 'substance' is itself the foundational category, substrata simply do not exist, and properties (whether universals or tropes) exist only as modifications of a substance. For instance an individual electron *just is* the instantiation of the substance-universal/kind 'electron' or 'electronhood'; it is not a construction out of more basic components and is thus not reducible to any collection of properties, even those taken to belong to it essentially.[6] Consult Broackes (2006), Ellis (2001; 2002), Fales (1990), Hoffman (2012), Loux (1974; 1978; 2002), Lowe (1994; 1998; 2000; 2006; 2012; 2013), Macdonald (2005), and Wiggins (2001). Heil (2003; 2012) also advocates for primitive substance theory, but his formulation is somewhat different insofar as he situates it within a nominalist ontology.

– ***Hylomorphism*** shares with primitive substance theory a commitment to the idea that every individual substance is the instantiation of a substance-universal/kind or (on the traditional terminology of hylomorphism) *substantial form*. From that shared base it adds the

[5] Relatedly: the four substance ontologies being summarized here are generally taken to be providing accounts of how to understand the precise metaphysics of substance; i.e., assuming that we already have some workable idea of what it would be to be a substance (whether defined in terms of existential independence or property-possession or fundamentality with respect to other ontological categories or some combination, etc.), they attempt to provide an account of the basic internal makeup of a substance. Insofar as these four seem to allow some neutrality with respect to the much-debated question of how best to define substancehood (such that two substratum theorists can disagree on whether to define substancehood in terms of existential independence while both remaining substratum theorists), and insofar as I only need work with these four in order to run the overarching argument of this chapter, I need not delve into the background debate over the definition of substancehood here. While a number of the sources already cited do discuss the issue of definition (as do several cited below), works targeted specifically at the issue include Ayers (1991), Denby (2007), Schnieder (2006), and Toner (2010).

[6] Primitive substance theory is thus committed to a fairly robust form of natural-kind essentialism of the sort noted towards the end of Section 4.3.

idea that substantial form is instantiated in (or, on the traditional terminology, *actualizes*) an underlying basic potency for the reception of substantial form. That underlying capacity persists in existence through the acquisition and loss of substantial forms; as such it amounts to a power to be transformed into objects belonging to other natural kinds. This power is viewed not as a property but as a substantial principle, traditionally known as *prime matter*. On hylomorphism then, every physical substance is a compound of two irreducible components: substantial form and prime matter, where the latter is essentially a *capacity to become a new kind of substance* via the reception of substantial form. (Hylomorphism thus has the interesting consequence of positing that dispositions cross-cut the ontological categories of 'property' and of 'substance' – there exist both dispositional properties and dispositional substantial principles.) To relate it back to our first theory, prime matter is vaguely akin to a substratum, since it plays a role in individuation (though a role rather different from that played by the substratum) and persistence, in particular persistence through changes in natural-kind membership. However, unlike standard accounts of substrata, prime matter does not function to unify the properties of a substance – that is part of the explanatory role of substantial form, which is taken both to entail and unite the essential properties of a thing. Historically there have been a variety of versions of hylomorphism, differing on a number of points,[7] but today most proponents of hylomorphism within substance ontology are either self-identified Thomists or heavily influenced by Thomism, and so defend the Thomistic formulation. These include Bobik (1961; 1965; 1998), Brower (2014), Clarke (2001), Feser (2014), Goyette (2002), Madden (2013), Oderberg (2002; 2005; 2007), Pruss (2013), and Toner (2011).[8]

---

[7] For example, there was much debate over whether prime matter can exist on its own or must always be paired with substantial form; whether a substance can have only one substantial form at a time, or several; whether prime matter is directly receptive only of substantial form or whether it can also directly receive properties, etc. See Pasnau (2011) for an overview of various debates on hylomorphism within mediaeval and early modern Scholasticism. Among the various Scholastic systems, Scotistic hylomorphism was among the more important and persistent competitors to the Thomistic version. See Cross (1998) for an in-depth account of Scotus' hylomorphism. A less technical presentation may be found in Bettoni (1961).

[8] Hylomorphism in the context of substance ontology should be distinguished from the quite different notions of hylomorphism recently deployed within the philosophy of mind, the metaphysics of special composition, and the ontology of artifacts. Contributions to those latter literatures include Evnine (2016), Fine (1999), Jaworski (2016), Johnston (2006), and Koslicki (2008).

Much more could of course be said by way of explicating the four versions of dispositionalism and the four major substance ontologies, and a really thorough review of them would require delving into the major arguments for and against each. But in the interests of space, the preceding will have to suffice.

Turning again to the relationship between laws and substance ontology: dispositionalists have been known to pair that theory of laws with each of the four main substance ontologies. For instance, Heil (2003; 2012) is a dispositionalist primitive substance theorist; Ellis (2001; 2002) had been a dispositionalist primitive substance theorist but in his (2009) converted to being a dispositionalist bundle theorist; Martin (1980) was a dispositionalist substratum theorist; and Oderberg (2007) is a dispositionalist hylomorphist.[9] None employs dispositionalism to argue for their favoured substance ontology or vice versa. (Similar diversity exists with respect to the other main ontologies of law and of substance; among nomological necessitarians for instance, Armstrong (1997) was a substratum theorist and Fales (1990) is a primitive substance theorist.) Prima facie then, one might incline to the view that theories about law and theories about substance function largely independently, and that this diversity of combinations indicates a lack of entailment relations between the various positions.

It is time to curtail this sunny ecumenism, for in fact these debates are more tightly interwoven than one might think from the preceding short survey of the current landscape. One might argue for this in various ways, but our focus will of course be on dispositionalism. In the remainder of this chapter I will concentrate on defending premise 1 of the following argument:

Premise 1 If any one of the four main substance ontologies is true, then dispositionalism is probably true.
Premise 2 At least one of the four main substance ontologies is true.
Conclusion Therefore dispositionalism is probably true.

Provided one adheres to any of the four main substance ontologies, the end result will be a novel argument for the probable truth of dispositionalism. But one could of course turn this modus ponens into a modus tollens, leading to the conclusion that it is not the case that any one of the four main substance ontologies is true. As such the chapter should still be of

---

[9] Or, to be more precise: Heil (2003; 2012) is an *identity theory* dispositionalist primitive substance theorist; Ellis (2001; 2002) was a *mixed view* dispositionalist primitive substance theorist but in his (2009) converted to being a *mixed view* dispositionalist bundle theorist; Martin (1980) defended *identity theory* dispositionalism paired with substratum theory; and Oderberg (2007) advocates *mixed view* dispositionalism along with hylomorphism.

considerable interest to categoricalists, providing them with the important result that they should either come up with a new substance ontology (one consistent with the plausible rejection of dispositionalism), or reject the irreducible reality of substances (perhaps by adopting one of the versions of eliminativist ontic structural realism discussed in Chapter 3).[10]

Each of the remaining sections of this chapter will focus on one of the four substance ontologies, defending premise 1 of the argument step by step. In the brief review above I laid out the four theories in order of familiarity – I suspect most readers are quite familiar with substratum theory and bundle theory (these being staples of undergraduate classes in analytic metaphysics) and perhaps a bit less familiar with primitive substance theory and hylomorphism. The arrangement below is different: hylomorphism, substratum theory, bundle theory, and primitive substance theory. I discuss hylomorphism first because its link with dispositionalism is uncontroversial and can be laid out quite briefly. Substratum theory is treated next, and the discussion there will build on one of the notions brought up concerning hylomorphism (specifically the idea that a disposition can cross-cut ontological categories). Bundle theory and primitive substance theory follow.

I will make no attempt to defend premise 2 ("at least one of the four main substance ontologies is true"), for several reasons: (a) arguably it is sufficient for present purposes to rely on the broad authority of the current and historical literature in metaphysics, which has settled on these four substance ontologies as the most promising options; (b) the task of trying to show that there are no other plausible alternatives besides these four most-discussed theories would be a daunting one, and I don't see any feasible way of accomplishing it here[11]; (c) as noted, I want this

---

[10] And of course some can sidestep the entire dialectic; ostrich nominalists for example deny the reality of *any* sort of property (whether categorical or dispositional and whether universal or trope), and so fall entirely outside the debate between categoricalists and dispositionalists. Consequently they are not really a party to the present discussion.

[11] Though I suppose one could attempt an argument to show that these four options exhaust the range of possibilities, with something like the following rough line of reasoning: *either substances are irreducibly real or they aren't. Say they are. Then they are either basic items in ontology ('basic' in the sense of not being composed of more primitive ontological ingredients) or not. This gives us the choice between primitive substance theory (where they are basic) and the rest. Say we reject primitive substance theory. Then the question becomes, granting that substances are composites of more primitive ontological ingredients, what could those ingredients be? Presumably two such ingredients would be properties and relations. But are those the only ingredients? If we say yes, then we arrive at bundle theory. If we say no (perhaps because we think that instantiated properties need grounds, something they must inhere in or belong to), then we have to ask what the further ingredient might be, and then the debate would be between substrata and prime matter (i.e., a ground-for-properties that is intrinsically particular and thereby automatically individuated vs. a ground-for-properties for which a further story about individuation is needed).* This rough line of reasoning is of course open to attack on multiple fronts, but perhaps something like it might work.

chapter (and of course the book as a whole) to be of interest to categoricalists. Perhaps I can encourage such interest by making explicit the fact
that this discussion (and others in the book) need not be seen as inherently inimical to categoricalism. Favouring as I do one of the four prominent substance ontologies, personally I do see the present chapter as
assisting dispositionalism; but I am just as happy to frame the discussion
simply as an exploration of the implications of dispositionalism, and to
invite categoricalists to develop the modus tollens alternative to my
modus ponens.

5.2   Hylomorphism and Dispositionalism

From the brief explication of hylomorphism above, the reader will
already have the general idea concerning its link to dispositionalism, but
it is worth making the point explicitly:

Premise 1 If hylomorphism requires a commitment to the reality of
prime matter and prime matter is a sort of disposition, then
hylomorphism entails dispositionalism.

Premise 2 Hylomorphism requires a commitment to the reality of
prime matter and prime matter is a sort of disposition.

Conclusion Therefore hylomorphism entails dispositionalism.

That hylomorphism requires a commitment to the reality of prime matter is uncontroversial. What it is to *be* a hylomorphist (at least in the
context of substance ontology) is to affirm that physical substances are
compounds of substantial form and prime matter. Moreover hylomorphists regard prime matter as a sort of disposition, namely an irreducible
potency or capacity for the reception of new substantial form. Given the
rough definition of dispositionalism laid out in the opening of Chapter 1
("dispositionalism is the view that there exist irreducible dispositions,
also called 'powers' or 'capacities' or 'potencies,' etc."), it would seem
obvious that hylomorphism entails dispositionalism.

   Still, some might resist that entailment on grounds that dispositionalism is a view solely about *properties*, and prime matter is not thought of
as a property by advocates of hylomorphism but rather as a *substantial
principle*. In Chapter 1, I had briefly noted that the question of whether
dispositions are necessarily properties is among the questions up for
debate in contemporary dispositionalism. Advocates of hylomorphism
take a stance on this: for them, powers cross-cut ontological categories.
On hylomorphism, most powers are properties while at least one other

power (prime matter) is an intrinsic component of physical substance without thereby being a property. Prime matter is the capacity to become a new kind of substance (via the reception of new substantial form), and as such is a dispositional *substantial principle* rather than a dispositional *property*. The basic idea that dispositions might belong to members of ontological categories other than that of 'property' is of course one we have encountered in this book already. Recall that in Chapter 3 we saw proponents of ontic structural realism like French (2006) and Esfeld (2009) putting forward the claim that fundamental relations are of themselves inherently dispositional, such that in their view 'disposition' at the very least cross-cuts the ontological categories of property and relation, or even applies *only* to the category of relation. So in advocating a cross-cutting formulation of dispositionalism, contemporary hylomorphists at least have some prominent company in the recent metaphysics of science literature. (Consult Jaeger (2014) for more on the cross-cutting aspect of hylomorphism. We'll return to this issue in the next section, since substratum theory will also be shown to be committed to cross-cutting.)

At any rate, *if* they are right and hylomorphism is true then so is dispositionalism. That entailment is all I need for present purposes. The aim is not to defend hylomorphism but simply to show that hylomorphism entails dispositionalism. (Regrettably, in the case of the other three substance ontologies the support for dispositionalism is weaker than entailment, such that the overall argument for dispositionalism laid out in the previous section has to be formulated in probabilistic terms.)

5.3   Substratum Theory and Dispositionalism

There have been nominalist substratum theorists (notably Martin (1980)), but most proponents of substratum theory have been realists about universals. This is unsurprising, insofar as one of the core justifications for substratum theory has been its alleged utility in providing a principle of individuation and/or concretization for universals. That is, by reference to substrata one can supposedly explain how it is that objects can possess all of the same sorts of intrinsic properties while remaining distinct individuals (e.g., how electron x and electron y can possess all the same sorts of intrinsic properties – the same negative charge, the same precise rest mass, the same spin, etc. – while still being distinct from each other) and, relatedly, one can explain how those *abstract* universals can be present to (in some sense of 'present to') the *concrete* realm of physical nature.[12] Substrata are inherently particular and concrete, and universals relate to the field of particular concreta through instantiation/participation/exemplification.[13] Since the explanatory role of substratum theory vis-à-vis realist accounts of universals has been such a prominent feature of discussions surrounding it (whether pro or con), for the most part in this section I will presuppose a realist formulation of substratum theory. However at least part of the argument below will also apply to nominalist substratum theory; I'll flag it when we arrive.

I should observe too that in this section my principal categoricalist dialogue partner is not regularity theory but nomological necessitarianism. That is, I am trying to show that substratum theory supports dispositionalism, but it will become obvious along the way that in doing so I am assuming the irreducible reality of causation (and the corresponding rationality of seeking out causal explanations), which regularity theorists either actively deny or remain sceptical of. Moreover, both historically and in the current literature regularity theorists have often tended towards one or another version of nominalism, so the fact that for much of this section I assume the falsity of nominalism will also render it less interesting to many regularity theorists. Finally, insofar as many regularity theorists are motivated at least in part by empiricist epistemological commitments, and insofar as substrata are prima facie inherently unobservable, regularity theorists have additional reason to be suspicious of substrata.[14]

Before presenting the argument, we need a bit of additional background: one of the longstanding debates among substratum theorists (and within metaphysics more generally) concerns the nature of the instantiation relation and the way in which it connects universals to

---

[12] While I say 'relatedly,' some would say either 'equivalently' or 'by entailment,' since some would claim that individuation is either identical to concretization or at least implies it. Take my 'relatedly' as neutral between those views. (The difference of opinion here rests at least in part on further issues in background ontology, notably the question of whether all abstracta are universals or whether there are also abstract individuals. If there are abstract individuals – the abstract haecceity of Socrates for instance – then the substratum's roles of individuator and concretizer may come apart in their case.)

[13] Note that some in the literature distinguish between these terms, whereas others treat them as synonyms. I will follow the latter practice. Note too that many deny that instantiation is literally a relation, preferring to conceptualize it as a 'non-relational tie,' by way of avoiding Bradley's regress. I do not wish to take a stance on that question, but for ease of reference I will call it a relation.

[14] On the other hand, some prominent empiricists have been substratum theorists (notably Locke). For more on the dialectic between empiricism and substratum theory see Loux (2002, pp. 102–103 and 119–121).

particulars. While there are of course a variety of debates surrounding instantiation, the one that is relevant here is that between so-called *relational* versus *constituent* ontologies. The precise nature of this distinction is contested, but on relational ontologies universals exist separately from particulars. Universals are not 'in' things, whether spatially or in some other *literal* sense of 'in.' Concrete objects have the properties they do because their substrata stand in the appropriate relation to transcendent universals – namely instantiation/participation/exemplification, where that is conceived of as a purely extrinsic relation. For instance, particular electron x has negative charge insofar as the substratum of x is a relatum standing in the instantiation relation, where the other relatum is the *transcendent* universal 'negative charge.' That transcendent universal exists independently, irrespective of whether or not it happens to be instantiated. Relational ontology is commonly thought to have its historical roots in Plato (rightly or wrongly). According to constituent ontology, by contrast, universals exist immanently in concrete objects, either spatially or in some other *literal* sense of 'in.' Particular electron x has negative charge insofar as the substratum of x is a relatum standing in the instantiation relation, where the other relatum is the *immanent* universal 'negative charge,' which immanent universal cannot exist uninstantiated. Constituent ontology is commonly thought to have its historical roots in Aristotle (rightly or wrongly).[15]

The debate between relational ontology and constituent ontology is longstanding and ongoing; it is so longstanding, in fact, that participants sometimes feel the need to encourage a large helping of epistemic humility in discussing it. Loux (2006, p. 212) writes:

> Finally, one might think that there are decisive reasons for favoring one of the two approaches over the other. Certainly, proponents of the two views try to convince us that this is so. It is in this spirit that relational ontologists accuse those constituent ontologists who make abstract entities constituents of concrete particulars of a category mistake. In the same

---

[15] For further explication of these two views see Armstrong (1989, ch. 5), Koons and Pickavance (2015, ch. 5), Loux (2006), van Inwagen (2011; 2016), and Wolterstorff (1970; 1991). Note that an actual Aristotelian, as an advocate of hylomorphism, would formulate the view in terms of prime matter rather than substrata. Note too that van Inwagen's version of relational ontology is importantly distinct from the standard one just provided – besides formulating the view independently of substratum theory, he maintains that although concrete objects stand in extrinsic relations to Platonic abstracta, those relations do not explain why those concrete objects are characterized by the properties we associate with those abstracta. For him, the fact of a particular electron's having negative charge is not subject to further metaphysical explanation, whether in Platonic or Aristotelian terms (though it may be subject to assorted scientific explanations).

spirit, constituent ontologists deny that it is possible for spatiotemporal particulars to stand in the required dependency relations to items completely outside space and time or for beings like us to acquire knowledge of such items. The charges on both sides are familiar, so familiar that they are likely to strike us as pieces of worn-out rhetoric rather than serious philosophy. In any case, it is difficult to believe that any of these charges can settle things one way or the other. If there is a moral here, perhaps it is the one Wolterstorff draws: the need for tolerance in ontology.[16] We should encourage proponents of both styles to lay out fully articulated versions of their respective approaches. Rather than raising a priori objections, we should attempt to understand how the styles work themselves out and to evaluate them in terms of their fruitfulness in illuminating metaphysically significant relations and in solving metaphysical problems on a variety of fronts.

Thankfully for present purposes no stated preference for one or the other framework is necessary. What I wish to argue is that substratum theory supports dispositionalism, though for somewhat different reasons depending on whether the theory is formulated as a relational or constituent ontology. To state the argument explicitly:

Premise 1 Substratum theory must be formulated either as a relational ontology or as a constituent ontology.
Premise 2 If substratum theory is formulated as a relational ontology, then it supports dispositionalism.
Premise 3 If substratum theory is formulated as a constituent ontology, then it supports dispositionalism.
Conclusion Therefore, either way, substratum theory supports dispositionalism.

'Supports' is obviously ambiguous – 'renders more probable' is scarcely better, and I am frankly unsure of the degree of positive probability that dispositionalism acquires on either version of substratum theory. What is clear (or rather will be made clear) is the *way* in which these theories support dispositionalism: the claim is simply that both versions of substratum theory are at their best, are most plausible, when paired with dispositionalism. In other words, advocates of both relational and constituent versions of substratum theory should favour dispositionalism (all other things being equal) given the important ways in which dispositionalism renders *their* theories more plausible. Much as with the probabilistic argument concerning atomism version 1 canvassed in the previous

---

[16] Here he footnotes Wolterstorff (1991).

chapter, I will simply leave it to the reader to decide what degree of support this dialectic ends up providing dispositionalism – how exactly to read 'supports' in the argument's conclusion.

The first premise should be uncontroversial. While there are substance ontologies identified by their advocates as sidestepping the relational versus constituent debate,[17] I am unaware of anyone who claims that substratum theory is among them. And though in both the contemporary literature and in the historical literature there are views that can plausibly be seen as hybrids of the two, even these can be divided between theories according to which universals are in *some* sense literally immanent and those according to which universals are in *no* sense literally immanent. For instance Moreland (1998; 2001; 2013) is a constituent ontologist in the sense that he thinks universals are genuinely (though non-spatially) present in concrete objects, but he also maintains that those same universals can and do exist independently of those concrete objects. He thus combines an element of Platonism (universals exist necessarily and outside space and time) with an element of the Aristotelian view (universals can also be literal constituents of concrete objects).

By way of justifying premise 2: first it is necessary to point out that relational ontology is compatible with dispositionalism. This may not be immediately apparent; after all, dispositions are typically understood as intrinsic properties, and one might initially think that relational ontology is inconsistent with the reality of any genuinely intrinsic properties. That however would be a misreading of the view. Certainly there is a sense in which a *substratum* has no intrinsic properties (at least on some conceptions of 'intrinsic,' a much-debated notion), since in and of itself it is wholly bare. It has no properties essentially, no properties as identity conditions. However, once the substratum has entered into the instantiation relation with a property, *the resulting substance* (the substratum + property, with the two connected via instantiation) can be said to have that property intrinsically. That is standardly taken to be the case whether one is talking about the relational or the constituent view. If a substratum x comes to be in the instantiation relation with the universal 'negative charge,' then whether that universal is viewed as transcendent or immanent, in either case the resulting concrete substance will be the possessor of an intrinsic property. In other words, even according to the relational ontology, by virtue of the substratum standing as a relatum in

---

[17] Lowe (2012) for instance argues that his version of primitive substance theory sidesteps (in a way) the relational vs. constituent debate.

the instantiation relation, the resulting compound substance has an *intrinsic* property.[18] And perhaps that intrinsic property is a disposition. So relational ontology in no way rules out dispositionalism.

Of course something stronger than compatibility is desired here, namely active support. One might try to get there by arguing that in order for the substratum to enter into the instantiation relation, it must after all be *able* to enter into the instantiation relation, and then cash out that 'ability' language in dispositionalist terms. This would involve re-conceiving the substratum as not quite bare, but instead as either *having* or *being* a power: namely the power to enter into the instantiation relation.

It is probably inadvisable to re-conceive it as *having* such a power, since that might be thought to involve the substratum instantiating a power and then one would be off on an obvious regress. On the other hand one might worry about re-conceiving the substratum as *being* a power, since one might think that would involve viewing the substratum as a dispositional property, thereby reducing substratum theory to bundle theory. However that second worry could be avoided if one were open to an idea mentioned above in the discussion of hylomorphism, namely the idea that dispositions cross-cut ontological categories; on this notion, the substratum would be viewed not as a dispositional *property* but as a *substantial* disposition, a power falling under the category 'substantial principle.' This would not automatically reduce substratum theory to hylomorphism,[19] provided one could uphold other important distinctions between substrata and prime matter, and it seems clear that one could; they do differ in some of their core explanatory roles, like the precise roles they play in individuation, which are quite distinct.[20]

A closely related worry might be that to re-conceive the substratum in this way would conflict with the substratum's explanatory role as individuator – after all, a power, whether thought of as a property or as a member of some other category, is typically understood by realists as a universal, as at least in principle multiply instantiable. In response, it is worth recalling one of the longstanding objections against substratum

---

[18] At least, this is so on the most charitable reading of relational ontology; in fact some do object to the theory based on the suspicion that it cannot accommodate the reality of genuinely intrinsic properties. For a concise review of some of the relevant dialectic see Koons and Pickavance (2015, pp. 108–109).

[19] Contrary to the suggestion in Dumsday (2012).

[20] For instance contrast Moreland's (1998) discussion of individuation with that provided by Bobik (1961).

theory: *all* substrata are particulars and are property-bearers,[21] and ipso facto seem to share several *universals*– 'particularity' or 'individuality' or 'property-bearer' – rendering problematic the very notion of an intrinsic principle of individuation/concretization. One of the traditional tasks of the substratum theorist has been to find ways of addressing this objection, ways which neither open her up to 'tu quoque' charges from the resemblance nominalist (e.g., it would appear slightly hypocritical to say that the prima facie shared 'particularity' universal is actually a primitive resemblance relation ungrounded by any type-identity),[22] nor drive her to the opposite extreme of a view according to which universals are all that is fundamentally real, and what we think of as concrete particulars are constructs out of them.[23] There are of course various strategies available to the substratum theorist for accomplishing this task,[24] and my suggestion would be that the substratum-reconceived-as-power simply hitch itself onto whichever of these seems most promising.

One might further object that the present proposal to re-conceive the substratum as a disposition is unsuited to substratum theory, at least as formulated within relational ontology. While it is a truism that in order to enter into the instantiation relation the substratum must be *able* to enter into it, given that the relation is conceived *extrinsically* (on relational ontology) it can be doubted whether any actual power must be invoked here. It is commonly thought that extrinsic relations can obtain without there needing to be any distinct disposition that is manifested thereby. For instance, it is true that I am currently in extrinsic spatial relationships with the Eiffel tower, the world's largest hunk of Swiss cheese, and my brother's pet rabbit, but at least prima facie the truth-makers for each of these truths need not include the manifestation of any distinct power to be in spatial relationship with these entities. If the world's largest hunk of Swiss cheese is eaten, I undergo no change in my intrinsic properties and do not cease manifesting any power. Likewise,

---

[21] Or at least potential property-bearers, for the minority of substratum theorists who suggest that substrata can exist without instantiating any properties.

[22] For an example of this dynamic at play see for instance the strategy taken up by Moreland and Pickavance (2003) and its critique by Morganti (2011a).

[23] Though such an ontology has certainly been entertained; see again the version of bundle theory developed by O'Leary-Hawthorne and Cover (1998).

[24] Sider (2006, p. 393) for instance writes:

> If there were a monadic universal of *being a particular*, a most inclusive genus under which each particular must fall in order to be a particular, then there could be no truly bare particulars. But substratum theory requires no such universal since it already admits thin particulars as a fundamental ontological category. Thin particulars do not need to instantiate such a universal in order to be thin particulars; they can just be thin particulars!

I am in the extrinsic relation 'much shorter than' with respect to Shaquille O'Neal, but would undergo no change in my intrinsic properties, and would not cease manifesting any power, if he were to meet a tragic end. By extension then, a substratum does not need to have (or to be) any distinct power in order to enter into the extrinsic instantiation relation, since entities generally do not need distinct powers to enable them to enter into extrinsic relations.

However, instantiation, on relational ontology, is no ordinary extrinsic relation. After all, when a substratum enters into the instantiation relation with a universal (or perhaps a set of universals), something genuinely new comes into being: a concrete substance is altered, perhaps even generated or destroyed (think of cases where the substratum undergoes a change in its natural kind membership). In this respect it is very much *unlike* the extrinsic relations referenced in the previous paragraph. A closer analogue might be a situation in which every time O'Neal sits down while I remain standing (thus bringing our occurrent heights closer to parity) I grow an extra limb. That change is not as radical an alteration as the coming-into-being of a new concrete substance, but it is at least more akin to what supposedly occurs when the extrinsic instantiation relation links a substratum to a new universal (especially a kind). And one might in consequence claim that the nature of the extrinsic instantiation relation is such that unlike other extrinsic relations, intuitively there must be *some* power possessed by (or identical to) the substratum which enables it to help give rise in this way to a novel entity in nature. Certainly in the case of my growing an extra limb on every occurrence of O'Neal's seatedness we would naturally be inclined to inquire what it was about me, or about him, or about both of us, which allowed for this, and would be frustrated by any claims to the effect that the limb growth was a matter of primitive fact or an obvious entailment of entering into this sort of extrinsic relation.

Moreover, by re-conceiving the substratum as a power one could side-step another worry facing relational ontology, namely the exceedingly robust sort of emergentism it appears to involve. Today it is usually thought that, considered qua uninstantiated, abstract universals are causally inert. Transcending time and space, they are unchanging and (as commonly understood today) cannot of themselves affect or be affected by anything. Substrata are also typically viewed as inert in and of themselves, being viewed as wholly bare and lacking any contentful nature. This gives rise to an extra worry for relational ontology, since now it is not merely making the prima facie counter-intuitive claim that the obtaining of an extrinsic relation can result in the appearance in the physical world of an altered or even new concrete object; in addition to that, it is also claiming that this unique extrinsic relation accomplishes this feat by relating two wholly *inert* relata. For some this may seem a bridge too far.

Note too that the instantiation relation itself is typically seen as abstract and therefore inert. So we have an inert relation linking together two inert relata and the product is supposed to be a powerful concrete substance. And even if one were to conceptualize instantiation as a concrete rather than abstract relation, it is far from clear that that would help – the consensus in the literature is that there is a sharp distinction between whatever sort of explanation is provided by the instantiation relation, on the one hand, and the sort of explanation provided by causation on the other.[25] As such it is not clear how concretizing the instantiation relation would help overcome the inertness of the relata (the substratum and universal) it is relating – unless one wished to conceive of instantiation as itself a *dispositional relation,* a power falling under the category 'relation' rather than 'property' or 'substance.' We encountered that idea in the treatment of OSR in Chapter 3 and saw it again in Section 5.2. That option would of course be grist for the mill of the dispositionalist, so for argument's sake let's leave it to one side and concentrate on the suggestion at hand, namely that of re-conceiving the substratum as a power.

By re-conceiving the substratum along dispositionalist lines, at least one party to the relation will not be wholly inert, and the resulting picture is liable to seem more plausible. That being the case, it might actually be better to characterize the substratum not as being the power to enter into the instantiation relation, but as *the power to become an altered or wholly new concrete substance* and then specify that this disposition's stimulus condition is (or at least always includes) being prompted into the instantiation relation with an appropriate universal or set of universals. At any rate, either formulation would serve to render whatever emergentism is involved here less extreme and more intelligible.

Perhaps some advocates of nomological necessitarianism could respond to this emergentism point by denying that abstract entities are inert. Indeed, one might think that for transcendent laws to play a genuine

---

[25] Cowling (2017, p. 80) reflects this consensus when he writes that "while [concrete] objects like the mug have causal powers that depend upon the properties they instantiate, the instantiation relation is not a causal relation either. Properly understood, these relations provide metaphysical rather than causal explanations. So, while the mug was dropped partly because it instantiates the property of *being hot*, the genuinely causal 'action' involves only concrete reality."

governing role wholly independently of concretely instantiated powers, such a denial is exactly what would be needed.[26] However, advocates of nomological necessitarianism rarely deny explicitly that universals or other abstracta are inert. Nomological necessitarians are generally intent on making laws of nature effective *prescriptive principles* without making them *efficient causes*, which latter move would undermine their status as genuinely abstract – at least on the common assumption that abstracta are necessarily inert.[27] The tension seemingly involved here, and the accompanying explanatory worry (i.e., *how* do purely abstract laws manage to govern events in the physical world even though those abstract laws and the universals figuring in them are all, qua abstract, inert) has received a good deal of attention in the literature on nomological necessitarianism, pro and con. (See for instance the conflicting treatments by Armstrong (1983, pp. 77–99) and Mumford (2004, ch. 6).) The dialectic is especially complicated in the case of Armstrong's specific version of nomological necessitarianism, in which there are no uninstantiated universals and all instantiated universals have spatiotemporal location, but the universal supplying the nomic force (the primitive N *relation*) is a second-order universal that directly relates first-order universals rather than concrete particulars. The dialectic is liable to be less complicated on versions of nomological necessitarianism where the laws are primitive and conceived along more Platonic lines. But the underlying concern remains much the same.

Moreover any nomological necessitarian who is wiling to entertain literally efficacious abstracta runs the risk of undermining the case against dispositionalism: for if abstract uninstantiated entities can be inherently causally significant, why can't concretely instantiated properties be inherently causally significant – i.e., what's wrong with irreducible powers in nature? Bird (2005; 2007, pp. 91–97), building on Tweedale (1984), makes a similar point against Armstrong's version of nomological necessitarianism, which implicitly relies on its nomic N *relation* being inherently

---

[26] By contrast, on the nomic dispositionalism I advocated in Chapter 2, abstract entities play a genuine governing role but only in *conjunction* with concretely instantiated powers. On that view abstracta could still be seen as inherently inert.

[27] As Bird (2007, p. 129) puts it, "on no metaphysics of laws do laws cause anything, although they may govern what causes what." However Latham's (2011, pp. 108–109) view seems an interesting exception; he favours an account according to which abstract laws determine particular states of affairs in what he terms a 'quasi-causal' fashion. Latham references Maudlin as holding a similar view, and indeed the latter does (2007, p. 30) speak of laws as being that by which later states of affairs are *generated* from earlier ones, and of the *operation* of laws leading to an event or state of affairs (2007, p. 36). Still, Maudlin does not quite say explicitly that laws, as abstract entities, are non-inert.

modally significant, a sort of unwitting second-order power; in other words, delve far enough into the ontological posits employed within nomological necessitarianism, and eventually one will hit upon a form of dispositionalism. At any rate, whatever one thinks about these issues as they manifest in the existing literature on the categoricalism vs. dispositionalism debate, the fact that this is hotly contested territory should perhaps make a would-be categoricalist substratum theorist reluctant to pursue this particular avenue of response to my justification of premise 2.

Note however that while admission of inherently causally significant abstracta would undermine the nomological necessitarian's case against dispositionalism, the reverse does not hold. That is, a dispositionalist could entertain the reality of such abstracta while also affirming the reality of irreducible concretely instantiated powers. In fact Vetter (2015, pp. 277–281) argues that on the correct understanding of 'potentiality,' abstract entities can legitimately be said to have potentialities (though not potentialities for direct interaction with concrete particulars). One might also make the case that the non-inertness of abstracta is implicitly required by Cowling's (2014) *locationism*, an ontology that is realist about properties but replaces the instantiation relation with the notion that substrata *occupy* properties. (That is, just as a substratum literally occupies a location in spacetime, it also literally occupies a location in abstract quality-space.) It seems to me that if locationism were true, then properties could be seen as the bearers of substrata rather than the other way round. So if what I've said in the main text concerning the dispositional nature of substrata is workable from the perspective of traditional substratum theory, then, transplanting the same basic idea to the very non-traditional framework of Cowling's locationism, we would end up with the view that abstract objects are powers for the reception of substrata.[28]

---

[28] Even some traditional substratum theorists occasionally sound as if they think of Platonic universals as non-inert. Consider Moreland (2001, p. 94), who writes: "When a property is exemplified by a bare particular, it is modified by being tied to that particular." And a bit later (2001, pp. 101–102):

> The universal is indifferent to any particular instance (a Platonist would add *all* its instances) since the universal can be a constituent *in* many instances through the non-spatiotemporal, inhomogenous nexus of exemplification. When redness has red1 as one of its instances, this is due to the fact that some entity (a bare particular) outside the nature of redness has entered into an exemplification relation with redness. Something happens to redness, namely, it is modified and becomes exemplified.

I should emphasize that I am not here advocating in favour of the hugely unpopular notion of non-inert abstract entities; rather I am merely noting the fact that dispositionalism could survive the admission of them, as its central commitment is to the reality of irreducible powers in nature, and the two notions are strictly compatible. By contrast the nomological necessitarian cannot admit the latter, and is placed in a difficult position dialectically should she entertain the former.

As a further objection to my justification of premise 2, some will resist the 'dispositions can cross-cut ontological categories' move this involves, despite the precedent in hylomorphism (and in the recent literature concerning OSR). But that idea is arguably less counter-intuitive than relational ontology + substratum theory as presently conceived in non-dispositionalist terms. Substratum theory understood as a relational ontology is thus most plausible when paired with dispositionalism (all other things being equal), and in that sense the view supports dispositionalism.

A separate worry relating to cross-cutting: isn't there a risk that by attempting to advocate for dispositionalism by reference to dispositional substantial principles (whether prime matter on hylomorphism or substrata on substratum theory) rather than dispositional properties, I might be equivocating on 'dispositionalism'? While, as already noted, dispositional substantial principles do count as 'dispositions' on the rough definition I provided in Chapter 1 (which definition accords with a common understanding of 'disposition' in the literature), is that really adequate for present purposes? Mightn't a categoricalist respond that what she is really concerned to exclude from her ontology is dispositional *properties*, but that these odd dispositional substantial principles are unobjectionable because irrelevant to the larger dialectic between the three main ontologies of law (dispositionalism vs. nomological necessitarianism vs. regularity theory)?

I do not think that reply will work. Recall the core question with which the present chapter began: fundamentally, why do objects behave

---

Moreland does not elaborate here on just what he means by this, but prima facie it sounds as if the abstract universal is literally being acted upon (modified) such that the result is its exemplification – i.e., that *the universal* is somehow the recipient of a causal input and the consequence is its entering into the exemplification relation. Later however he reaffirms the immutability of abstracta (2001, p. 132):

> For one thing, if we pay attention to the intrinsic nature of redness and compare it to the coming-to-be and perishing or altering of red particulars, we learn that redness, and universals in general, are ingenerable, incorruptible, timeless and unchangeable (except in their relational features). Red particulars come-to-be and so forth, but it is a mistake – indeed, a category fallacy – to apply these notions to the universal itself.

the way they do? Or, phrased differently: what most fundamentally accounts for why things act and react in the ways they do? For regularity theorists, there is ultimately nothing *about* objects that determines the regular patterns in their actions and reactions. Regularities in nature are ultimately basic and not subject to further metaphysical explanation. That includes regularities in minor property-changes (e.g., the growth of hair in a human body) and regularities in major property-changes that we associate with shifts in kind-membership (e.g., when a human body is cremated and thus transformed into ashes). Try to tell a regularity theorist that there is something intrinsic to the human body (and the materials composing it) that enables it to be transformed into a radically different kind of thing, and the regularity theorist will deny this. Try to tell a regularity theorist that there is something *about* a fundamental particle that enables it to be transformed into a different kind of particle – a more foundational, metaphysical constituent like prime matter or a substratum – and the regularity theorist will deny this. She must deny this, because admitting the existence of an inherently causally significant principle in nature is clearly incompatible with regularity theory. Prime matter and substrata, while not dispositional *properties*, are certainly *dispositional*, because like dispositional properties they are inherently causally significant; moreover, like dispositional properties their identity conditions involve stimulus condition(s) and manifestation condition(s) and (perhaps) ceteris paribus clauses.[29] Similarly, the nomological necessitarian cannot admit the existence of inherently causally significant principles in nature, let alone principles with stimulus and manifestation conditions, etc. For nomological necessitarians, objects act and react in the ways they do because of extrinsic governing laws. They cannot allow that there exist dispositional substantial principles any more than they can allow that there exist dispositional properties. What they find objectionable about the latter they will also find objectionable about the former. And the reality of either suffices to establish the truth of dispositionalism.[30]

---

[29] Though CP clauses have not come up in the discussion of this chapter thus far, it is not unreasonable to think that it is possible to block prime matter's reception of substantial form, or to block the substratum from entering into the instantiation relation with a new property.

[30] While I am confident that that last sentence holds, if needs be I could go for a weaker claim: granting for the sake of argument that dispositional substantial principles and dispositional properties do not fall under a common genus 'disposition,' nevertheless the reality of dispositional substantial principles would provide strong evidence for the possible reality of dispositional properties, given how similar they are. So even if one wants to restrict the meaning of 'dispositionalism' to a commitment to dispositional *properties*, the arguments I'm making in Sections 5.2 and 5.3 will certainly contribute towards defending dispositionalism.

By way of concluding the defence of premise 2, I should stress that I am not using any of the preceding points as part of an argument against relational ontology. I have no interest in taking a side in that debate here. Moreover, seen as an attempted argument against relational ontology, the preceding would be redundant – the claim that the extrinsic instantiation relation is very unlike other sorts of extrinsic relations, and at least prima facie counter-intuitive in certain respects, is among the unoriginal 'pieces of worn-out rhetoric' alluded to by Loux above. My point is different: I am simply claiming that the unique nature of the extrinsic instantiation relation on relational ontology is such as to motivate a re-conception of the substratum as something other than wholly characterless and de-natured. By viewing it instead as a sort of power, along the lines suggested above (lines already standard and unexciting within hylomorphism), counter-intuitive aspects of relational ontology can be defused (or at least lessened) without relinquishing any essential elements of the view. I should likewise stress again that I have not claimed that substratum theory + relational ontology entails dispositionalism, or that it would be unworkable without the suggested re-conceptualization of the substratum as a power. Rather I have argued that the theory works better, is more plausible, when thus re-conceived.

Moving on to premise 3 of the overarching argument of this section: while it has taken a good bit of effort to motivate the idea that entering into an extrinsic relation requires a disposition (even the unique extrinsic relation that is instantiation, for the relational ontologist), it should take less work to motivate the idea that for something to function as a receiver/bearer/ ground of properties, a disposition is required. And on substratum theory understood within constituent ontology that is exactly what is going on. Within the framework of constituent ontology, the substratum functions as a ground – i.e., the substratum bears the properties instantiated in it or inhering in it, which instantiated properties depend on that substratum for their existence. The notion that instantiated properties need grounds, such that they cannot exist by themselves/freestanding/independently, constitutes one of the core dividing lines between substratum theory and bundle theory. Consequently, substratum theorists should not give it up without a struggle.

In fact for the nominalist substratum theory advocated by Martin (1980), this grounding role is the *only* explanatory role played by substrata, and yet he saw this as by itself a sufficiently weighty point to justify belief in substrata. If one concurs with Martin in finding the notion of freestanding properties (with Martin taking 'properties' as tropes) highly counter-intuitive, this will seem an especially powerful motivation – instantiated properties *need* something to inhere in, something to ground them, and substrata fulfill that role. So while my defence of premise 2 pre-supposed realism about universals, the defence of premise 3 should also be of interest to nominalist substratum theorists. And for realists, note that the constituent ontologist who is a substratum theorist is committed to the impossibility of freestanding *instantiated* properties. That still leaves room open for the constituent ontologist who is a substratum theorist to affirm the reality of *uninstantiated* properties. Again, the hybrid Platonic/constituent ontology advocated by Moreland (1998; 2001; 2013) is of this sort. At any rate, for the remainder of this section the nominalist can read 'properties' as referring to tropes, and the realist can read 'properties' as referring to instantiated universals. The argument should go through either way.[31]

So: while it might seem initially plausible to maintain that a wholly bare, characterless, inert entity might enter into extrinsic relations, it is decidedly less plausible to maintain that such an entity might function as a receiver/bearer/ground for anything. The substratum theorist thus has considerable prima facie motivation to affirm that the substratum is able to ground properties either by *having* a power to do so or (much more plausibly) *being* a power for property reception.

A substratum theorist eager to avoid a connection to dispositionalism will wish to stop short of that conclusion, and the obvious option for doing so is to claim that even though a substratum can truly be called 'receptive' of properties, this receptivity is not explained by any literal causal power on the part of the substratum; or, to put it in the terminology of contemporary truthmaker theory, the truthmaker for this disposition-ascription is not a disposition. Rather, the substratum is itself the truthmaker for the disposition-ascription, and primitively so. There is nothing *about* the substratum that makes it receptive of properties – it just *is* receptive of properties, and there is nothing more to be said. Every ontology needs primitives, and this is simply one of the (hopefully few)

---

[31] Though in fact, I suspect Moreland's hybrid view implies dispositionalism for reasons more closely tied to those provided in the defence of premise 2. That is, even though Moreland identifies as a constituent ontologist, his particular version of constituent ontology (affirming as it does the independent existence of transcendent universals and the purely extrinsic nature of the instantiation relation) requires dispositionalism because it faces the same issues relational ontology does with respect to excessive emergentism. Re-conceiving the substratum as a power is more plausible than maintaining that one can obtain a novel concrete substance by way of a purely extrinsic relation tying together two wholly inert entities.

that must be admitted by substratum theorists working within the framework of constituent ontology.[32]

Yet while it may be that any ontology needs primitives (depending on how one understands 'primitive'), primitive counterfactuals are specially worrisome. To say that substratum x would, if acted upon in manner y, bear property z, is to assert a counterfactual of the substratum. And in this case, it is to do so while claiming that nothing really *explains* why this counterfactual obtains rather than not. To many, this sort of move will seem unsatisfactory. Indeed, contemporary truthmaker theory developed partly out of the desire to formulate a more precise objection against primitive counterfactuals, specifically Rylean disposition-ascriptions. To employ a concrete example, take for instance the (roughly stated) counterfactual truth that a bucketful of water would help put out a campfire if dumped on it. Pace regularity theory, most would find it unsatisfying to be told that this counterfactual holds true not because of the active and passive causal powers of water and fire, or the obtaining of governing laws of nature, but instead that it holds true simply as a matter of primitive fact, subject to no further explanation. Yet we are being asked to accept something comparable of the substratum.

Granted, some are already committed to primitive counterfactuals – Molinists, for instance, given their belief in primitively true counterfactuals of creaturely freedom; likewise, some recent views in the metaphysics of science literature posit primitively true counterfactuals, notably the ontology of laws advocated by Lange (2004; 2009; 2009a) and the similar theory defended by Whittle (2009). However, it is the very positing of such counterfactuals that has prompted one of the more important criticisms of these theories,[33] such that if a substratum theorist must rely on primitive counterfactuals this will, for many at least, count as a mark against the theory (though hardly a decisive one, and we'll discuss primitive counterfactuals further in Chapter 6). A more promising perspective might be the one suggested above: the substratum is receptive of properties not because this receptivity is a primitive fact obtaining of the substratum, and not because it has some dispositional property making it receptive, but because the substratum *just is* a power for the reception of properties.

---

[32] See LaBossiere (1994, pp. 368–369) and Moreland (2001, pp. 153–154) for clear statements of this reply.
[33] See for instance Handfield (2005a).

Formulating substratum theory in this dispositionalist manner also allows the theory to sidestep the common concern that it is deeply counter-intuitive to posit the existence of something that is utterly characterless – a worry especially pressing for the minority of substratum theorists who maintain that substrata can exist on their own, without instantiating any properties.[34]

So, as with the relational formulation, substratum theory understood as a constituent ontology is most plausible when paired with dispositionalism (all other things being equal), and in that sense supports dispositionalism.

Having now run through the justifications for the argument's three premises, I think the whole holds up reasonably well. Though part of me wishes to press for a more robust formulation of premise 3 – I suspect a case can be made that substratum theory understood within constituent ontology actually entails dispositionalism, based on the idea that it is *impossible* for a truly bare, utterly characterless substratum to function as a ground for properties (i.e., as a bearer of tropes or instantiated universals, the existence of which depends on being thus borne). However, doing so would require an in-depth exploration of grounding, a topic whose associated literature has so exploded in recent years ('exploded' both in the sense of 'expanded very rapidly' and in the sense of 'expanded in a chaotic and confusing manner') that it would be an act of hubris to try and engage with it here. Moreover a good deal of the recent work on grounding is arguably of tangential relevance to the specific sort of grounding under discussion in the context of substratum theory (i.e., grounding as another label for the necessary dependence of a property on the entity to which it belongs). I will therefore rest content with a weaker formulation of premise 3. In any case, the weaker 'support' formulation for the argument as a whole is unavoidable, since a stronger conclusion regarding substratum theory formulated in terms of relational ontology is not available.

---

[34] Though Sider (2006, p. 392), who belongs to that minority, has an interesting reply to this concern, writing that:

> it does not follow that to have a nature, a thing must instantiate at least one monadic universal; for a thing could have a nature simply by *failing* to instantiate monadic universals. On an intuitive level: to have a nature is to 'be a certain way'. There must be answers to such questions as 'what is the thing like?', and 'to what is the thing similar, and to what is it dissimilar?' Truly bare particulars *do* have natures in this intuitive sense. Indeed, they all have the same nature, and that nature is exhausted by the fact that they instantiate no monadic universals. That is the way that they are. 'What is a truly bare particular like?' Answer: 'It is not charged. It does not have any mass. It does not have any spin. And so on.'

5.4   Bundle Theory and Dispositionalism

This argument is a bit different from the two preceding, insofar as the conclusion is not to dispositionalism in general, but to one of the more specific versions of dispositionalism described in Section 5.1:

Premise 1 If bundle theory is true, then pan-dispositionalism is probably true.
Premise 2 Bundle theory is true.
Conclusion Therefore pan-dispositionalism is probably true.

There is no need to defend premise 2, since the truth of bundle theory is simply being taken on board provisionally, as one of the four disjuncts we are working through in our treatment of the major options in substance ontology. The task is to justify premise 1. To begin: prima facie, bundle theory can be combined either with categoricalism or with any of the four versions of dispositionalism. But in fact bundle theory does not sit well with categoricalism, or indeed any sort of robust realism about categorical properties.[35]

The central examples of familiar categorical properties in the literature are geometrical/structural properties like shape or size.[36] But historically there have been two main ways of thinking about geometrical/structural properties: **(a)** one can think of them as boundary conditions/limits on stuffs or qualities. For example, to have a square is to have a some stuff (gold, say) bounded in a certain way, namely squarely; or, if one does not want to speak of stuff (and the bundle theorist will not want to speak of stuff, at least not as irreducible, since stuff is not a property or reducible to properties),[37] one can speak of some *quality* bounded in a certain way. For example, to have a square is to have some amount of greenness bounded in a certain way, namely squarely. Or, **(b)** one can think of geometrical/structural properties in a different way, as arising from the determinate spatial locations of disparate particles. For example, to have a square is to have some group of (ultimately) extensionless

---

[35] It is worth noting that unlike the two previous sections, this argument should be of interest to regularity theorists, since bundle theory is a comparatively popular substance ontology amongst regularity theorists (specifically trope bundle theory, where all the tropes are categorical). That is unsurprising, since this sort of bundle theory is apparently compatible both with nominalism and empiricism. Moreover the argument of this section does not presuppose causal realism, though it does conclude to it, insofar as any version of dispositionalism entails causal realism.

[36] The 'familiar' qualification will be explained presently.

[37] The object vs. stuff distinction was discussed in detail in Chapter 4, in the context of the atoms vs. gunk vs. extended simples debate. The most plausible account of extended simples involves a commitment to irreducible stuff.

point-particles arranged in such a way as to compose a square.[38] Think of children's 'draw-by-the-numbers' art books, where at first glance one just sees a bunch of numbered dots, but they are arranged in such a way that a shape emerges when one draws lines between them. If nature bottoms out at extensionless point-particles, then the shaped macro-level world is derived in an analogous way, substituting fundamental forces connecting particles for drawn lines. Consequently, depending on one's ontology of macro-level objects, on model (b) categorical properties like shape can either be seen as intrinsic properties of irreducible/emergent macro-level objects (e.g., a molecule has shape as an intrinsic property because a molecule is an emergent substance irreducible to its component atoms) or shape falls away altogether as an intrinsic property and is replaced by relations obtaining between distinct objects.[39]

Both models of geometrical/structural properties clash with bundle theory. Model (a) is problematic because the bundle theorist cannot view structural properties as boundary conditions on stuff, given that stuff is in turn viewed as a sort of irreducible substance or substantial principle. (By contrast, a primitive substance theorist or hylomorphist would seem to have no difficulty in principle in accepting a stuff-version of (a).) Moreover, geometrical/structural properties cannot ultimately be understood as boundary conditions on qualitative properties, because there are no good candidates for irreducible physical qualitative properties, unless perhaps one is a primitivist about colour.[40] Model (b) would likewise be problematic on a categoricalist bundle theory, since an extensionless particle seems to lack any irreducible positive categorical features – it has no shape or determinate size or other structural properties, and there are no good candidates for irreducible physical *qualitative* properties for such

---

[38] This latter understanding of geometrical/structural properties in terms of the arrangement of parts is the more common one in the recent literature. In fact sometimes it seems to be taken for granted that it is the *only* available conception of such properties – see for instance the discussion by Skow (2007).

[39] In other words, mereological nihilists who also affirm atomism version 1 as their account of fundamental material entities must reject the reality of intrinsic geometrical/structural properties as *properties* and re-conceive them as extrinsic structural *relations*. By contrast, mereological nihilists who affirm atomism version 2 or the theory of extended simples can still admit fundamental intrinsic geometrical/structural properties into their ontology (and in fact have to). I am not sure how to think about the property-status of shape on the theory of gunk.

[40] In the metaphysics literature, the nature of colour is most commonly cashed out either in terms of the reflective power of surfaces or in terms of the ability of bodies to prompt conscious colour-experiences in percipients or some combination of these. However, there are advocates of *colour primitivism* (sometimes also called *naive realism* about colour), according to which colour is an irreducible quality belonging to bodies and existing independently of percipients. Recent proponents include Allen (2011; 2015) and Gert (2008). For critique see Byrne and Hilbert (2007).

a particle to possess (including colour – even granting colour primitivism, it is dubious whether an unextended object could be coloured). In short, it is not at all clear what sorts of categorical properties could be bundled together to make up an extensionless particle.

Moreover, neither model (a) nor model (b) of geometrical/structural properties can gain any assistance by resorting to a class of categorical properties much-discussed in the literature: *quiddities*. While the understanding of 'quiddity' varies somewhat, at least in the context of the dispositionalism vs. categoricalism debate the meaning is fairly well-established: quiddities are categorical (i.e., non-dispositional) properties, each of which is identical to itself and distinguished from all others. A quiddity can be seen as the property-analogue of a bare substratum: its intrinsic nature consists wholly in self-identity and numerical distinctness from other quiddities, and that is all there is to be said.[41] While not all categoricalists affirm the reality of quiddities, for some they play a key role in the metaphysics of laws. Among regularity theorists for instance, Lewis (2009) was an advocate for quiddities. Among nomological necessitarians, Armstrong (1983; 1997) employed them prominently in his system. Whatever may be said in favour of quiddities, they are far from familiar; they cannot be perceived and they play no explicit role in any scientific law (however important a role they may be alleged to play in the underlying *metaphysics* of laws). Unsurprisingly, they have been the subject of critical comment.[42] Still, let us grant their possibility for the sake of argument. Quiddities would still not help with model (a), since they are utterly characterless. As such they are not the sorts of properties that could be spread out in space such that their boundaries would constitute the determinate shape of an object. *What* would be getting spread out? Self-identity? That just seems nonsensical. And quiddities would likewise be helpless to assist with model (b). Even granting that extensionless particles can possess spatial location despite being devoid of shape, to think that they can possess spatial location despite being devoid of shape *and any other sort of positive character besides self-identity* seems difficult to believe. How does a unique instance of self-identity manage to occupy space – even a spatial point? Again, the notion seems borderline nonsensical. It may appear still more unbelievable for someone who

---

[41] Somewhat confusingly, quiddities are sometimes labeled 'qualities.' Here I'll reserve the latter term for properties like colour. Also, usage here should be distinguished from meaning of the term as it appears in scholastic philosophy, where 'quiddity' is sometimes used as a synonym for 'nature' or 'essence.'

[42] See for instance Black (2000) and Bird (2007, pp. 70–79).

is a relationist about space, for then the quiddities would be tasked not only with occupying spatial locations but with *constituting* the spatial manifold itself, with the manifold consisting of the relations between instances of bare self-identity.[43] If the categoricalist replies that quiddities are never instantiated bare, that they are always compresent with other intrinsic qualitative properties (reminding us again of the analogy with substrata),[44] then the question again becomes whether there are any plausible candidates for irreducible physical qualitative properties with which the quiddity could be conjoined. And as we have seen already there are no such candidates, so no progress has been made.

Is the bundle theorist in trouble then? Only if she tries to include irreducible categorical properties in her system. If she jettisons them, she can carry on. And what does she end up with after jettisoning irreducible categorical properties? Pan-dispositionalism. (Why pan-dispositionalism instead of neutral monism? Because the dialectic leading to the conclusion took for granted the real distinction between categorical and other epistemically possible sorts of property. If the neutral monist wanted to appropriate this argument she would have to do it with a 'kick away the ladder when you're done' strategy in mind, and that would be problematic here. And why pan-dispositionalism instead of identity theory? Because identity theory would run into the same problem regarding the lack of plausible candidates for fundamental physical qualitative properties – though more on that in a moment.)

There are at least four ways one might challenge this argument: first, by finding a plausible candidate for an irreducible physical qualitative property. I could of course be missing something here, and welcome

---

[43] Recall that in the debate over the ontology of space, relationists maintain that space is reducible to the distance relations obtaining between physical objects. If there were no physical objects, there would be no space. By contrasts, substantivalists maintain that space is itself an object, over and above what we think of as physical bodies. This distinction will be treated in more detail in Chapter 7. Note that the idea of the spatial manifold being constituted by relations between instances of bare self-identity might initially seem reminiscent of one or another version of ontic structural realism discussed in Chapter 3. However, none of the extant versions of the theory canvassed there actually envisions objects with intrinsic natures consisting solely of self-identity + distinction from other such natures. Rather, they all envision the objects either being devoid of intrinsic identity altogether (with their natures being exhausted by their functional role as nodes in the structure), or, on some of the moderate versions, as having natures consisting both of intrinsic features and functional role in the structure. Moreover some prominent advocates of OSR reject quiddities (under the label of 'haecceities,' which in this context is used in an equivalent manner to indicate a bare individual essence or instance of self-identity) – see Ladyman and Ross (2007, p. 134).

[44] I take it that Armstrong (1983; 1997) believes quiddities are never instantiated as bare quiddities (i.e., instantiated outside of any nomic connections with other properties), just as he maintains that substrata never exist without properties.

suggestions for candidate irreducible physical qualities (*unambiguously irreducible physical qualities*). But I am sceptical that they will be found.

Second, and relatedly, one might challenge the connection to pan-dispositionalism by biting the bullet and accepting colour primitivism (and perhaps also analogous perspectives on other qualities traditionally classed as 'secondary properties' like sounds or textures or tastes). This is hardly a crazy idea – again, that sort of robust realism about colour retains some defenders in the current metaphysics literature. In fact a categoricalist could take much of the same reasoning above and apply it to justify premise 1 of the following:

> **Premise 1** If bundle theory is true, then colour primitivism is true.
> **Premise 2** Bundle theory is true.
> **Conclusion** Therefore colour primitivism is true.

The justification for premise 1 would be the fact that bundle theory seems to lead to pan-dispositionalism, unless colour primitivism can intervene to save bundle theory from that grisly fate. And only colour primitivism can manage it (or colour primitivism + analogous accounts of other perceived qualities), given that there are no other candidates for irreducible physical qualitative properties. For someone who comes into this debate already thinking that the wider case against pan-dispositionalism is strong, and already thinking that robust realism about perceived qualities is potentially workable, this line of reasoning could be appealing.

It would be interesting to speculate how advocates of colour primitivism might further develop this line of argument. But for those of us who remain sceptical of their position, this second strategy will not go through.

Third, one might seek out a third model (or more) of geometrical/structural properties, distinct from models (a) and (b) above, which sidesteps the problem. While I do not want to rule this out, and I invite suggestions, I think it a tall order. Historically, accounts of geometrical/structural properties have cashed out their basic nature either in terms of boundaries on something else (whether substance or some other kind of property) or in terms of the spatial relations obtaining between simples. Even when this is not always made explicit, the accounts can be boiled down to one or the other of these two basic models.

Fourth, one might try to press the case for irreducible physical qualitative properties by assigning them an irreducible *explanatory role*. That is, while we may lack any unambiguous examples of such properties, taken either from everyday experience or from the sciences, perhaps they can do work in metaphysics. While I do not wish to rule this out, again I think it a tall order. One strategy might go like this: suppose one is an identity theorist dispositionalist, but that one does not think that there are any geometrical/structural properties at the fundamental level. Perhaps atomism version 1 is favoured as the best account of material composition, such that at the bottom level of natural objects, objects lack any shape or size or other such properties, but still possess powers. Yet according to identity theory dispositionalism, all properties necessarily have both dispositional and categorical identity conditions. Since in this case there are no geometrical/structural candidates to serve in the latter role, something else must do so, and the only remaining candidate is an irreducible physical qualitative property. While this would be an interesting approach, it would at worst force me to revise premise 1 to read: "If bundle theory is true, then either pan-dispositionalism or identity theory is probably true." So we would still end up with some version of dispositionalism being probably true. Of course, the categoricalist could run the same sort of argument for the reality of irreducible physical qualitative properties, perhaps something like this:

> **Premise 1** If categoricalist bundle theory is true and there are no geometrical/structural properties at the fundamental level, then there must be irreducible physical qualitative properties.
> **Premise 2** Categoricalist bundle theory is true and there are no geometrical/structural properties at the fundamental level.
> **Conclusion** Therefore, there must be irreducible physical qualitative properties.

The obvious worry about the categoricalist running this line of reasoning is that it seems at best to result in a stalemate with dispositionalism, or at worst to beg the question against the latter.

Clearly I have not provided a knockdown refutation of categoricalist bundle theory. From the perspective of the proponents of such a view, I have at worst presented them with a to-do list: (A) come up with some unambiguous examples of irreducible physical qualities, (B) shore up colour primitivism, (C) develop a new account of the nature of geometrical/structural properties, or (D) find some explanatory role for irreducible physical qualitative properties that does not end up either relying on dispositionalism or begging the question against it. But for the moment, lacking the fulfilment of any of those tasks and (in my view) being warranted in provisional scepticism towards the prospects of completing them successfully, I think the modest conclusion stands: namely that pan-dispositionalism is probably true given bundle theory.

5.5   Dispositionalism and Primitive Substance Theory

As noted during the brief explication of this theory in Section 5.1, most of its current defenders are realists about universals. Heil (2003; 2012) is an exception, pairing primitive substance theory with nominalism. I believe the argument of the present section is effective on either the standard formulation or Heil's. For the most part I will develop the support connection between primitive substance theory and dispositionalism with the majority, realist perspective in mind, but I will from time to time note how the relevant claims can be re-stated to fit Heil's nominalist version. I should also observe that, as with the argument of the previous section (but unlike those pertaining to hylomorphism and to substratum theory in Sections 5.2 and 5.3), the categoricalist competition I am targeting includes *both* nomological necessitarianism and regularity theory.

Before formulating the argument I would first like to set aside what might initially seem like a promising alternative route. For at first glance it might appear as if a comparable line of reasoning could be employed in this section as was employed for the constituent ontology version of substratum theory. After all, both theories are committed to the following two claims: (a) there is an irreducible distinction between a substance and its properties; (b) instantiated property-universals (or, for the nominalist primitive substance theorist, tropes) are always possessed by a substance, in some sense of 'possess.' For the constituent ontology version of substratum theory, the concrete electron x possesses negative charge as an intrinsic property because its substratum contingently instantiates the universal 'negative charge,' whereas on primitive substance theory the concrete electron x possesses negative charge because it is itself an instantiation of the substance-universal/kind 'electron,' which substance-universal/kind is necessarily associated with the distinct property-universal 'negative charge.' (For the nominalist: the concrete electron x possesses negative charge because its individual substantial nature entails the presence of that trope.) So while the two theories cash out the notion of property possession differently, they agree that instantiated properties are always possessed by a substance – there cannot exist freestanding properties, thereby ruling out bundle theory.[45] So, given (a) and (b), one might think that primitive substance theory leads to dispositionalism because just as the substratum must be *capable* of grounding properties (thus explaining how the concrete substance possesses its properties), on primitive substance theory the substance itself must be *capable* of property possession.

Yet to draw that conclusion would be a mistake. While on primitive substance theory the substance is indeed distinct from its properties (even its essential properties), there is no need to explicate this distinction using dispositionalism, as there is on substratum theory. Again, on the latter theory the tie between any substratum and its properties is always a contingent one. The substratum is a power for the reception of properties, and in principle it can gain or lose any mutually consistent set of properties. By contrast, on primitive substance theory the tie between a substance and at least some of its properties is a necessary one. A concrete object instantiating a substance-universal/kind cannot cease being a member of that kind without ceasing to exist altogether. If it stops instantiating that kind then it simply ceases to exist, for there is no other, more basic ontological ingredient (like a substratum or prime matter) that could allow a concrete substance to persist through a change in its basic natural kind. Moreover, the substance-universal/kind entails the presence of a set of essential properties, such that any concrete object lacking any of those properties is ipso facto not an instantiation of that substance-universal/kind. A substance and its essential properties are an inseparable package on primitive substance theory, even while remaining distinct. (That is, on this view 'inseparable' is not synonymous with 'identical.') And they are distinct in part because there is a priority relation between them – instantiating a kind explains why an object must have certain properties, not vice versa. On primitive substance theory, substance-universals/kinds are not simply aggregates of property-universals, and by extension their concrete instantiations are not simply

---

[45] That is, primitive substance theory and the constituent formulation of substratum theory are both committed to the idea that there cannot exist instantiated properties which fail to be instantiated *in* or *by* something. They are thus both committed to the falsity of bundle theory, as one would expect. However, as I noted above with reference to Moreland's (1998; 2001; 2013) version of constituent ontology + substratum theory, the claim that there cannot exist instantiated properties which fail to be instantiated *in* or *by* something is consistent with the view that there can still exist *uninstantiated* properties – i.e., according to Moreland one can be a constituent ontologist while also believing in Platonic abstracta. The same can be said for primitive substance theory. And there are those who affirm both primitive substance theory and Platonism – see Fales (1990) and Loux (1978).

aggregates of their instantiated properties. The irreducibility of the kind to its associated property-universals (and of the concrete particular to its instantiated properties) is emphasized repeatedly in the literature on primitive substance theory.[46] All of which is to say: on primitive substance theory, the substance cannot properly be thought of as a passive power, simply receptive of properties, because in fact the nature of the substance *necessitates and explains* the presence of those properties (at least its essential properties). That is why, prima facie, primitive substance theory is compatible both with nomological necessitarianism and regularity theory. For a primitive substance theorist could claim that the essential properties of the fundamental natural kinds are all *categorical*, and that the substance's abilities to act and react in various ways are not ultimately made true by reference to intrinsic dispositions, but rather by reference to external laws of nature governing that propertied substance,[47] or that they are matters of primitive fact permitting no further explanation.[48]

So another, more circuitous route will be needed to try and draw out a connection between primitive substance theory and dispositionalism. I suggest the following:

Assumption 1 Of the four principal competing ontologies of material composition (atomism versions 1 and 2, the theory of extended simples, and the theory of gunk), only the theory of gunk can be plausibly combined with categoricalism.

Assumption 2 At least one of those four principal competing ontologies of material composition is true.

Premise 1 If categoricalism is true then the theory of gunk is true.

---

[46] Lowe for instance (2006, pp. 92–93) writes that:

> a particular thing's being an instance of a certain substantial universal can never be 'reduced to,' or 'analysed in terms of,' that thing's being characterized by modes of certain properties. It may indeed be the case that things of certain kinds necessarily exemplify certain properties, but that does not imply that their being of those kinds simply consists in their exemplifying certain properties.

[47] The substratum theorist by contrast cannot adopt nomological necessitarianism – contra Armstrong (1997) and others – because as shown in Section 5.4 she needs to re-conceive of the substratum as a power in order to make plausible sense of the instantiation relation, and nomological necessitarianism assumes the reality of the instantiation relation.

[48] Many regularity theorists would be loath to speak of genuinely *essential* properties, whether categorical or dispositional; the point is simply that for those who can find a place for them (on some account of modality) in their particular version of regularity theory, the sort of argument for dispositionalism from substratum theory seen in Section 5.4 – and which they would reject anyway on account of its implicit causal realism – is *doubly* problematic when one attempts to employ it in favour of primitive substance theory.

Premise 2 It is probably the case that primitive substance theory is incompatible with the theory of gunk.

Conclusion 1/Premise 3 Therefore it is probably the case that primitive substance theory is incompatible with categoricalism.

Premise 4 If it is probably the case that primitive substance theory is incompatible with categoricalism, then primitive substance theory supports dispositionalism.

Final Conclusion Therefore primitive substance theory supports dispositionalism.

Assumption 1 reflects one of the key findings of Chapter 4. To recap the general idea very briefly: recall that in the debate over fundamental material composition there are four main alternatives, namely *atomism version 1*, *atomism version 2*, the *theory of extended simples*, and the *theory of gunk*. According to *atomism version 1*, any process of material division, carried out long enough, will eventually come to a definite end. (For example, take a rock and split it into two. Then split each of those smaller rocks. Keep splitting, again and again, until you've reduced them to pebbles, then to sand, then to their constituent molecules, then down to the atoms, then the sub-atomic particles, etc.) Physical nature bottoms out at a level of indivisible objects[49] wholly lacking in spatial extension and thereby wholly lacking actual or potential parts. These are atoms ('atoms' here functioning as a philosophical term of art distinct from the 'atoms' referenced in modern chemistry). On *atomism version 2*, the process comes to an end, but ends at objects that are extended yet still indivisible. Atoms, on this variant of the theory, are fundamental and lack actual proper parts, but are spatially extended. According to advocates of the *theory of extended simples*, processes of material division can in principle go on forever. There is no bottom layer of indivisible objects. The reason why there is no bottom layer is that all physical objects are spatially extended, and hence in principle divisible. But that extension (and divisibility) does not entail that the object has *actual* parts (i.e., parts that are themselves real objects); rather it merely entails that the object has *potential* parts, in the sense that if the object were to be divided, a new, smaller object (constituted out of the same stuff as the original object) would thereby be brought into being. The *theory of gunk*, finally, can be motivated by the rejection of the idea of potential parts. If all physical objects are spatially extended and hence divisible (no atoms allowed), and

---

[49] 'Object' in Chapter 4 was taken as neutral between the competing substance ontologies discussed in the present chapter. In this section we're seeing one way of revoking that neutrality.

extension and divisibility entails that the object has actual parts, then this implies that every physical object is composed of smaller physical objects, which are in their turn composed of still smaller physical objects, which are in their turn, etc. ad infinitum. On the theory of gunk there is no bottom layer to nature, rather there is an infinite descent into ever-tinier objects.

Chapter 4 was principally a defence of what is here labeled assumption 1; it was argued that atomism version 1 supports dispositionalism and that the theory of extended simples entails dispositionalism. Moreover it was observed that atomism version 2 faces a particularly strong objection, widely seen as decisive against it. That left gunk as the only plausibly available option for categoricalists – or rather, the only option provided one also accepts what is here labeled assumption 2, namely that at least one of those prominent theories of material composition is true. I did not defend assumption 2 in Chapter 4 in great detail, merely outlining how there is a decent case to be made that these four options are exhaustive (at least for realists about material objects), which would also accord well with the way the literature on the topic has played out. (That is, the fact that these four options are exhaustive, if it is a fact, would nicely explain why they have been the ones most commonly discussed in both the recent and the historical literature on fundamental material composition.)

It would be difficult to attempt in this section a suitably brief recap of the somewhat complex chains of reasoning employed in Chapter 4. For those readers who have not yet worked through that chapter, but who are reluctant to take assumptions 1 and 2 on board for the sake of argument, I'm afraid there's no substitute for flipping back there.

Premise 1 is really just a concise re-packaging of assumptions 1 and 2, so I will likewise not attempt to justify it here. Premise 2 is the heart of the argument; if it can be shown that primitive substance theory is likely incompatible with the theory of gunk, then the proposition that primitive substance theory supports dispositionalism follows readily enough, as laid out in the latter half of the argument. So premise 2 will be the focus of the remainder of this section.

Why think that primitive substance theory is likely incompatible with the theory of gunk? The basic idea runs as follows: as noted above, primitive substance theory is committed both to the real distinction between a substance and its properties (whether those are conceived as instantiated property-universals or as tropes), and to the ontological priority of the substance vis-à-vis those properties. The nature of the substance entails the presence of its properties – or, more precisely, its *essential* properties. The specifics of how this works is a matter of discussion within primitive substance theory.[50] But that there is this explanatory priority is a common commitment of primitive substance theorists. Now, according to our best current physics, among the defining properties of fundamental particles (e.g., electrons and quarks, which so far as we know do not have lower-level component parts) are properties with determinate quantitative values. An electron for instance doesn't just have the determinable 'rest mass' as a defining property, but rest mass of a precise quantity: 9.109×10^{-28} g. The primitive substance theorist will want to cash this out by saying that the substance-universal/kind 'electron' is necessarily characterized by 'rest mass of 9.109×10^{-28} grams.' (For the nominalist primitive substance theorist, re-phrase in terms of the individual nature of the concrete electron.) Of course, if the theory of gunk is true, then our best current physics is incomplete – electrons are not really fundamental, rather they have lower-level component parts, because all physical things have lower-level component parts. Assume that is the case. Then presumably the precise rest mass of an electron, regarded within physics as a defining property of an electron, is not actually entailed by the substance-universal/kind 'electron' (or the individual nature of the concrete object), but rather is derived from the ever-smaller determinate mass values of the constituent objects making up the electron. Just as the determinate mass of the globe on my desk (say, 1 kg) is derived from the determinate masses of its component parts,[51] so the electron's determinate mass, if it has lower-level constituent parts, is presumably the sum of the determinate masses of those constituent parts. And much the same can be said for any intrinsic property of the electron properly expressed as a determinate quantitative value. But that conflicts with a core commitment of primitive substance theory, according to which the essential properties of a substance are entailed by that substance's nature. Put succinctly: if the theory of gunk is true, then not all of the essential properties of a substance are entailed by the nature of that substance (whether that nature is conceived in realist terms as *universal* kind-essence like 'electron' or in nominalist terms as an *individual* nature). But the claim that all of the essential properties

---

[50] More broadly, it is also a matter of discussion within natural-kind essentialism, which primitive substance theory is committed to (at least on its realist rather than nominalist formulation). We'll discuss natural-kind essentialism further in Chapter 6.

[51] Clearly it has lower-level component parts that are themselves objects – few would claim that the globe on my desk is an irreducible substance instantiating a natural kind.

of a substance are entailed by the nature of that substance is a core commitment of primitive substance theory. Therefore the theory of gunk is incompatible with primitive substance theory.[52]

That conclusion, as just stated, is more robust than what is actually given in premise 2. The weaker formulation there is on account of the objections available against this line of reasoning. For it is open to at least two:

(A) Perhaps in the case of the electron, its defining rest mass is not actually derived from its lower-level parts. Maybe it is in the case of the globe on my desk, but not in the case of the electron. Perhaps once we get to the quantum level, intrinsic properties properly expressed in determinate quantitative terms simply work differently – one has hit upon a level which, while not fundamental in terms of its *parts* (there is no fundamental level in that sense, on the theory of gunk), is nevertheless fundamental in terms of its *properties*. That way, the substance-universal/kind 'electron' could still entail its determinate rest mass directly, even though concrete electrons are composed of an infinite number of ever-smaller objects.[53]

In reply, I have to grant that I don't see this as obviously impossible (assuming that gunk is not obviously impossible). Perhaps there is some sort of decisive split in nature, whereby the hierarchy of physical objects has no endpoint (things are composed of smaller things which are composed of smaller things …) but the hierarchy of intrinsic properties *does* – even intrinsic properties with determinate quantitative values. However, I also don't see any easy way of motivating such a split, let alone a principled way to motivate the positing of a specific site for the cutoff. Clearly the level of nature represented by my desk globe is not where we would want to posit the cutoff, but why then is the cutoff at the level of sub-atomic particles like electrons rather than the level of molecules? After all, both are composite entities having lower-level

---

[52] For the regularity theorist: note that nothing in this argument that explicitly presupposes robust realism about causation. Entailment is typically seen as a *non-causal* relation, and certainly within primitive substance theory (and natural-kind essentialism) it is *not* claimed that the substance-universal/kind (or the concrete individual nature) is the *efficient cause* of the presence of the essential properties associated with the kind. Moreover there is no need to see the derivation of determinate mass from component parts as a causal relation.

[53] Bird (2007, pp. 14–15) discusses something akin to this.

component parts. At any rate, I am not claiming that such a 'primitive substance theory + gunk' model is impossible, but I am claiming that it would require a good deal of additional effort to round it out and motivate it. In the meantime I think we are warranted in remaining sceptical concerning the workability of the project.

(B) Perhaps rest mass is simply a poor candidate for a defining, intrinsic property. Perhaps it is a poor candidate precisely because it does involve a determinate quantitative value. Perhaps only determinable properties are among the essential properties of any physical object, or at least determinates specified in qualitative rather than quantitative terms.

In reply I will just observe that this would place 'primitive substance theory + gunk' in an awkward spot. The theory of gunk is already in prima facie conflict with our best current physics, which seems to suggest that objects like electrons do not have lower-level component parts. This position is worsened if the theory of gunk also has to claim that what physicists typically take to be a defining property of electrons is not really such. Of course this is not a knockdown argument; our best current physics might be wrong on both fronts, and given how much these sorts of claims within physics have changed over time, those working in metaphysics of science are hardly obliged simply to read off their metaphysics from current physics. We are however obliged to take current physics seriously in our theorizing, and to the extent that a metaphysical theory clashes on multiple fronts with current physics, that is rightly seen as a downside for that theory – hardly a death blow, but a downside nonetheless.[54]

So while I think there are plausible replies to these two objections, I also think these replies are not decisive. As such, the proposition that is

---

[54] Note that rest mass may or may not be an intrinsic property of electrons; the discovery of the Higgs boson in fact suggests that it is not, but rather is derived from electrons' interaction with the Higgs boson. However, that would not really affect the dialectic here, for then it just turns out to be the case that the really fundamental intrinsic property at play in the electron is not mass but rather whatever property enables the electron to interact with the Higgs boson such as to acquire mass, and more specifically to acquire that *precise* mass via that interaction. But then the argument above could be run just as well on that other, unspecified property, which presumably will also have to be defined in determinate quantitative terms.

premise 2 is most plausibly stated in probabilistic terms: it is probably the case that primitive substance theory is incompatible with the theory of gunk. Since the remainder of the argument follows readily enough, I will leave the discussion there.

I would however like to make a final observation about the relationship between primitive substance theory and dispositionalism. The focus of this section has of course been on showing that the former supports the latter, in keeping with this section's place within the overall argument of this chapter, laid out in Section 5.1 and recapped in the conclusion below. Yet one might also argue that dispositionalism supports (or even entails) primitive substance theory. How? Consider the commonsensical claim that dispositions are not really the actors in causal relations, despite the sometimes inexact language of dispositionalists. That is, while dispositionalists sometimes speak of negative charge attracting or repelling particles, or solubility prompting dissolution, etc., this is plausibly regarded as non-literal. Powers don't literally *do* things, rather *things* do things *by virtue of* their powers. The electron attracts the proton by means of its negative charge, the salt dissolves in water by means of its solubility, etc. Dispositionalists sometimes make this point explicit; Dumsday (2012a, p. 53) for instance writes:

> It is ubiquitous in the literature to see talk of one power acting on another power. I have been cavalier about such language myself in this article. But of course it can only be a convenient shorthand for the more stilted and inconvenient, but true, 'one *object* acts on another object *by virtue of* its power'. I never act on a disposition, I act on an object. I step on a vase, and, as a result of that vase's fragility (plus a swathe of background conditions, unmanifested *ceteris paribus* clauses etc.) the vase breaks. Nevertheless, I did not step on the vase's fragility. I stepped on the vase. Objects act and are acted upon through their powers. It is not the powers that do the acting and being acted upon. [Emphases in original]

Consider also Ellis (2002, p. 3):

> The forces of nature are the kinds of causal influences that things exert on each other, and the things themselves are always the agents of these influences. Thus, if one thing causes another to do something, then this is because it has the causal power to do so, and it achieves its effect by the exercise of this power. It acts, and the other thing reacts. Or, perhaps, they interact, so that each responds to the other. Essentialists thus suppose that the inanimate objects of nature are genuine casual agents ...

Or consider Armstrong (1978, p. 132): "If the world consists simply of particulars having properties and relations, it is particulars and particulars alone which can act and be acted upon. But we must add: they act and are acted on solely in virtue of their properties, non-relational and relational; in virtue of their nature." Whittle (2016, p. 14) makes a similar point when she writes that the "function of properties is not to stand in causal relations, but rather to 'enable' their bearers to be causes ... Their properties are what make substances powerful, causally efficacious entities that cause things. But properties are not themselves powerful entities that cause things. Properties are the kingmakers, substance is king." This is at least prima facie a plausible picture of the relationship between substances and their powers, one that remains plausible whether powers are taken as irreducible ingredients in ontology (as on the dispositionalism affirmed by Dumsday and Ellis), or as reducible to categorical properties + laws (Armstrong) or as reducible to categorical properties + primitive functional facts (Whittle).[55] The question is whether this picture is sustainable on the substance ontologies discussed in this chapter. And a case can be made that it is not sustainable on hylomorphism, substratum theory, or bundle theory.

Briefly: (a) hylomorphism involves commitment to the irreducible reality of prime matter, which is conceived as a *substantial disposition*, namely the power to become different kinds of substance by taking on new substantial forms. Prime matter, in other words, is a power. It is not a power *of a pre-existing substance* (it is not a property), rather it is a basic ontological ingredient of substances, a substantial principle. Prime matter is acted upon, and a compound substance (prime matter + substantial form) results. That prime matter is both a power and what is acted upon is made more evident when we recall one of its core explanatory roles: to function as a source of continuity across radical change, i.e., change in natural kind membership/substantial form. The compound substance (the form + matter) cannot be that which is acted upon throughout that whole process of change, because the compound does not persist through the whole process of change – when the one substantial form is replaced by another, there is a different compound. That which is acted upon *when this change is effected* must be that which remains through the process of change, and in this case that is the prime matter. Thus prime matter is both a power and prime matter is what is acted upon (at least in such cases of change in kind-membership), contradicting the prima

---

[55] We'll discuss Whittle's account further in chapter 6.

facie plausible picture just laid out.[56] **(b)** Much the same can be said of substratum theory, or rather substratum theory as re-conceived in Section 5.3 above. For now the substratum is itself a power, much like prime matter, and just like prime matter is the direct object of causal interaction, the direct recipient of causal activity. The substratum is not a power of a pre-existing substance (it is not a property) rather it is a basic ontological ingredient of substances. The substratum is acted upon, and a compound substance (substratum + properties qua tied together by instantiation) results. As with hylomorphism, in the case of substratum theory the compound substance cannot be that which is acted upon throughout a whole process of radical change, because the compound does not persist through the whole process of radical change – when the properties are replaced by others (most clearly in cases where *all* the properties are replaced by others) there is a different compound. That which is acted upon when this change is effected must be that which remains through the process of change, namely the substratum.[57] **(c)** The unsustainability of the prima facie plausible picture is perhaps most obvious on bundle theory, for dispositionalist bundle theory openly embraces freestanding powers (or complexes of compresent powers) that act and are acted upon. What we think of as substances just are collections of connected properties – and on pan-dispositionalism (probably the only workable form of bundle theory, if the argument of Section 5.4 is sound) all of those properties are powers.

In short, if we want to maintain the commonsensical picture that powers are never themselves the actors in causal interactions, the only

---

[56] Note that while prime matter must be the recipient of causal activity here, this does not automatically imply that there is ever a time when the prime matter exists wholly devoid of any form. One might try to model substantial change as the instantaneous replacement of one substantial form with another, such that there is no actual temporal interval where the matter is formless. The point is simply that the original compound (the substantial form + prime matter) cannot be the subject of the change, since the compound does not persist through the change – only the matter persists. (However, if *formless* matter is invoked – and it is on some historical versions of hylomorphism, though not on the currently more popular Thomistic version – then the fact that matter can be the direct recipient of causal activity follows even more readily than it does on the argument I've just provided. Whether that makes the view more or less problematic in the present context might be debated; in fact one might argue that to affirm the possibility of independently existent prime matter is actually to affirm a sort of primitive substance theory, since prime matter on this view looks more like a substance on its own accord than a substantial principle. In some historical variants of these substance ontologies, the walls between theories seems to become thinner. And these historical variants are not *merely* historical; Scotistic hylomorphism for instance, on which prime matter can exist independently of substantial form, still has advocates.)

[57] As with hylomorphism, radical change on substratum theory need not be seen as automatically entailing the proposition that a substratum ever exists at a time utterly devoid of all properties.

way to do so is to pair dispositionalism with primitive substance theory. To put it more formally:

Premise 1 If dispositionalism is true and substances are always the literal subjects of causal interaction, then primitive substance theory is true.

Premise 2 Dispositionalism is true and substances are always the literal subjects of causal interaction.

Conclusion Therefore, primitive substance theory is true.

Granted, we may not want to maintain that commonsensical picture; indeed one might take the plausibility of hylomorphism, or of the other two substance ontologies, as an implicit indictment of that commonsensical (mere folk-metaphysical?) picture. Or one might maintain that although the commonsensical picture holds most of the time, instances of radical change (change in kind-membership) in which prime matter and substrata are implicated as causal subjects constitute a narrow exception. (Though that is not a point the bundle theorist can rely on.) Or one might maintain that the commonsensical picture is correct, and that because prime matter and substrata are dispositions falling under the category of 'substance' or 'substantial principle' rather than 'property,' they actually adhere to that picture. (That would however require at least an adjustment of the usual terminology at play in these substance ontologies; as noted above in Section 5.1, the typical practice is to reserve the designation 'substance' for the compound of substratum + properties (or prime matter + substantial form) rather than the substratum itself.) Still, as there has been very little by way of discussion of this issue in the existing literature on dispositionalism, this would be a fitting topic for future work. In particular, if primitive substance theorists could shore up the intuitive plausibility of the commonsensical picture (i.e., the second conjunct of premise 2), perhaps some way of arguing for its metaphysical necessity, then they would end up with a more pressing, novel argument for the truth of that substance ontology – at least, a novel argument for it given the truth of dispositionalism.

5.6   Conclusion

To recap, the principal aim of this chapter has been to justify premise 1 of this argument:

Premise 1 If any one of the four main substance ontologies is true, then dispositionalism is probably true.

Premise 2 At least one of the four main substance ontologies is true.
Conclusion Therefore dispositionalism is probably true.

As noted in Section 5.1, not much effort is made here to justify premise 2, and I am (mostly) content to see the categoricalist take the arguments of this chapter and use them as fuel to run a modus tollens and conclude to the falsity of these four main substance ontologies. Regardless then of whether this chapter is taken as an argument in favour of dispositionalism or as the springboard for some new projects for categoricalists, I hope at least to have succeeded in showing that there are some interesting and largely neglected connections between dispositionalism and substance ontology.

CHAPTER 6

Dispositionalism and Natural-Kind Essentialism

6.1   Introduction

As we've seen, with respect to the ontology of laws the two main competitors to dispositionalism are regularity theory and nomological necessitarianism. In citing advocates of the latter, I have repeatedly drawn attention to the important accounts of Lange (2004; 2009; 2009a) and Whittle (2009), whose theories are more akin to nomological necessitarianism than to the other two options, and yet do not fall strictly within it. They argue that laws are ultimately reducible to primitive subjunctive facts (on Lange's terminology) or primitive causal or functional facts (on Whittle's). As we shall see, this form of reductionism presents an especially tricky challenge to the dispositionalist.

I wish to put forward a response to this challenge, one which requires situating dispositionalism within a robust form of natural-kind essentialism. On this view, dispositions are dependent on ontologically prior natural-kind essences. I will show how the positing of such essences allows the dispositionalist to sidestep Lange and Whittle's anti-dispositionalist arguments.

The remainder is structured as follows: in the next section I outline the reductionist strategies of Lange and Whittle, explaining how they differ from the more common categoricalist arguments and why they constitute a particularly forceful objection to dispositionalism. Then in Section 6.3 I lay out a potential reply, one which will be deemed unsound but which will be instructive and lead naturally into a more workable strategy. This I present in Section 6.4.

6.2   Lange and Whittle On Dispositionalism

Dispositionalists typically hold that the laws of nature in some way reduce to (or are eliminable in favour of) dispositions. So it is hardly surprising that Lange's objection to dispositionalism is tied in with his broader view concerning the truthmakers for nomic truths. I lack the space to do justice to Lange's account of laws, but I believe the nuances of that account can be put to one side for the present. The important thing to note is that for Lange, part of what guarantees the obtaining of stable regularities in nature are primitive subjunctive facts. It is these, rather than primitive laws or dispositions, which do the real ontological work. "In other words, rather than holding that the lawhood of p, q, etc. is responsible for various subjunctive facts (namely, those that make stable the set spanned by p, q, etc.), I suggest the opposite order of onto-logical priority: those subjunctive facts make it a law that p, a law that q, etc." (2009, p. 311). Lange contrasts his perspective with that of disposi-tionalists, writing that "rather than taking the laws to be determined by the essences of the properties figuring in them, this approach takes the laws as determined by various non-nomic actual and counterfactual truths. These counterfactuals are ontologically prior to the facts about what the laws are" (2004, p. 240). With primitive subjunctive facts in place, there is no need to posit dispositions as basic entities in ontology (2009, p. 316):

> Whereas Cartwright and Mumford place capacities (a.k.a. causal powers, 'natures') at the bottom of the world, I locate subjunctive facts there. Just as Cartwright and Mumford see little or no work for laws to do, once capacities are admitted, I see no work for capacities to do once primitive subjunctive facts are admitted. I ask Cartwright and Mumford: Are capa-cities supposed to be ontologically distinct from subjunctive facts? If so, then how do capacities make the subjunctive facts turn out a certain way? If not, then a capacity cannot scientifically explain subjunctive facts, since a capacity just is a collection of subjunctive facts.

With respect to the dilemma Lange is presenting, the dispositionalist will likely wish to respond with her own appeal to a sort of primitiveness. It is generally thought that the identity conditions of a disposition involve at least: (a) a manifestation or range of manifestations, and (b) a condi-tion or set of conditions according to which that manifestation or those manifestations will come about (including any ceteris paribus stipula-tions). Dispositionalists hold that the truthmaker for the possible mani-festation will involve a real and irreducible disposition, such that when faced with Lange's question of why dispositions make the subjunctive facts turn out a certain way, the response will likely consist in simply affirming that that is just what dispositions are for – that is their basic role. However, this does not really impact Lange's underlying point:

if the role of a disposition is simply to serve as the ground or truthmaker for a counterfactual truth, such that it is taken as basic and the counterfactual as derived, what is to stop someone from dropping the disposition and making the counterfactual truth itself basic, and itself the truthmaker for law-statements and disposition-ascriptions?

Granted, the notion that there could be ontologically primitive subjunctive facts has struck some as being odd and counterintuitive, as was noted in the previous chapter. But in fairness, there is no shortage of Humeans and others who find dispositionalism odd and counterintuitive, so one might maintain that all sides can play the oddness card. Dispositions do have the advantage of longstanding philosophical pedigree and a clear link to ordinary language, but Lange's theory is not without advantages of its own. Moreover, one might think it more parsimonious: rather than have an ontology of dispositions and the subjunctive facts they ground, there is now just the subjunctive facts.

Whittle's (2009) case is similar to Lange's. She reduces dispositions to primitive causal or functional facts rather than to primitive subjunctives, which seems a purely terminological difference. However, the broader ontology in which she situates her case is importantly different from Lange's. She advocates a non-Humean causal nominalism, one in which there are no real properties (whether conceived as universals or tropes),[1] but in which there is still real causation. The causal facts are not grounded in causal powers, or any other sort of property; rather, they are primitive. Lange, by contrast, is not committed to nominalism, and allows for the reality and irreducibility of categorical properties. However, they are agreed in the basic strategy for reducing dispositions, and my discussion will focus on what they hold in common.

Whittle and Lange's proposal may strike the reader as reminiscent of Rylean inference tickets, and Whittle openly acknowledges the association (2009, p. 268):

"It is similar, at least in spirit, to Ryle's account of dispositions, because the powers of objects ultimately get reduced to facts about what would and could happen to objects." That account is typically thought by dispositionalists to founder on its lack of truthmakers. Whittle

---

[1] "In this paper, it [nominalism] is taken to be the conjunction of two theses. The first is the standard claim that everything that exists is particular, so there are no entities that exist in more than one place at the same time. The second asserts that there are no basic property instances or tropes" (2009, p. 244).

sketches out a few possible replies to this worry, before settling on the following (2009, p. 283):

> Realists might interject that this violates the truthmaking principle, since there is nothing that makes this counterfactual true of its object. But at this level, it is not clear how seriously causal nominalists need take this complaint. After all, realists such as Armstrong or Shoemaker also posit irreducible facts. Realist causal theorists, for instance, claim that what makes it true that a Xs in circumstances C1 is that a instantiates an irreducibly powerful universal or trope … Causal nominalists, then, can respond to these objectors by turning the tables and fairly questioning the explanatory value of such metaphysical posits. They can argue that appealing to sui generis powerful universals or tropes, as the realist causal theorist does, or powerful laws and causally inert individuals, as Armstrong does, offers us no real advancement. For, either way, we still have to make do with irreducible causal facts.

The challenge being raised here is a powerful one. A number of the usual replies that the dispositionalist would make against a Humean anti-dispositionalist have no application here, since both Lange and Whittle admit the reality of causation and posit truthmakers for nomic truths that involve necessary connections, by way of primitive subjunctive facts. And even if one is leery of taking such facts as ontologically primitive, the dispositionalist is still obliged to explain how exactly she can block the reduction of dispositions to primitive subjunctive facts.

That is the task I attempt in what follows. As part of this attempt, I will first take the reader through a potential solution that, while ultimately unsound, will pave the way for a more promising strategy.

6.3   'Dispositional Properties' versus 'Behavioural Dispositions'

One of the in-house disputes among dispositionalists concerns whether we should think of there being a distinct disposition for each possible determinate stimulus/manifestation pair, or if we should think of at least some dispositions as generic or determinable, serving to ground a *range* of subordinate stimulus/manifestation pairs. In a somewhat idiosyncratic fashion Ellis refers to dispositions of the first sort (dispositions having only a single determinate stimulus/manifestation pair) as *behavioural dispositions* and dispositions of the second sort (any that ground a range of stimulus/manifestation pairs) as *dispositional properties*. I will follow his usage for the remainder of this chapter (and only for this chapter).[2]

---

[2] His distinction is similar to the division between single-track vs. multi-track dispositions mentioned in earlier chapters, though not quite equivalent.

Ellis (2001, ch. 3) and Shoemaker (1998) are among those who defend the irreducibility of dispositional properties, while Mumford (2004, pp. 170–174; 2007), and Shoemaker (1980) are among those who maintain that they can be rejected in favour of clusters of behavioural dispositions. To clarify, consider the following passage from Ellis (2001, p. 120):

> The causal powers, capacities, and propensities that feature in scientific explanations, for example, are all dispositional properties ... For each is supportive of a wide range of specific behavioral dispositions, often an infinite number of them, and for each of them it is true that their identities depend on the sets of behavioral dispositions they support. The refractivity of a certain kind of glass, for example, is a dispositional property of the glass that grounds infinitely many behavioral dispositions. The dispositions it grounds are characterized by a range of quantitatively different circumstances (different angles of incidence, different frequencies of incident light, different refractivity of the medium, and so on) resulting in a range of quantitatively different effects (different angles of refraction, total internal reflection, and so on). This is the sort of thing we have in mind when we speak of a dispositional property. It is a causal power, capacity, or propensity that underlies a range of behavioral dispositions.

So although there is a certain dependence of a 'dispositional property' on its 'behavioural dispositions,' in the epistemic sense that we can identify a dispositional property only by the behavioural dispositions it grounds, from a metaphysical perspective the dispositional property grounds the behavioural dispositions. The dispositional property is thought to play an important explanatory role, grounding and serving to bundle together diverse but interrelated behavioural dispositions.

By contrast, Mumford argues that there is no such property over and above the behavioural dispositions. The latter have no ground. Rather, they function as causal grounds by themselves. What we think of a dispositional property (in Ellis' sense) is really just a cluster of behavioural dispositions (2004, p. 171): "The cluster view is that there is nothing more to a property than its powers and that the powers fix the identity of the property."

My aim in laying this out is not to begin adjudicating between these two positions; rather, it is just to point out that if the dispositionalist adopts the Ellis/later Shoemaker view here, it might be thought to supply an escape route from Lange and Whittle's argument. For although their reduction might apply to a behavioural disposition, it is not clear that it could apply to a dispositional property. The reason is that the property's

identity does not consist in giving rise to certain behaviours (under certain circumstances etc.). Rather, it is a further step removed from the
relevant counterfactuals – it grounds the diverse dispositions that in turn
supply the particular manifestations. In consequence, the property might
be thought to remain out of reach of reduction to such subjunctive facts.

I think this reply is unsuccessful. Lange and Whittle could respond
by suggesting that to possess the so-called dispositional property is for
yet another subjunctive fact to obtain, just a more fundamental one.
The notion of nested subjunctives plays an important role in Lange's
ontology of laws, and he would have no difficulty accommodating the
idea that a certain primitive subjunctive fact could be in a relation of
ontological priority with respect to a set of subordinate subjunctive
facts.[3] For him, the ontological category 'subjunctive fact' is primitive
in the sense that its members have a causal base in the members of no
other ontological category (such as laws or dispositions). This does
not mean that there can be no relations of priority among subjunctive
facts themselves. Furthermore, the more basic subjunctive facts can
play just the same grounding and bundling roles as that played by
dispositional properties. In consequence, this potential reply on the
dispositionalist's behalf is unsuccessful. But the preceding discussion
will still prove profitable, as it points the way to a more promising
alternative.

6.4   Turning to (Robust) Natural-Kind Essentialism

I want to turn now to another, closely parallel debate, namely the question of whether natural kinds are reducible to their associated properties
(whether categorical, dispositional, or both). As one might expect, opi-
nions are divided. Armstrong (1997, pp. 65–68) is among the reduction-
ists, and holds that they are reducible to nomically governed categorical
properties instantiated in substrata. For instance what we might initially
think of as an irreducible kind like 'electron' is on this view reducible to
a law-governed conjunction of fundamental properties: negative charge +
half-integral spin + precise rest mass of 9.109×10^{-28} g, etc. There
is no such thing as a kind or nature of electronhood over and above
those nomically connected properties being instantiated in a substratum.
Along similar lines, Bird (2007, pp. 208–211; 2012) and Hawley and
Bird (2011) suggest kinds are reducible to sets of dispositions reliably

---

[3] See for instance Lange (2009a, pp. 37–42).

linked together by laws of nature.[4] Elder (2004, p. 26; 2007), though a self-identified natural-kind essentialist, likewise views them as consisting of clusters of properties connected nomically or causally. On this view then, there are no irreducible substance-universals/kinds like 'electron' or 'proton' that play an explanatory role in nature; rather, basic properties like negative charge and half-integral spin link up together with other properties in certain reliable ways, and given their reliable clustering we find it convenient to denominate these clusters as 'kinds.' A natural kind is thus not a fundamental ingredient in ontology, over and above the clustered properties. This position on kinds vis-à-vis their associated properties is analogous to the Mumford/early Shoemaker perspective on the reducibility of dispositional properties to behavioural dispositions.

On the non-reductionist side one finds more robust versions of natural-kind essentialism, in which kinds are not reducible to collections of properties. We have already encountered this sort of essentialism in Chapter 5, insofar as commitment to it is a feature of both primitive substance theory and hylomorphism. On these views, the *substance-universal* or *kind* (terminology commonly employed by recent primitive substance theorists like Lowe (2006)) or the *substantial form* (the preferred language of hylomorphists) is real and irreducible to the properties necessarily associated with it; moreover it serves to ground those properties, explaining their presence and coherent unity. So for an advocate of this view, there is a distinct universal 'electron' whose instantiation entails the subordinate instantiations of properties such as mass, charge, etc. Importantly, this holds not just for the dispositional properties, but for the fundamental categorical properties as well (if there are any). In what follows I'll use *kind* to refer to this sort of universal, taking it as neutral between the typically associated substance-ontologies,[5] and I'll use *robust natural-kind essentialism* to refer to any theory that accepts the irreducible reality of kinds.[6]

---

[4] "The laws of nature will explain why-necessarily-there are no members of chemical and microphysical kinds that lack certain properties, why of necessity certain properties cluster together in a partially or fully precise manner" (2007, p. 211). This appeal to laws as playing an apparently robust and independent governing role with respect to properties arguably does not sit comfortably with Bird's larger dispositionalist ontology.

[5] Note that this robust natural-kind essentialism is compatible also with substratum theory and bundle theory, though these combinations are not as commonly seen in the literature.

[6] The terminology is variable; Dumsday (2016b) for instance calls it *priority natural-kind essentialism* (to signal that on this view the kind is ontologically prior to the properties necessarily associated with it), while Ellis (2001) calls it *scientific essentialism* and Oderberg (2007) *real essentialism*. Still others refer to it as *Neo-Aristotelianism*.

To bring this back to our earlier contrast, the position of robust natural-kind essentialism with respect to the irreducibility of kinds to their associated properties is parallel to the position of Ellis and the later Shoemaker with respect to the irreducibility of what Ellis terms 'dispositional properties' to 'behavioural dispositions.' For them, dispositional properties ground behavioural dispositions. For the advocate of robust natural-kind essentialism, the kind grounds the range of dispositional and categorical properties definitive of that kind.

The upshot: I wish to argue that if the dispositionalist situates her theory within this form of essentialism, she will thereby obtain an effective counter to the reductionist argument proposed by Lange and Whittle.

Think again of the failed reply we examined in Section 6.3. The problem with it was that even though dispositional properties are thought (by their advocates) to play an important explanatory role over and above the role played by subordinate behavioural dispositions, Lange and Whittle's primitive subjunctives can satisfy that explanatory role, since their position allows for priority relations among subjunctive facts. More basic subjunctive facts can account for the presence of and ordering among less basic subjunctive facts. Dispositional properties, as much as behavioural dispositions, simply collapse into primitive subjunctives.

One might suppose that kinds would succumb to a similar problem. They ground fundamental dispositional properties, just as dispositional properties ground behavioural dispositions, so what is to prevent their reduction to (still higher-level) primitive subjunctives? In other words, just as Lange and Whittle take dispositions to be redundant posits once primitive subjunctive facts are admitted into ontology (both behavioural dispositions and the grounding dispositional properties), one might think that the kinds supposedly grounding the dispositions are likewise rendered redundant. So why think that kinds exist, any more than dispositions? Both might seem redundant.

In reply, it is important to note that the kind cannot itself be reduced to a primitive subjunctive fact, since it plays a wider explanatory role than that played by a primitive subjunctive – even one of Lange's aforementioned higher level subjunctives. To see this, recall the wider explanatory role traditionally ascribed to kinds. They ground not only a variety of dispositions, but also the fundamental categorical properties that a member of that kind instantiates. Robust natural-kind essentialism thus provides an account of the relationship between dispositional and categorical properties, grounding them in a single principle. This stance automatically drives a wedge between the notion of a natural-kind essence and that of a primitive subjunctive fact, since the scope of its explanatory role is wider. A primitive subjunctive fact is ordered to a possible future state of affairs, and cannot, in and of itself, explain the present instantiation of a categorical property like shape or size. By contrast, the kind-essence, as traditionally conceived, does exactly that.

In short then, by situating dispositionalism within robust natural-kind essentialism, the dispositionalist is provided a way of avoiding the reduction of those dispositions to Lange and Whittle's primitive subjunctives. This is because although the dispositions are real and irreducible (hence preserving dispositionalism), they are not ungrounded, but instead are rooted in the kind. Consequently dispositions cannot be reducible to primitive subjunctives. And the kind in its turn is not reducible to a primitive subjunctive fact, as its explanatory role goes beyond that of such a fact.

So someone committed to dispositionalism has good reason to take robust natural-kind essentialism seriously. It may not be the only way to reply to Lange and Whittle's reductionism; however, it may be the only plausible way to do so that does not involve an a priori ruling out of the possibility of primitive subjunctive facts (on account of their oddness or whatnot). To put the point a bit more formally:

> **Premise 1** If dispositionalism is true, then it is probably the case that robust natural-kind essentialism is true.
> **Premise 2** Dispositionalism is true.
> **Conclusion** Therefore, it is probably the case that robust natural-kind essentialism is true.

The justification for premise 1 rests on the argument that linking dispositionalism to robust natural-kind essentialism supplies a good way to defuse an important objection facing dispositionalism. If it could be shown that it is the best way to do so, then the force of premise 1 would be increased. And of course if it could be shown that it is the only way to address the objection, then the argument could be reformulated so as to conclude to an entailment relation rather than a probabilistic one.

I leave it to those dispositionalists who reject kinds to develop alternative replies. And some will have to develop alternative replies. For the argument I've made assumes that there are fundamental dispositions and fundamental categorical properties, with neither sort of property being reducible to the other and both being grounded in kinds. Recalling the distinctions drawn in Chapter 5 between *mixed view dispositionalism*, *identity theory dispositionalism*, *pan-dispositionalism*, and *neutral monism*, it is clear that pan-dispositionalists cannot employ my reply to Lange and Whittle, since pan-dispositionalists maintain that what we think of as categorical properties are either reducible to dispositional properties or that they are (contrary to initial appearances) actually dispositional in nature. By contrast, mixed view dispositionalists explicitly accept the irreducibility of categorical properties to powers, while identity theorists accept categorical properties as equally fundamental (insofar as every property necessarily has both dispositional and categorical identity conditions). And a neutral monist could re-formulate the argument by saying that the really fundamental sort of property (itself neither dispositional nor categorical but serving to ground predicates of both sort) is grounded in the kind. So to the extent to which one finds Lange and Whittle's objection pressing, and in the absence of other replies, dispositionalists have some new reason to favour one of the other three versions of the theory over and against pan-dispositionalism.

By way of potential objections, the more obvious concern facing the argument is that a great many still look askance on robust natural-kind essentialism. It has taken several decades for robust causal powers to once again become respectable topics of debate in analytic philosophy, having been snatched from the Humean bonfire. Trying to pair them up with irreducible kinds, with all the additional historical baggage they might be thought to carry, could be seen as a case of the cure being worse than the disease.

By way of reply I will note a few quick points: first, a kind grounding multiple properties is no odder than a dispositional property grounding multiple behavioural dispositions, which as we have seen is an idea that has received attention in recent literature. Second, it is no odder than the primitive relation of nomological necessitation existing between universals in Armstrong's version of nomological necessitarianism. Third, even if such 'innocence by association' points do not move one's intuitions, and one's reservations happen to centre around the precise relationship between the kind and its associated properties, it can still be noted that there are various options available for explicating this relation. Up to this point I have referred to it as 'grounding,' but obviously that notion is itself much disputed in current metaphysics. Historically, how exactly to understand the explanatory relation obtaining between a kind and the properties necessarily associated with it has been a source of discussion among advocates of robust natural-kind essentialism. Is it akin to conceptual entailment, with the kind entailing a particular set of properties? Is it instead more akin to causation, with the kind-essence causally giving rise to the set? Or might it be a primitive sort of grounding relation? I will not review the various options that have been taken here, historically and in the recent literature. For present purposes the important point is that, provided one can motivate the need to posit kinds (and I believe that the essentialists cited have provided plausible motivations), the further clarification of the precise ontological relationship between the kinds and their associated properties can be regarded more as an in-house task for advocates of robust natural-kind essentialism to undertake than as an objection against the view.[7] Of course, if further efforts were to reveal that all of these options were unworkable, that would constitute an objection, but that state of affairs is far from obtaining. Fourth and finally, I suspect that for many the underlying concern about admitting kinds is less about how to formulate the surrounding metaphysics and more a reaction against the whiff of pre-modern, unscientific mediaevalism some associate with it. Here I would just observe (in line with Ellis (2001; 2002) most especially) that if one believes conformity with common conventions of scientific terminology and conceptualization is an advantage for theories within the metaphysics of science (if only a small one), then acceptance of kinds should be looked up on favourably. Kind-talk is utterly ubiquitous across all the natural sciences; and I would suggest that a great many physicists (for instance) would be loath to admit that the massive efforts devoted to the classification of apparently fundamental types of particle must automatically fail to carve nature at its deepest joints insofar as no *kinds* really belong there.

6.5 Conclusion

I have argued that although the reductionist strategy pursued by Lange and Whittle constitutes a unique and important challenge to dispositionalism, advocates of the theory can meet that challenge by pairing it with robust natural-kind essentialism. Insofar as the latter theory has undergone a notable revival in recent philosophy of science and metaphysics (much like dispositionalism), and insofar as their pairing has been quite a common one historically and remains so today, hopefully most dispositionalists will be willing to see it as a live option.

---

[7] For a recent discussion devoted to this issue see Oderberg (2011).

CHAPTER 7

Dispositionalism and Spacetime

7.1 Introduction

Dispositionalism intersects with a number of debates concerning the metaphysics of spacetime, and in this chapter we will touch on three of these. The first is taken up fairly briefly and pertains to the ongoing debate over whether spacetime is to be conceived as a substance. I point out that, in light of the conclusion reached in Chapter 5, whichever of the major alternatives one adopts an argument for dispositionalism becomes available. Then in Section 7.3 I explicate and critique an argument by Koons and Pickavance (2015, pp. 196–197) according to which dispositionalism can play an important role in showing that time travel is impossible. In Section 7.4 I turn to Mumford's (2009) argument that dispositionalism is most naturally paired with endurantism and is probably incompatible with perdurantism (these being the principal competing views concerning the nature of persistence). After explicating Mumford's arguments for this thesis, I proceed to suggest two strategies for rendering dispositionalism compatible with perdurantism. The first relies on turning to a less-often discussed version of perdurantism, one formulated in such a way as to allow for irreducibly extended temporal parts and causal processes within them. The second strategy works within the formulation of perdurantism Mumford focuses on (a formulation more common today, according to which temporal parts are instantaneous and discrete). I tentatively suggest a strategy that would permit even this version of perdurantism to be paired with dispositionalism.

7.2 Dispositionalism and the Substantivalism versus Relationism Debate

There are two main types of theories concerning the metaphysics of space: substantivalism and relationism (often termed 'relationalism').

On the former, space is an existent thing, a substance (reading 'substance' here as neutral between the four main competing substance ontologies discussed in Chapter 5). On the latter, space is not a substance; rather, the nature of space is exhausted by relations between material substances like particles. Space consists of the relations obtaining among material substances.

The distinction between these positions can be further clarified by noting a couple of their uncontroversial consequences: if substantivalism is true then in principle there could exist a universe consisting of nothing but the spatial manifold itself – pure empty space would still be a real substance. By contrast, if relationism is true then a hypothetical 'universe' devoid of material substances like particles would not be an existent universe at all – 'empty space' is a synonym for 'nothingness.' Likewise, if substantivalism is true then in principle intrinsic properties can be attributed to space. For instance space can rightly be spoken of as having a structure of its own, perhaps even as having causal powers. Space can also be a subject of change, insofar as those intrinsic properties may be alterable; think for instance of the idea in contemporary cosmology that space has been expanding continually since the big bang. By contrast, it is typically thought that if relationism is true then in principle only such intrinsic properties as can be attributed to relations can be attributed to space (e.g., formal properties like self-identity),[1] and whatever changes can be attributed to space must supervene on changes taking place among physical objects.

That basic characterization of the distinction demands two qualifications. First, while historically speculations concerning the nature of space were often seen as separable from speculations concerning the nature of time, since the advent of relativity theory it has become common both in physics and philosophy to view space and time as unified in a four-dimensional spacetime manifold; consequently most of the recent debate concerning substantivalism versus relationism has been framed not in terms of space but in terms of spacetime.[2] The widespread acceptance of

---

[1] Recall however our previous mentions of those in the ontic structural realism literature (like French (2006) and Esfeld (2009)) who entertain the idea that relations might themselves be dispositional or bearers of dispositions. If such an idea were workable, this particular contrast between substantivalism and relationism might have to be reconsidered.

[2] Though it is worth keeping in mind Nerlich's (2003, p. 282) admonition:

> A cloud obscures … both substantivalist and relationist. Theories of motion usually progress conservatively. Much of Newton remains in GTR [the general theory of relativity]. However, quantum theory and GTR cannot both be true as they stand. Reconciling them is a major problem for contemporary physics. A quantum theory of gravity is expected to change the face of GTR radically and unforeseeably. The metaphysical themes which have dominated space-time metaphysics may change markedly, too.

a strong linkage between space and time has resulted in some options seen in the history of philosophy being largely (though by no means completely) sidelined. These are positions where the ontologies are decoupled, i.e., metaphysical systems that are substantivalist about space but relationist about time or vice versa, or where space and time are both seen as substances but are held to be *wholly distinct* substances. Second, the above characterization takes for granted realism about substance; substantivalism is realist insofar as it claims that space (or spacetime) at least is a substance, and relationism is realist insofar as it claims that space (or spacetime) amounts to a web of relations between substances. The debate would of course need to be re-conceived somewhat on antirealist views of substance, such as the versions of eliminativist ontic structural realism canvassed in Chapter 3.[3]

The debate continues, and while it is safe to say that substantivalism is the majority view today,[4] relationism retains considerable support.[5] For present purposes our interest is not with the debate itself but with its relationship to dispositionalism. One such relationship presents itself readily enough, given the argument of Chapter 5 and given that both relationism and substantivalism, as typically formulated, assume realism about substance. Recall the overarching argument of Chapter 5:

Premise 1 If any one of the four main substance ontologies is true, then dispositionalism is probably true.

Premise 2 At least one of the four main substance ontologies is true.

Conclusion Therefore dispositionalism is probably true.

The thought was that each of the four main substance ontologies (substratum theory, bundle theory, primitive substance theory, and hylomorphism) either entails dispositionalism or at least supports it. Now, given that relationism and substantivalism both take on board substance realism, they will ultimately be cashed out in terms of one of those four ontologies. As a result, both of these ontologies of spacetime end up supporting dispositionalism:

Premise 1 With respect to the ontology of spacetime, either relationism is true or substantivalism is true.

---

[3] For further discussion of eliminativist OSR in relation to the metaphysics of spacetime, see Dorato (2008) and Greaves (2011). For another sort of substance antirealism in this context (one not motivated by OSR), see Le Bihan (2016).

[4] Advocates include Baker (2005), Hoefer (1998), Maudlin (1993), and Pooley (2013).

[5] See for instance Belot (1999), Dieks (2001; 2001a), and Huggett (2006).

Premise 2 Both relationism and substantivalism will have to be paired with one or another of the four main substance ontologies.

Premise 3 If any one of the four main substance ontologies is true, then dispositionalism is probably true.

Conclusion Therefore, whether relationism is true or substantivalism is true, dispositionalism is probably true.

Since premise 3 is clearly the most controversial, the soundness of this probabilistic argument rests mainly on the soundness of the chain of argumentation laid out in Chapter 5. I will not attempt to recap here the rather complicated lines of reasoning employed in that chapter. But if the alleged connection between the four main substance ontologies and dispositionalism holds, then this establishes an interesting if indirect link between dispositionalism and the two main ontologies of spacetime. (And for the convinced categoricalist, this argument will provide new motivation either to formulate substantivalism and relationism in terms of substance antirealism, or to come up with a fifth option in substance ontology.)

7.3   Dispositionalism and Time Travel

This section will require some additional preliminary background, in this case concerning the debate between A-theory and B-theory in the philosophy of time. While there are disputes concerning how best to characterize these views, Gilmore, Costa, and Calosi (2016, p. 105) provide an admirably concise rundown:

(1)   B-THEORY. This term is usually reserved for the following package of views: *Eternalism.* Past, present, and future all exist.

Realism about time and tenseless relations. Time is real and mind-independent, and things in time stand in mind-independent temporal relations (e.g., *being simultaneous with* and *being earlier than*).

Anti-realism about passage. There is no metaphysically robust passage of time. Nothing instantiates presentness, and no such property flows from one time to another.

Next, we will consider three versions of the A-theory of time. As Smart (2008, p. 227) put it, the A-theory is a gerrymandered 'syndrome, rather than having a very tight definition.'

(2)   MOVING SPOTLIGHT. Eternalism is true, and yet time passes, in that different times successively have the property of presentness, which flows from earlier to later times.

(3) GROWING BLOCK. Past and present things exist, whereas (wholly) future things do not. The presage of time is robust and should be construed as the coming into existence of new entities.

(4) PRESENTISM. Only present things exist. The passage of time is robust and consists of new things coming into existence and old things ceasing to exist.

Each of these versions of the A-theory entails that the present is *objectively special*. This seems also to be the A-theory's main virtue: it respects the allegedly common sense belief that the present is, in some not-merely perspectival way, different from other times. They also note that these three versions do not exhaust the range of options within A-theory: "There is, for example, the THINNING TREE (McCall 1994), according to which reality consists of a branching universe with a single past and present (the trunk) but many possible futures (the branches), all equally real, and the passage of time is robust and should be construed as the ceasing to exist of the lower branches" (1994, p. 115). Hudson (2014, p. 79) adds the 'shrinking block theory' to the list, according to which reality encompasses the present and the future but not the past.

Note that the terminology used in this literature is variable; Koons and Pickavance (2015, pp. 185–186) for instance observe that the thinning tree model is also called the 'falling branches theory' (which others, like Rea (2003, p. 247), in turn label as the 'shrinking tree theory'), and that 'minimal A-theory' functions as another name for the moving spotlight theory (which Haslanger (2003, p. 321) calls the 'flashlight' theory). And some, like Deasy (2015, p. 2074) use 'permanentism' in place of 'eternalism,' while Cameron (2016, pp. 110–114), explicitly rejects treating those two terms as synonymous. It should also be noted that 'four-dimensionalism' is often used as a collective label for B-theory and the non-presentist versions of A-theory, all of which have in common the proposition that more than just the present exists.[6]

The links between the A-theory versus B-theory debates on the one hand, and the debates between substantivalists and relationists on the

---

[6] Rea (2003, p. 246) for instance writes: "Presentists say that only present objects exist. There are no dinosaurs, though there were such things; there are no cities on Mars, though perhaps there will be such things. Four-dimensionalists, on the other hand, say that there are past or future objects (or both); and in saying this, they mean to put such things ontologically on a par with present objects. According to the four-dimensionalist, non-present objects are like spatially distant objects: they exist, just not here, where we are." As we shall see later though, this usage of 'four-dimensionalism,' while common, is not universal.

other, are (unsurprisingly) complex and controversial; however it is common in the literature on time travel to presuppose substantivalism, at least for ease of formulation, and I'll follow that practice in this section. Now, on the plausible principle that travel into x requires the existence of x, presentism seems to preclude travel into the past or future, since neither the past nor the future are real on presentism.[7] For this same reason it seems difficult to entertain the prospect of travel into the future on the growing block theory, since on that theory the future does not exist. However, time travel into the past seems prima facie conceivable. Travel into the past is ruled out on the shrinking block theory, but not travel into the future. The moving spotlight and B-theories appear most liberal, conceivably permitting travel into both past and future.

Let's focus on the prospect of time travel into the past. Even those theories that posit the existence of the past face arguments to the effect that such a voyage is impossible. The most famous of these is the 'grandfather paradox.' The basic idea is well-known: even on the assumption that the past exists, it would not be possible to travel into it, since such travel would open up the prospect of causal scenarios entailing contradictions. If I travel into a past time when my grandfather is a child and kill him, then I wipe out the causal chain leading to my own conception. But if I am never conceived, how could I be there to kill my grandfather? (The parallel case of killing one's own younger self is sometimes called the 'paradox of autoinfanticide.')

There are a range of options for the defender of time travel to attempt to address this seeming paradox, familiar both from the philosophical literature and from science fiction. (A nice example from the latter is found in Daphne du Maurier's (1969) novel *The House on the Strand*, where the protagonist ingests a drug that allows him to go back to the middle ages, but only as an ethereal witness with no capacity for causal interaction.) In the philosophical literature it is often thought that the possibility of backwards time travel can be preserved on the assumption that *something* would always have to happen to prevent the killing of my grandfather: every time I try, necessarily the gun jams or a bystander jumps me or I slip on a banana peel, etc. Assuming that such interventions must always occur seems to save the possibility of backwards time travel, but at the cost of supposing possible worlds in which some prima

---

[7] At least, this is one of the stock arguments against the possibility of presentist time travel – see Grey (1999) for a detailed presentation. Still, some have tried to make a case for the compatibility of presentism and some sort of time travel, including Daniels (2012), Hall (2014), and Keller and Nelson (2001).

facie bizarre coincidences occur – perhaps routinely, should attempts at ancestor-killing prove a popular hobby for time travelers. One can then argue that backwards time travel, even if *possible*, comes out looking quite *improbable*. Arntzenius (2006, p. 605) puts the point succinctly (though he goes on to dispute it):

> There is a simple argument that the grandfather paradox implies that it is unlikely that time travel occurs in our universe. We know that if there are time travellers they will fail to kill their ancestors before they are born. This requires bizarre coincidences such as banana peels lying around in just the right spots. But it is implausible that our world is set up in such a conspiratorial way.

Are there ways of avoiding having to countenance these bizarre coincidences? One option is to bite the bullet and argue that in fact it *is* possible to kill one's own youthful grandfather, thereby sidestepping the concerns surrounding banana peel scenarios. Goddu (2003) argues that contradiction is avoided provided one is willing to countenance the reality of hypertime – the idea that there is more than one temporal dimension, and that changes might occur to the past in our temporal dimension (a portion of the past being wiped out and replaced) so long as they are registered eternally in a higher temporal dimension. This is an exceedingly controversial notion.[8] So let's assume the prevailing view that it is indeed impossible to kill one's own youthful grandfather.

Another option is to suggest that rather than having to reference a whole range of bizarre preventative scenarios, one simply posits that a relevant law (or laws) of nature self-adjust to prevent temporal paradoxes. For instance, perhaps the normal laws governing the neurology of choice are automatically adjusted such that the time traveler is always rendered incapable of forming the intention to pull the trigger. However, this solution is liable to seem less appealing on a dispositionalist account of laws. Koons and Pickavance (2015, p. 197) write:

> It seems reasonable to suppose that, if time travel is possible at all, it is possible for the time traveler to arrive in the past possessing all of his or her intrinsic powers and capacities. We can easily suppose that Mr. X possesses, as, sadly, do most of us, the natural capacity to kill another human being at will. When Mr. X arrives in the past, he will find plenty of implements with the natural capacity of ending his grandfather's life prematurely. If we suppose that such casual powers and capacities are

---

[8] For more on hypertime (and for motivations for entertaining its possibility that are quite distinct from the dialogue surrounding the grandfather paradox), see Hudson (2014).

intrinsic to the traveler and his immediate environment (which we should do if we are either Powerists or Nomists),[9] then we have to acknowledge the possibility of their exercise, and so the possibility of Mr. X's successful killing of his grandfather. Since we know this to be impossible, we can refute (by *reductio ad absurdum*) the hypothesis that time travel is possible.

And presumably recourse to improbable coincidence scenarios is not on the table here, insofar as it might be supposed that from a dispositionalist perspective there would be nothing in the powers of the traveler or the immediate environment that would intelligibly ensure the coincidences – nothing in the power of the gun to ensure that it would jam or in the power of the environment to issue a consistent supply of well-placed banana peels, etc. Koons and Pickavance conclude that dispositionalism and nomological necessitarianism both support the force of the grandfather paradox and by extension the idea that backwards time travel is not merely improbable but impossible. They then draw the further conclusion that dispositionalists should favour those versions of A-theory (like presentism) that preclude travel into the past.

I will leave to one side the claim that nomological necessitarianism tells against backwards time travel and focus on dispositionalism.[10] It is not very common in the literature on time travel to see dispositionalism explicitly invoked, so this brief argument by Koons and Pickavance is significant; and since my principal aim in this book is to draw attention to neglected connections between dispositionalism and other areas of debate within the metaphysics of science, it would work to my advantage to be able to get behind their argument. However I am not persuaded that dispositionalism supports the grandfather paradox argument against time travel. Furthermore I am not persuaded that, if it were to do so, that this would be to the benefit of dispositionalism. As Sider (2001, p. 109) points out, the physical possibility of time travel is much-discussed in current physics, which provides philosophers with at least some (defeasible) motivation to refrain from dismissing it: "This is not just a fringe movement: time travel is currently discussed in major physics journals.

---

[9] These are the terms they use for what I've been calling dispositionalists and nomological necessitarians, respectively.

[10] Though there are certainly versions of nomological necessitarianism in which it is not the case that the relevant 'powers' are intrinsic to the traveler and her environment. (Recall that on NN powers are reducible, or eliminable in favour of, to categorical properties + laws.) Rather, the laws are wholly external to the objects involved and could be adjusted independently of them, assuming that the laws are contingent.

It would be rash to rule out, a priori, the possibility of a physical hypothesis that is taken seriously by physicists."

How then might a dispositionalist address the grandfather paradox and thus defend the possibility of backwards time travel? And might there be a way to do so without countenancing reams of bizarre coincidences? I think the simplest, least ad hoc way of accomplishing both tasks is to suggest that at least some dispositions have ceteris paribus clauses relevant to time travel. For example, suppose for the sake of argument that a person's ability to pull a trigger is a genuine, fundamental causal power (rather than a being derivative ability arising from fundamental causal powers). In a world where time travel is physically possible this ability must then include among its identity conditions something akin to the following (stated very roughly): 'person x will pull the trigger upon choosing to do so, unless *these circumstances* obtain ...' where the specification of *these circumstances* incorporates 'the pulling of the trigger would prompt a temporal paradox.' In other words, if time travel is physically possible then any disposition that could figure in the causing of a temporal paradox will include in its ceteris paribus clauses whatever is necessary to block that from occurring. So if I were to travel back in time and attempt to shoot my grandfather, I would perhaps find myself unable to move my trigger finger, or find myself unable to form the mental intent to carry out the act, etc. Note that this would *not* be a case of the laws of nature *changing* in a time travel scenario; rather, the blocking of the temporal paradox is already built into the ceteris paribus clauses of the relevant power(s). And perhaps only one or a few such powers are involved (such as those pertaining to the neurology of choice) so that the bizarre coincidence scenarios (fortuitous banana peels and whatnot) needn't be admitted. As such the grandfather paradox argument for the impossibility (or improbability) of time travel is defused, and the dispositionalist need not reject time travel, and by extension need not favour those versions of the A-theory that rule it out.

I have suggested that this seems the least ad hoc option for the dispositionalist; that does not mean it is entirely free from the odour of the ad hoc. However the lingering stench might be lessened somewhat when one recalls the point made in Chapter 2 that the identity conditions of a disposition (including its ceteris paribus clauses) can be sizeable, incorporating reference to a whole range of alien (i.e., uninstantiated) universals. A real object like an electron thus has the capacity to interact with a range of physically possible but unactualized kinds of particles which are themselves possessed of a range of physically possible but unactualized dispositions. On this expansive sort of picture, it will seem less strange to suggest that a real object might also include amongst its capacious identity conditions some ceteris paribus clauses relevant to time travel. In particular, it will seem less strange to suggest this if one is already inclined towards any of those versions of four-dimensionalism which seem prima facie to be friendlier to the physical possibility of time travel.

Another potential option: perhaps the relevant ceteris paribus clauses are located not in the individual objects implicated in grandfather-type scenarios (e.g., the brain physiology of the time travelers), but rather in the overarching spacetime manifold itself. That is, suppose we already take seriously the notion that at least some global laws (i.e., laws applying uniformly across a universe, to all members of all natural kinds) are not grounded in powers of individual objects within a universe, but rather in the powers of the universe itself. Then it might seem plausible to locate a power or powers to exclude temporal paradoxes within the latter. Bigelow, Ellis, and Lierse (1992, p. 385) make use of this sort of idea in trying to provide a dispositionalism-friendly account of the law of conservation of energy:

> It is not essential to the category of events that they should be energy-conservative, or angular-momentum-conservative, or conservative in any other respect. Changes which were not in accordance with these conservation principles would still be events. But it seems to be of the nature of the universe we live in that such events should never, or at least very rarely, occur. A universe in which the forbidden changes did occur sufficiently often would not be our kind of universe … Therefore, if the reason for the necessity of the conservation laws is like the reason for the necessity of other less general laws, we must suppose it to be essential to the nature of the universe that its source be one in which these quantities are at least very nearly conserved. Without the assumption that the universe is one of a kind in which certain basic quantities are conserved in this way, we do not see any satisfactory way of giving an ontological explanation of their necessity. There is no equally plausible rival bearer of essential properties which could explain the necessity of the conservation laws. Therefore, we conclude, conservation laws are best understood as ascribing properties to the world as a whole, properties which are essential to the natural kind to which our world belongs.

The notion that universes have kind-essences has proven a controversial strategy for explaining global laws, even amongst dispositionalists.[11] Still, if a case can be made for it, it might then plausibly be referenced by the

---

[11] See for instance the critiques by Bird (2007, p. 213) and Elder (1994, p. 665). Naturally enough it has also been critiqued by categoricalists, such as Katzav (2005) and Lange (2009a, pp. 82–86).

dispositionalist seeking a way to sidestep temporal paradoxes. It will seem an especially plausible idea for those who accept spacetime substantivalism; for if the universe as a whole is a substance, and one is a natural-kind essentialist who thinks that every substance is the instantiation of a natural kind, well then of course the universe is too. And perhaps among the universe's essential dispositions are the requisite ingredients for excluding temporal paradoxes.[12]

7.4 Dispositionalism, Endurantism, and Spacetime

Preliminary to outlining Mumford's (2009) argument, we need to cover some additional background concerning the metaphysics of persistence and how it relates to debates in the philosophy of time (and by extension spacetime). The current debates on persistence employ vocabulary popularized by David Lewis (1986, p. 202):

> Let us say that something *persists* iff, somehow or other, it exists at various times; this is the neutral word. Something *perdures* iff it persists by having different temporal parts, or stages, at different times, though no one part of it is wholly present at more than one time; whereas it *endures* iff it persists by being wholly present at more than one time.

Lewis here provides names to two models for how something might persist in existence. On *perdurantism*, just as an object can have distinct spatial parts (my head and arms and legs, etc.) it can have distinct temporal parts (the part of me that existed on May 12 of 2005, the part of me that existed on May 13 of 2005, etc.). The divisions into temporal parts are just as real as the divisions into spatial parts. I exist at different times in the sense that I am ultimately a composite of all my temporal parts, just as I exist in different regions of space because I am a composite of all my spatial parts. I never exist wholly in any one of my spatial parts (I am not identical to my arm), nor do I exist wholly in any one of my temporal parts (the 'me' that existed on May 12 was not the whole me). Or, put in terms of spacetime: I am the composite of all my spatiotemporal parts. By contrast, on *endurantism* there is no need to reference such thing as temporal parts of objects when explaining persistence.[13] I exist

---

[12] Kutach (2003), though not working explicitly within dispositionalism or natural-kind essentialism, puts forward a similar suggestion according to which the constraints on temporal paradox are grounded at the global level, in the spacetime manifold itself.

[13] The 'of objects' is worth highlighting, since as Sider (2001, pp. 100 and 211–212), Hawley (2001, p. 29), and Lowe (2005, p. 105) observe, an endurantist might allow the idea of *events* or *processes* having temporal parts.

at different times because I am multi-located with respect to times. I was temporally located at May 12 of 2005 and also temporally located at May 13 of 2005. The *whole* of me existed at both of those times, not a *part* of me.

Haslanger's (2003, pp. 317–318) characterization of the distinction should provide further clarity:

> Roughly, an object persists by *enduring* iff it is *wholly present* at different times. For example, the candle endures iff the candle itself is wholly present at *t* (in the morning when I set it on the shelf), and it is also wholly present at a distinct time *t'* (in the afternoon when I return ... and presumably in the intervening times). The notion of being 'wholly present' may become clearer by contrast with the perdurantist's notion of being 'partly present'. On the perdurantist's conception of persistence, an object persists through time in a way analogous to how an object is extended through space. The candle is spatially extended through its 7-inch length not by being wholly present at each spatial region it occupies, but by having parts at the different regions. Likewise, according to the perdurantist, the candle extends through time not by being wholly present at different times, but by having parts or stages at distinct times ... On the perdurance account, the persisting object does not undergo alteration by 'gaining' or 'losing' properties; instead, it changes in a way analogous to how a painting changes colour across the canvas. The canvas is green at this part and blue at another; the candle is straight at this part and bent at another ... On this account, persisting things are temporally extended composites, also known as space-time worms.

She then draws attention to a third option, closely related to perdurantism (often classed as a version of it) known as *stage theory* or *exdurantism.*[14] On this view, an object persists insofar as each of its temporal parts or stages, though existing only for an instant, has a counterpart at an earlier or later time, and the counterpart relation is supposed to suffice for continuity. Haslanger (2003, p. 318) writes: "Although on this view ordinary objects are stages and so (strictly speaking) only exist momentarily, they can nonetheless persist by virtue of having counterpart antecedent and/or successor stages. The idea behind this view is to treat identity over time as analogous to identity across possible worlds in modal counterpart theory."

An important difference between perdurantism and exdurantism is that on the former, some types of property (including sortal properties/ natural kinds) are properly attributed only to the composite, the sum of

---

[14] Still others label it 'stage-theoretic perdurantism' (e.g., Crisp (2003, p. 216)), while Koons and Pickavance (2015, p. 212) call it alternatively 'extreme perdurantism' or 'eliminative perdurantism.'

the temporal parts.[15] This is because perdurantism can accommodate a genuine composite meaningfully distinct from its components, and because it is normally considered problematic to attribute a sortal property to a mere part of a thing. (I am a human being, but my left hand is not a human being. Likewise, the spatiotemporal whole that is me is a human being, but none of my temporal parts is strictly speaking a human being.) By contrast, on exdurantism such properties are attributed to the individual temporal stages because there is no genuine larger spatiotemporal whole, in the sense of there being a composite entity which could literally bear properties. Hawley (2001, p. 42) writes:

> Perdurance and stage theorists share a common metaphysical picture – the world is full of very short-lived objects existing in succession ... But the two accounts differ over what we talk about when we use phrases like 'the tennis ball', and about which objects satisfy sortal predicates like 'is a tennis ball'. According to perdurance theory, it is long-lived sums of stages which are tennis balls, whereas according to stage theory, it is the stages themselves which are tennis balls (or bananas, or human beings, as the case may be).[16]

So far then the three options on the table for explicating the nature of persistence are endurantism, perdurantism, and exdurantism. I will not attempt here to cover the many arguments for and against these views, but to give some idea of what is motivating the debate consider for instance a puzzle involving change, sometimes referred to as the 'problem of temporary intrinsics.' Say I decide to dye my hair green, and carry out the act. I transition from being non-green-haired at time t1 to being green-haired at time t2. This is a change from one intrinsic property to a distinct and contrary property, yet prima facie we want to say that I am still me even after the change. My identity remains intact even while green-haired. That is, commonsensically we want to say that 'me at time t1' is identical to 'me at time t2.' Yet presumably we also want to affirm the principle of the indiscernibility of identicals. According to this principle, identity entails that there be no difference in intrinsic properties;

---

[15] Note that while I follow convention in speaking here of temporal parts, most parties to the debate would grant Balashov's (2000, p. 551) point that given the truth of relativity theory "the perdurantist notion of a temporal part will have to give way to that of a spatiotemporal part." Sider (2001, p. 80) makes the same observation.

[16] This account is later made somewhat more complex when Hawley (2001, pp. 54–56) clarifies that a sortal property can be attributed to an instantaneous stage only when that stage stands in appropriate relations to other stages; that is, the individual instantaneous stage can properly be the bearer of a sortal property, but the sortal will necessarily be a relational property rather than an intrinsic one.

that is, if x = y then x and y must share all the same intrinsic properties. Yet 'me at t1' does *not* share all the same intrinsic properties as 'me at t2,' because 'me at time t2' has the intrinsic property 'green-haired.' So what are we to say here? Do we deny that I am the same person pre-and-post-green-hair? Or do we drop the indiscernibility of identicals? Or is there some other way out?[17]

Endurantists can offer a distinctive set of strategies for dealing with this. They want to affirm that I exist at t1 and at t2 and remain genuinely me at these different times, despite the change. One way for them to do this is by reference to time-indexed properties. Thus the property I possessed at t2 was not 'green-haired' but rather the more complex, partly relational 'green-haired at time t2.' Provided that seemingly intrinsic properties are inherently ordered to times, the conflict evaporates: the same identical 'me' can without contradiction have both 'not-green-haired at time t1' *and* 'green-haired at time t2.' The perdurantist, by contrast, can offer a very different sort of solution. For her, there is no single, genuinely identical 'me' at those two times. Rather, there is the time-slice of me at t1 and the time-slice of me at t2, both of which are merely parts of the larger four-dimensional spacetime worm that is the whole me. And there is no contradiction involved in distinct parts of a thing having contrary properties, so the fact that one temporal part of me lacks green hair and another has green hair is in no way problematic.

The exdurantist can offer a comparable solution, and in one sense more parsimoniously since she can deny that there is any whole, over-arching space-time worm composed of the time-slices. Rather, there are *just* the individual time-slices standing in relations to successor counterpart time-slices.[18]

---

[17] For more thorough statements of this problem of change see Haslanger (2003, pp. 315–317), Hawley (pp. 14–16), and Sider (2001, pp. 4–5; 92–98). Mumford's own concise summary is also very clear (2009, pp. 226–227).

[18] Hawley (2001, p. 52) emphasizes this parsimony:

> Perdurance theory has as much need of instantaneous things as stage theory does … Moreover, perdurance theory takes on extra commitments that stage theory need not. Perdurance theory is committed to the existence of sums of temporal parts, for it is these very sums which are supposed to be the ordinary objects of everyday life … Stage theory can remain neutral here. If it makes sense to think of instantaneous stages as having extended fusions, or sums, then stage theorists can recognize those sums. But if not, then no problems arises, since, according to stage theory, sums of stages play no significant role in our everyday ontology. Perdurance theorists, on the other hand, must establish the existence of such fusions, for those very fusions are supposed to be familiar objects.

Later she offers an account for how stage theorists who want to include sums of stages as distinct items in their ontology can best do so (ibid., pp. 189–191).

The preceding remarks showcase a common way of characterizing and motivating these three positions. Unsurprisingly however, the landscape of this literature is more complicated and contentious than this initial description might indicate. For instance, there are ongoing disputes concerning how best to define these three views, with some maintaining that endurantism may be compatible with the existence of temporal parts of objects and so should not be defined in terms of their denial.[19] Hawley argues that while perdurantism (unlike endurantism) is compatible with the reality of temporal parts, it is better defined in terms of objects being temporally *extended*.[20] Some argue that the puzzle of change helping to motivate the debate is misconceived and dissolves once a more traditional form of the principle of indiscernibility of identicals is employed.[21] And there are also important disputes about how these three views relate to the debate in philosophy of time between A-theorists and B-theorists.

[19] See again Koons and Pickavance (2015, p. 212). See also Wasserman (2016), who argues that endurantism should be understood in negative terms as the denial of the *explanatory aspect* of perdurantism (i.e., as the denial that the reality of temporal parts *explains* how things persist) rather than as the denial of the *ontological aspect* of perdurantism (i.e., as the denial of the mere existence of temporal parts). On this understanding, endurantism is strictly compatible with the reality of temporal parts. Donnelly (2011) likewise argues for a characterization of the persistence debate that allows those often classed as endurantists to affirm the reality of temporal parts.

[20] The disagreement between perdurance and endurance theorists is often glossed as a disagreement about whether ordinary persisting objects have temporal parts. But at a more fundamental level, it is a disagreement about whether ordinary persisting objects are temporally extended (as perdurance theorists believe) or whether they occupy times in a rather different way (as endurance theorists believe). The claim that an object is temporally extended – that it endures – is not analytically equivalent to the claim that it has temporal parts, for it is not trivial that an extended object must have parts (Markosian 1998). It is at least conceivable that an object could be spatially extended without having spatial parts – and it ought to be equally conceivable to a perdurance theorist than an object could be temporally extended without having temporal parts. (pp. 27–28)

A view of this sort, according to which an object is extended in time but lacks temporal parts, is defended by Parsons (2000), who actually considers it a form of endurantism. (This is of course analogous to the theory of extended simples in the material composition literature, which we discussed in Chapter 4.) The view is further developed (but ultimately rejected) by Miller (2009), who sees it as occupying a middle ground between endurantism and perdurantism and labels it *terdurantism*. Pashby (2013) in turn calls this sort of view *temporal holism*. Hudson (2014, p. 93) assigns the name *regionalism* to a view where one affirms that an object is extended in time but remains neutral on whether it has temporal parts.

[21] Oderberg (2004, p. 691) writes:

The principle of the Indiscernibility of Identicals must mention the possession by objects of the same property *at the same time*. In other words, for any two objects and any time, if the objects are numerically identical then they share all their properties at that time ... The reasons PII needs to be formulated in terms of the times at which properties are possessed, and hence the reason it is a basic metaphysical truth, is that it is entailed by the Law of Non-Contradiction. Stated in its traditional general form as applied to the realm of the concrete, the laws holds that nothing can both be and not be *at the same time and in the same respect*. An application of it is that no object can both possess a property and lack it at the same time and in the same respect. [Emphases in original]

Let's dwell on that last issue for a few moments. Haslanger observes that it is common to characterize the endurantist vs. perdurantist split as a split principally between presentists and four-dimensionalists. However she herself rejects this characterization and argues that each of endurantism, perdurantism, and exdurantism is compatible both with presentism and with four-dimensionalism (2003, pp. 320–326). Part of the dispute here revolves around the issue of whether it is coherent to think of something as possessing non-existent parts, a notion that would be required by a presentist perdurantist. (This is because the presentist maintains that only the present exists, but the perdurantist think that an object is a spacetime worm composed of past, present, and future temporal parts. So a presentist perdurantist would have to maintain that some of an object's temporal parts – namely its past and future temporal parts – are genuine parts despite their lack of existence.) Haslanger defends the coherence of this idea, while others (like Merricks (1995) and Benovsky (2009)) deny it. In addition to the debate over whether presentism requires endurantism, there is the debate over whether endurantism requires (or accords best with) presentism. While many endurantists are presentists, there are certainly advocates of the view that endurantism can be combined with B-theory or the non-presentist versions of A-theory.[22]

With that background in place, we can now proceed to Mumford's argument. His primary thesis:

> Ultimately, it would be satisfying if the powers ontology were able to deliver for us a verdict on the endurance/perdurance debate. I will argue that it doesn't quite do that – not conclusively anyway – but that a powers ontologist nevertheless has some reason to favour endurantism as sitting most comfortably with their ontology. I will argue that if one is to be a casual powers theorist, one will have difficulty defending a perdurance theory of persistence. (2009, pp. 225–226)

He begins by outlining perdurantism, noting that he is working with Hawley's (2001) formulation of the view. (Mumford does distinguish between perdurantism and stage theory (2009, p. 226) but since both include a commitment to short-lived entities related to each other by

---

[22] For instance Gibson and Pooley (2006, p. 160) write:

> Endurance involves persisting objects being wholly present at different times. For tenseless eternalists, therefore, endurance involves persisting objects existing at multiple times by being tenselessly and wholly located at these times. But note that the kernel of tenseless eternalism is that all times are on a par. Since the endurantist is not committed to regarding any time – any particular temporal location of any particular enduring object – as special, endurantism and tenseless eternalism are entirely consistent.

succession – whether temporal parts of a larger whole or temporal stages that are themselves considered objects – and since it is *this* feature that Mumford focuses on in his analysis, he takes that analysis to apply to both and opts to speak simply of perdurantism.) On that formulation, an object's temporal parts are fleeting and extremely fine-grained, with each being as short as needed to preclude possible change.[23] So if time bottoms out at *unextended* instants then so do temporal parts; if instead time bottoms out at *extended* instants then so do temporal parts. Regardless, the individual time-slices are each of them inherently static. Mumford (2009, p. 227) writes that "the perdurance theory posits for each thing, a large number of changeless and fleeting temporal parts of that thing. They will also be entirely distinct and discrete from each other, permitting no overlap." Consequently what we think of as change is cashed out in terms of different temporal parts having different properties – recall Haslanger's analogy of the painting.[24] According to Hawley the sort of changes we think of as *causal processes* are distinguished by their standing in particular sorts of relations to each other. Mumford summarizes (2009, p. 229):

> To account for processes, the perdurance theorist can only offer a sequence of parts or stages, each of which is static. Such parts must be suitably related if they are to genuinely form a sequence. Not any old collection of temporal parts forms a sequence. They must be suitably related so that they are temporal parts of the same thing. Changes in the same thing could then constitute what I am calling a sequence or process. What kind of relation must the parts bear to each other to be a sequence? Without saying exactly what the appropriate relation is, for perdurantists to posit in order to stick stages together, Hawley does tell us that it is a non-supervenient relation. This is because she cannot see how facts about

---

[23] This is important for preserving the perdurantist's solution to the problem of change. Hawley (2001, p. 48) writes:

> To account for change, stages and temporal parts must be as fine-grained as change: a material thing must have as many stages or parts as it is in incompatible states during its lifetime. If it were in more incompatible states than it had stages or parts, then at least one of its stages or parts would be in incompatible states without itself having parts or stages, and the problem of change would re-emerge.

That is, if my irreducible temporal parts or stages included one sufficiently lengthy as to incorporate me-without-green-hair *and* me-with-green-hair, then the problem of change remains unresolved.

[24] Sider (2001, p. 2) offers another nice analogy: "A road changes from one place to another by having dissimilar sub-sections. Route 1 changes from bumpy to smooth by having distinct bumpy and smooth subsections. On the four-dimensional picture, change over time is analogous: I change from sitting to standing by having a temporal part that sits and a later temporal part that stands." Hawley (2001, p. 11) also uses the road analogy: "You are a single object which exists at different times by having different parts at different times, just as a road exists at different places by having different spatial parts at those different places." Both are drawing on Lewis' (1986, p. 210) earlier use of it.

processes of a thing could supervene on the facts about the static properties of the changeless temporal parts of that process. A non-supervenient
relation is thus an external relation: one that does not hold merely in virtue of its relata existing.[25]

This relation, because external, is also going to be contingent; and
because it is contingent, Mumford concludes that for the perdurantist
there can be no satisfactory explanatory relation between the time slices
in the sequence. To see why, he asks us to imagine a three-stage process
S1–S3, where each stage instantiates a different property – property F at
S1, property G at S2, and property H at S3. He then writes (2009,
pp. 230–231):

> If the relations between S1 and S3 are non-supervenient, as Hawley
> insists, there is nothing about the mere existence of S1–S3 that makes it
> that they are indeed so related. We have seen that the relation is an exter-
> nal one. S1–S3 could, therefore, exist without being suitably related,
> which means that it is a contingent matter that they are so related. There
> is, therefore, nothing more than contingency in this process. There is
> nothing that makes S3 instantiate property H, even if the stages S1 and
> S2 of the same particular thing have instantiated F and G. The disposi-
> tionalist, in contrast, believes in real dispositions towards natural kinds of
> process. If a particular instantiates G, having previously instantiated F, it
> may well be naturally and essentially disposed towards H.

The dispositionalist picture of the explanatory relation between the stages of
a causal process is thus markedly different from that supposed by the perdurantist. This point is reiterated in Mumford and Anjum (2011, p. 116):

> With perdurantism tends to go the view that it is essentially contingent
> what follows what. The reason for this is that it is no part of the essence
> of the temporal parts that they be arranged in any particular order. They
> could preserve their identity through rearrangements such that, as
> Humeans intend, there is no reason in principle why they could not occur
> in a different order to the one in which they actually occur.[26]

---

[25] He is drawing here on Hawley (2001, ch. 3).
[26] It's worth noting that a nomological necessitarian perdurantist could posit that external laws of
nature govern the relations between discrete time-slices, such that their relationship remains
strictly contingent (provided the laws are contingent) yet not arbitrary. Armstrong (1980; 1983,
pp. 79–81; 1997, pp. 74 and 99–107) presents just such a perdurantist view, and that would certainly be one way of cashing out Hawley's idea of non-supervenient external relations. In fact,
though Hawley explicitly (2001, p. 87) wants to allow for a Humean reductive account of causation, her conception of 'Humean' is a bit non-standard (at least from the standpoint of much of
the literature on laws), permitting the reality of robustly real extrinsic governing laws of the sort
nomological necessitarians favour. At any rate, none of this directly affects Mumford's main point,
namely that the perdurantist picture seems to conflict with dispositionalism.

I believe Mumford's first argument may be stated more formally as follows:

Premise 1 If perdurantism is true, then the stages of a causal process are related merely contingently.

Premise 2 If the stages of a causal process are related merely contingently, then dispositionalism is false.

Conclusion Therefore, if perdurantism is true, then dispositionalism is false.

In addition to the worry over the pure contingency of the relationship between temporal stages (in contrast to the more robust relations obtaining between the stages of a causal process that obtain when a disposition is manifested), Mumford questions whether a single, static temporal part could ever be an appropriate vehicle for the instantiation of a disposition – or at least of a key *type* of disposition. That is, Mumford distinguishes here between passive powers and active powers, where the former are powers that merely enable an object to receive a change (like fragility permitting an object to be broken) and the latter are powers that enable an object to prompt a change. Now, passive powers might well be instantiated in a static temporal part, but it makes little sense to think of an active power being instantiated there, because the manifestation of an active power is only intelligibly situated within a larger causal process. The example he uses is the power of an alarm clock to ring: it does so because as an object it is undergoing a process – in this case perhaps the arm of the clock being shoved towards a trigger point – that concludes with the bell ringing. But it makes little sense to think of an active power like this being realized without that embedding in a larger process. Active powers are manifested because of their relationship to prior changes undergone by the object, within the context of a larger process. While perdurantism may be able to accommodate passive powers, it seems to leave no room for active powers, insofar as the latter are grounded in irreducible, temporally extended processes. And given the crucial importance of active powers in our world, an ontology permitting only passive powers would be so hollowed-out a form of 'dispositionalism' as to be unworthy of the name. (I am inferring that last claim; Mumford does not state it explicitly, but it follows from his explicit claims that perdurantism does not fit with dispositionalism even while perdurantism does allow for passive powers. If the reality of passive powers sufficed for 'dispositionalism' properly speaking, then perdurantism would be compatible with dispositionalism. I am inclined to disagree; passive powers are still powers, and any ontology that admits them should count as a form of dispositionalism – a weaker form, if *only* passive powers are admitted, but a version nonetheless. One might develop the point further as an alternative strategy for addressing Mumford's argument and defending the compatibility of dispositionalism and perdurantism, but I'd rather try for the more ambitious aim of showing that perdurantism also allows for active powers.)

The upshot is that dispositionalism involves a commitment to irreducible, temporally extended causal processes, and that the reality of such processes accords with endurantism but not perdurantism. Or to put it a bit more formally:

> **Premise 1** If dispositionalism is true, then there are irreducible temporally extended causal processes.
>
> **Premise 2** If there are irreducible temporally extended causal processes, then perdurantism is false.
>
> **Conclusion** Therefore, if dispositionalism is true, then perdurantism is false.

In the final portion of the piece, Mumford turns to the relationship between endurantism and four-dimensionalism, and by extension dispositionalism and four-dimensionalism. As I noted above, four-dimensionalism is often used simply to refer to the denial of presentism (in favour of B-theory or one of the non-presentist versions of A-theory). In that usage it is at least prima facie neutral between endurantism and perdurantism. But Mumford rightly observes that some, including Sider (2001), equate four-dimensionalism with acceptance of temporal parts.[27] Such an equivalence claim (and likewise the related view that four-dimensionalism *entails* perdurantism) would be problematic for any dispositionalist who inclines towards four-dimensionalism but wants to reject perdurantism. So Mumford briefly makes a case against it (2009, p. 234):

> Accepting the reality of the four-dimensional manifold is one thing but committing to that manifold being populated by fleeting existents with

---

[27] Sider makes this clear in the very first sentence of his (2001, p. xiii): "This book articulates and defends four-dimensionalism: an ontology of the material world according to which objects have temporal as well as spatial parts." However he is certainly cognizant of the fact that the meaning of the label has varied: "I feel a bit apologetic for retaining the term 'four-dimensionalism' as a name for the thesis that things have temporal parts. That is one standard usage of the term, but the term is also sometimes used (particularly in Australia) for the B-theory of time, or for the conjunction of B-theory and the doctrine of temporal parts" (2001, pp. xiii–xiv). Others who equate four-dimensionalism with the acceptance of temporal parts include Balashov (2000, p. 550), Brogaard (2000, p. 341), and Hales and Johnson (2003, p. 524).

their static properties is another. Instead, the four-dimensional world, in which all places and times exist and are equally real, could be populated by particulars and their dynamic properties, with natural powers and processes doing the work of producing change. Atemporally, there may well be no change in the four-dimensional manifold, but there is change when one considers the temporal perspective – the temporal facts – within that world. The powers ontology, in my views, paints a more convincing ontological picture of how that change occurs than does the perdurantist alternative.

These remarks are suggestive and should serve to prompt further reflection by dispositionalists on how exactly the theory relates to four-dimensionalism, and whether dispositionalism might have anything unique to contribute to the longstanding debate between A-theory and B-theory over whether the latter allows for genuine change. The question of how to accommodate change is commonly thought to be less worrisome for the four-dimensionalist versions of A-theory than it is for B-theory, so I expect one strategy for the dispositionalist would be to pair dispositonalism with four-dimensionalist A-theory rather than B-theory. In particular, A-theorists (unlike B-theorists) can accept the reality of the four-dimensional manifold while also attributing change *to the manifold itself* – e.g., on the growing block theory the manifold itself is expanding, and on the moving spotlight theory the property of presentness proceeds across the manifold. (This is most apparent for A-theorists who are also spacetime substantivalists, though perhaps there are ways to run this on relationism as well.) The A-theorist therefore need not restrict the realm of change to facts *within* the manifold, to use Mumford's distinction.[28]

Summing up, Mumford has developed an original set of arguments to the effect that dispositionalism carries an important and heretofore unnoticed implication for the metaphysics of persistence.[29] Once again, given

---

[28] Williams (forthcoming, p. 182) is substantially more optimistic about the consistency of dispositionalism with standard B-theory, and with the reality of change *within* the spatiotemporal manifold on eternalism. He writes that:

> the truth of eternalism is not incompatible with a robust account of causation (that is, one that is not typical of neo-Humeanism). Adopting eternalism does not require one to reject theories of causation wherein states are causally necessitated by one another, and where some of those states explain the presence of those states, precisely because they are responsible for them ... Even if you have very different ideas about the nature of the causal relata, there is nevertheless a place for robust causal connections in the four-dimensional manifold ...

[29] Oakes (2004) had earlier made the case that perdurantism has a difficult time accommodating *any* form of causal realism (presumably including dispositionalism), but the arguments he offers are somewhat different from (though I think complementary to) Mumford's. And Wahlberg (2009) arrived independently at an argument for the incompatibility of dispositionalism and perdurantism that is similar to Mumford's second argument.

that my goal in this book is to draw out precisely these sorts of implications, it would be to my advantage if I could get behind this argument. However, I am not entirely convinced that dispositionalism is incompatible with perdurantism. (Neither for that matter is Mumford; recall that he is not claiming to establish *conclusively* that the two are incompatible (2009, pp. 225–226), though he has certainly made a forceful case.) In the remainder of this section I would like to try out two strategies for reconciling dispositionalism with perdurantism: the first involves turning to a different, less common formulation of perdurantism, while the second works with the version Mumford is targeting.

On to the first strategy then. Recall that on Mumford's conception of perdurantism (whether perdurantism proper or exdurantism/stage theory), the theory involves a commitment to non-overlapping and inherently static time-slices: "… the perdurance theory posits for each thing, a large number of changeless and fleeting temporal parts of that thing. They will also be entirely distinct and discrete from each other, permitting no overlap" (2009, p. 227). Now it is true that Hawley (2001) accepts this picture, as does Sider (2001) and others in the literature. Moreover, as noted above there is some motivation for doing so, insofar as it seems necessary for the preservation of the perdurantist's solution to the problem of change. However, while Sider favours instantaneous temporal parts, he is open to their being conceived instead as extended (2001, p. 60):

> Some may wish to avoid commitment to instantaneous parts. An *extended* temporal part of x during interval T may be defined as an object that exists at, but only at, times in T, is part of x at every time during T, and at every moment in T overlaps everything that is part of x at that moment. Four-dimensionalism may then be reformulated as the claim that spatiotemporal objects have temporal parts during intervals of certain sorts, perhaps extended continuous intervals. But unless otherwise noted I will think of temporal parts as being instantaneous.

He does *not* specify here that these hypothetical extended continuous intervals would have to be so short as to rule out change occurring within them. This may be intentional, since, while Sider thinks perdurantism (and in particular his favoured version, stage theory) can effectively address the problem of change, on the whole he does not think this constitutes a particularly forceful portion of the larger case for perdurantism (2001, p. 97). That is, he thinks that there are substantially better reasons for being a perdurantist than that supplied by the argument from the problem of change.[30] So perhaps he is open to the prospect of a temporal part that could admit change (and by extension a causal process) within it.

If so, he would be following in the footsteps of some earlier prominent figures in the literature. Lewis (1983, p. 76) writes:

> A person-stage is a physical object, just as a person is. (If persons had a ghostly part as well, so would person-stages.) It does many of the same things that a person does: it talks and walks and thinks, it has beliefs and desires, it has a size and shape and location. It even has a temporal duration. But only a brief one, for it does not last long … Hence a stage cannot do everything that a person can do, for it cannot do those things that a person does over a longish interval.[31]

This is significant, insofar as Lewis is allowing for temporal stages of sufficient duration as to include at least some sorts of apparently causal processes, like those involved in walking. Heller (1990, p. 6) is also open to the idea of non-instantaneous temporal parts:

> One question about four-dimensional objects is whether it is possible to have zero extent along the temporal dimension – Can there be instantaneous objects? I do not have a strong opinion about this one way or the other. What should be noted is that this is no more an issue with respect to the temporal dimension that with any of the spatial dimensions …

Later he indicates a preference (1990, p. 27): "Personally, I am more certain of the existence of temporally extended temporal parts than I am of momentary ones." And he nowhere specifies that these extended parts must nevertheless be small enough to rule out change within them; this may be because he does not rely heavily on the problem of change as part of his case for perdurantism.[32]

The upshot: while perdurantists typically suppose that temporal parts (or temporal stages) are instantaneous, with an instant being of sufficiently short duration as to rule out the possibility of change taking place within a single temporal part, this is *not* an essential commitment of perdurantism; at least, it is not an essential commitment if one's justification

---

[30] Sider (2001, chs. 4 and 5) covers ten distinct arguments for perdurantism, and places special emphasis on the solution it provides to the paradoxes of coincidence.

[31] Cited in Heller (1990, p. 1).

[32] Williams (forthcoming, p. 188) notes that in addition to Lewis and Heller, C. D. Broad (1923; 1925) and Bertrand Russell (1915) also affirmed versions of perdurantism on which the temporal parts were seen as non-instantaneous. On Williams' view though, the dispositionalist perdurantist should still affirm that change does not take place within a temporal part, even one that is longer than an instant. This issue also receives attention in Williams (2017, pp. 155–161).

for favouring it rests on something other than the solution offered by it for the problem of change. And since there are a variety of other justifications available, it is open to the perdurantist to allow for temporal parts/ stages in which change occurs. Moreover, it is open for the perdurantist to think that the change occurring within that temporal part/stage is the manifestation of a disposition, and thus not contingent. Taking all of that into account, premise 1 of Mumford's first argument and premise 2 of his second (as I've reconstructed them above) become problematic and perdurantism can be seen as compatible with dispositionalism.

However, in a way this does not get at the core of Mumford's case, because his principal target is not really perdurantism in general, but the specific formulation he is addressing: namely, a formulation in which temporal parts/stages are instantaneous, discrete, and of themselves static, being of insufficient duration to permit any processes of change. And this is in fact the better target, insofar as no one in the more recent literature explicitly advocates for perdurantism of the sort I just suggested was upheld by Lewis and perhaps also Heller. (At least, I have not yet encountered anyone advocating explicitly for temporal parts or stages being such as to admit internal change – perhaps I have missed someone.) So while it is worth noting that in principle at least there is an alternative form of perdurantism available to dispositionalists, the more important task is to try and show that the formulation Mumford is actually targeting can sidestep his critique.

On then to my second strategy. Let's consider Mumford's arguments separately, beginning with his argument pertaining to contingency. Recall that the first premise of Mumford's first argument (at least as I've reconstructed it) says that perdurantism entails that the stages of a causal process are related merely contingently. I wonder though if this entailment really obtains. As noted above, a nomological necessitarian might invoke external laws to govern the relations between the stages of a perdurantist process. And while such laws are often viewed as ultimately contingent (Armstrong for instance certainly thought of them as contingent), they need not be viewed that way, and some nomological necessitarians maintain that laws are necessary – e.g., Fales' (1990; 1993) ontology of laws, while generally similar to Armstrong's, departs from him on this point. Again, this observation does not directly help the would-be dispositionalist perdurantist. But it should get us thinking: why can't the perdurantist suggest a model whereby two *distinct but simultaneously existing* temporal parts (i.e., for the perdurantist proper these two parts are portions of different spacetime worms, and for the exdurantist they are distinct stages) are causally related such that one instantaneously acts on the other, with the outcome then showing up in an immediately succeeding temporal part? What would be problematic about such a picture?

One might reply that it is problematic because it supposes that an active power can be exercised at a durationless instant, whereas Mumford has demonstrated in his second argument that this is impossible. However, this would imply that Mumford's first argument implicitly relies on his second – that they are not really independent arguments. But I think he intends them to be taken as independent. So let's bracket this worry about the feasibility of the instantaneous manifestation of an active power, and come back to it when we consider Mumford's second argument.

What else, then, might render my suggestion problematic? Perhaps the idea, which Mumford defends at length elsewhere (see Mumford & Anjum (2011, ch. 5)), that a cause must be simultaneous with its effect. By contrast, it seems that on the perdurantist picture the effect obtains at a succeeding, disjoint temporal part/stage.

I suggest two possible avenues of response. One is to argue that Mumford is incorrect in thinking that a cause must be simultaneous with its effect. While historically this was a popular view amongst dispositionalists (it was taken for granted by many mediaeval scholastics, at least with respect to causation within the physical world), one might argue that it is not a core commitment of dispositionalism. And though Mumford and Anjum ably defend the idea, it may remain open to further objections, even by those sympathetic to dispositionalism.[33]

Still, that is a much larger debate that I would be prudent to avoid here. So as a second possible response, consider that the perdurantist dispositionalist might grant that a cause must be simultaneous with its effect, *in the sense that a passive power is acted upon only when an active power is acting upon it,*[34] while yet maintaining that the change may not register until a subsequent moment. So suppose that temporal part A is distinct from but exists simultaneously with temporal part B (i.e., they are parts of distinct spacetime worms, say one of a cat and the other of a dog). Suppose further that instantaneous temporal part A exercises

---

[33] See the critique by Wahlberg (2017). Moreover, denial of the simultaneity of cause and effect plays a role in Williams' argument for the compatibility of perdurantism and dispositionalism (forthcoming, pp. 186–196 and 211–215).

[34] Or, more properly: an *object* is acted on by means of its passive power only when a distinct object is acting upon it by means of its own active power.

(instantaneously) its active power on instantaneous temporal part B. One object acts and another is simultaneously acted upon. Remember though, both objects are perfectly static: the action/reception pairing is simultaneous and occurs at a durationless instant. So an activity occurs, but no change occurs.[35] The change occurs insofar as an immediately succeeding temporal part/stage registers that prior disposition manifestation, such that it loses or acquires some intrinsic property. What I am suggesting is that the perdurantist dispositionalist decouple the notion of an effect from the notion of the *registering* of an effect. The former (an effect) is, as Mumford thinks, necessarily simultaneous with its cause, where both are cashed out in terms of powers (one passive and the other active). The latter (the registering of the effect) is an outcome of a causal activity without itself being a direct party to that activity.

The obvious objection to positing a real distinction between an effect and the registering of an effect will be the worry about an explanatory gap: if temporal part B is impacted at time t1, but the change does not register until disjoint time t2, how can the latter have anything to do with the former? (This worry is rendered more pressing for the perdurantist, for whom the entity in which the change is registered is strictly speaking distinct from the one impacted – it is a numerically different temporal part or stage.) Here I think the dispositionalist perdurantist will have to invoke a primitive fact: necessarily, the manifestation conditions of powers are structured in such a way as to include an orientation to a subsequent temporal part/stage in which the manifestation (the effect of the causal interaction) is *registered*. Because rooted in a power, the connection between the initial and successor temporal parts is necessary rather than contingent. This is just an aspect of the identity conditions of powers in a perdurantist world, and there is nothing more to be said. (Though it might help to recall that for the perdurantist eternalist – and most if not all perdurantists in the current literature are eternalists – a temporal gap does not entail a gap in *existence*. That is, although temporal part B at time t1 is disjoint from a subsequent temporal part at time t2, both temporal parts exist equally, since all times exist equally. On four-dimensionalism, more than just the present exists, and on eternalism, the past, present, and future are all equally real. So if part of what motivates Mumford to affirm the simultaneity of cause and effect is a

---

[35] Historically it has been pretty widely held that activity need not entail change. Recall for instance Aristotle's Unmoved Mover, eternally engaged in an act of contemplation, which act involves no change whatever. Or consider Kant's example of a ball sitting stationary on a cushion. It is compressing the mattress so long as it sits there, but this compression is (arguably) a static activity.

concern about a temporal gap involving an *existence* gap between past and future, that particular concern needn't trouble a perdurantist dispositionalist.)

Admittedly, that is not a response liable to generate enthusiasm. Invocation of primitive fact ought to be a last resort. But while the invocation of primitive fact may reek somewhat of desperation, remember that the modest goal here is to defend the compatibility of perdurantism and dispositionalism – the *compatibility*, not the matchmaker's ideal. It seems to me that the model just suggested is not obviously incoherent, so perhaps an unhealthy relationship is good enough for present purposes (at least for convinced dispositionalists who also happen to think that the case for perdurantism is strong).[36]

Turning to Mumford's second argument, let's grant its premise 2, namely that the reality of *irreducible* temporally extended causal processes would entail the falsity of perdurantism. (The sort of causal process described just above is temporally extended, but not irreducibly so – the disposition manifestation occurs at t1 but is not registered as a change until t2, with the temporal parts at t1 and t2 being distinct and non-overlapping. The temporally extended causal process is thus broken down into individual, static temporal parts.) Focus then on premise 1: is it true that dispositionalism entails the reality of irreducible temporally extended causal processes? Here it is worth drawing attention to a seemingly minor concession Mumford makes just after working through his alarm clock example of an active power (2009, p. 232):

> The way we think the clock can do this [ring] is that it is undergoing a process – such as its short arm being moved towards a trigger – that will in the end produce the alarm. We would, however, by mystified by the idea of something having an active power that had no grounding in that particular's movements or changes. The only cases we can think of are spontaneously manifested powers such as radioactive decay or the spurious case of spontaneous human combustion. But could we countenance a power that was manifested in a spontaneous but reliable and regular way? It seems hard to think why we would or should …

---

[36] Or one might turn to Williams' (2017; forthcoming) very different strategy for rendering them compatible – different insofar as he rejects a good deal of the background at work in Mumford's argument, including, again, the simultaneity of cause and effect, and also the sharp division between active and passive powers. By contrast, I have opted to work within the same background as Mumford. For the dispositionalist perdurantist, hopefully either Williams' approach or my own will be seen as workable.

The concession is that the manifestation of an active power can occur – and in the case of radioactive decay actually *does* occur – even outside the context of an irreducible temporally extended causal process. But he takes this to be a minor point since spontaneous manifestations are not at issue in the natural regularities normally referenced in discussions of the laws of nature. But elsewhere he is a bit more liberal with respect to the breadth of spontaneous manifestations. Thus Mumford and Anjum (2011, p. 36) write:

> Radioactive decay is an example of a power that is understood to manifest itself without any further stimulation. Particles are disposed to decay at a certain time, though their actual lifespan can vary. They do indeed tend to manifest this disposition but not because anything stimulated them to do so. Momentum is also characterized in Newton's First Laws as a power that will operate without further stimulus, unless stopped from doing so. Spontaneous human combustion, so feared in the 1980s though now believed to be spurious, shows that we can at least accept the idea of a spontaneously manifested power.

The significant addition is that momentum is here added to the list of spontaneously manifested powers. Given the central role that momentum plays in causal interactions in nature, this is worth highlighting: Mumford and Anjum take it that momentum can plausibly be conceived as a spontaneously manifested power.[37] And it is a spontaneously manifested power that, contra his supposition in the previous citation, *is manifested reliably and regularly.*[38]

The momentum case might be thought insignificant in the context of the present dialectic, provided one conceive of momentum as intelligible only within the context of an irreducible temporally extended process. And this is precisely how Mumford (2009, pp. 232–233) conceives of momentum:

> A billiard ball rolls across a table. Its force drives it forward, though it is gradually lost through friction. This is a process through time. In the perdurance view, there are no moving parts or stages, only a series of suitably connected static parts or stages. Presumably, then, there is no momentum

---

[37] Note that this is a controversial claim amongst dispositionalists; for instance Wahlberg (2017, p. 113) questions whether momentum can properly be conceived as a disposition, on the grounds that it is arguably not an intrinsic property of an object. Feser (2015, ch. 1) argues that a dispositionalist need not understand inertial motion as the manifestation of a power, but that if she does, she should not conceive it as a *spontaneously* manifested power.

[38] One might make a case for further examples here: perhaps exercises of libertarian free choice are also the spontaneous manifestations of an active power, which nevertheless occur with regularity?

in any of the static parts. A scientist may well be able to construct a model in which an unmoving billiard ball can be ascribed a force and momentum, but can we as metaphysicians accept that this is the way the world actually works? If we accepted a hypothesis that there are active powers, which in being exercised and merely in being held involve change, movement and dynamism, then perdurance theory cannot seriously accommodate them.

Perdurantists might at this point object that this is too quick, insofar as they have argued at length that processes involving momentum can be reduced to processes involving individually static temporal parts – in fact the discussion of 'instantaneous velocity' plays an important role in the dialectic on perdurantism, with both Sider (2001, pp. 224–236) and Hawley (2001, pp. 73–85) attempting such reductions. Mumford is clearly not impressed with the results, but what he has provided here does not strictly show that momentum is irreducible to features of static temporal parts. And the sort of model I tentatively suggested above might apply: in the case of the billiard balls, a dispositionalist perdurantist might interpret this as a case of two simultaneously existing temporal parts, A and B (belonging to two distinct spacetime worms), where A's active power to transmit force to B is manifested at time t1, with the effect registering in a change evident in B's successor temporal part existing at t2. And with respect to inertial motion, the dispositionalist perdurantist might model it as a case of the temporal part A spontaneously manifesting at time t1 a power to transmit momentum, with the effect registering in a successor temporal part in the form of its occupying a different spatial region at t2. (Remember, on the common combination of perdurantism + eternalism, the successor temporal part, while distinct, is just as real as its predecessor. A presentist perdurantist might not be able to run this analysis of momentum, since for the presentist there is no successor temporal part in existence to act upon.)

At any rate, I believe there is at least something to be said for the idea that one can be a dispositionalist without also committing to the irreducibility of temporally extended causal processes, and that more is needed show that such a combination of views is either incoherent or beyond the pale. This is admittedly a modest claim, but perhaps one worth making, for the sake of those who find plausible both dispositionalism and perdurantism.

7.5 Conclusion

To sum up, in this chapter we have examined three areas of debate relating to the metaphysics spacetime: the substantivalism versus relationism debate in Section 7.2, the time travel debate in Section 7.3, and the debate over persistence in Section 7.4. If sound, the argument of Section 7.2 of course favours dispositionalism. The take-aways of my efforts in Sections 7.3 and 7.4 are more ambiguous. If one is enamoured with the prospect of backwards time travel and also a fan of dispositionalism, then one will be encouraged by the conclusion of Section 7.3. By contrast if one is a dispositionalist who hoped to obtain from the theory a novel argument against the possibility of backwards time travel (and perhaps in favour of presentism), one may be discouraged by the conclusion of Section 7.3. – at least if one finds the material there at all plausible. Similarly if one is a perdurantist seeking to find some way of reconciling that view with dispositionalism, my arguments in Section 7.4 will hopefully be seen as a step in the right direction. By contrast if one is a dispositionalist who hoped to obtain from the theory a novel argument in favour of endurantism, one may be discouraged.

CHAPTER 8

Dispositionalism and Essentially Active Objects

8.1 Introduction

Could a physical object not only be constantly active, but *necessarily* constantly active? And if so, what is the best way to understand the metaphysics of this constant activity – what, if anything, serves to ground it? Besides having a long historical pedigree, these questions have arisen repeatedly in the recent literature on dispositions. I wish to argue that such an object is possible, and that the constant activity would be grounded neither in a distinct disposition which is necessarily constantly manifested, nor that it would be an *ungrounded* primitive activity – these two options being the ones discussed in the recent literature – but rather that it is grounded in the natural-kind essence of the object. That is, I will argue that the two recently discussed models for how a necessarily constantly active object might operate are unworkable. It will further be shown that this is a good thing for dispositionalism, insofar as it has been suggested that by reference to primitive activities one might eliminate dispositions as irreducible components of our ontology. However a third model of necessarily constantly active objects is potentially workable; on this model, an object is necessarily constantly active because it is *essentially* active – that is, its activity is grounded directly in its kind-essence, in its nature as a certain sort of object. This third model thus relies on the robust natural-kind essentialism discussed in Chapters 5 and 6. Taking this third model seriously means taking seriously the idea that there may be activity in the physical world that is *not* the manifestation of a disposition, thereby blocking attempts to use dispositionalism to provide an exhaustive account of physical activity. Some dispositionalists may balk at this; however, the notion of activities grounded directly in kinds rather than in powers need not be seen as conflicting with dispositionalism, and certainly provides no route to reducing powers to kind-grounded activities (let alone eliminating powers altogether). Moreover there is an indirect way in which this third model, if seen as independently plausible, can support dispositionalism.

The remainder of the chapter is divided as follows: I begin by laying out some important distinctions between different modes of disposition-manifestation. This is a needed preliminary to the discussion of necessarily constantly manifested dispositions, the main focus of Section 8.3. There I argue that such dispositions are impossible. Then in Section 8.4 I review and critique Corry's (2009) notion of primitive activities, and his important argument for the possibility of eliminating dispositions in favour of such activities. (As we'll see, though he does not actually endorse such elimination, he maintains that primitive activities raise the prospect of elimination and rightly remarks that, at the time of his writing, this important fact had gone unnoticed among dispositionalists.) Having argued against those two models for conceptualizing necessarily constantly active objects, I then spend Section 8.5 outlining and defending the third alternative, according to which some objects are by their very natures constantly active. Finally, in Section 8.6 I briefly remark on how admitting such objects into our ontology can lend indirect support for dispositionalism.

8.2   Preliminary Distinctions

For clarity's sake, consider first a macro-level example: a fire hydrant. A well-functioning fire hydrant has the power or disposition to spray water. Now, imagine a fire hydrant installed at a street corner. It sits there for twenty years and during that time there is never a fire on the block. After twenty years it is scrapped and replaced. Consequently, the hydrant's power to spray water was never manifested. As such, we can say that it had a *permanently unmanifested* power to spray water. If on the other hand there was a fire, and the previously dormant hydrant was turned on and its power manifested, and then turned off again, we can say that it had a *variably manifested* power to spray water. Finally, if the mechanism of a hydrant is so designed that it constantly sprays water (think of a toy hydrant at a water park), we can say that it has a *constantly manifested* power to spray water.

Let's consider the last category more closely. Presumably there would have to be a time lag between the manufacture of the functioning hydrant and its water-spraying mechanism being put into action. Consequently, its power to spray water would be constantly manifested in a temporally restricted fashion: it was unmanifested, and then, upon becoming manifest, the power remained constantly manifested. Call this a *temporally restricted* constantly manifested disposition. And the temporal restriction could work in the other direction. Imagine God creates a fire hydrant *ex nihilo*, and in such a way that as soon as it comes into being its water-spraying power is operative. Then, after a few months, someone interferes with the mechanism and the spray is halted. This too would be an instance of a temporally restricted constantly manifested power, but one in which the temporal restriction comes at the back end rather than at the front, as it were.[1] And in theory we could also have a temporally *non-restricted* constantly manifested disposition. This would be a case in which the disposition is exercised from the very moment that the disposition comes into being, and remains in exercise for the duration of its existence. In the real world there will likely be no examples of such dispositions in the macro realm, but there seem to be cases in the realm of fundamental physics, examples of which will come up shortly.

Within the category of temporally non-restricted constantly manifested dispositions, there is a further distinction between these dispositions as *contingently* versus *necessarily* constantly manifested. The hydrant's constantly manifested power to spray water is clearly a case of a *contingently* constantly manifested power. Someone at the water park could easily stop up the hole through which the water sprays, thereby blocking the disposition's manifestation. Now, as we've seen in previous chapters it is generally thought that the identity conditions of a disposition involve at least: (a) a manifestation or range of manifestations, and (b) a condition or set of conditions according to which that manifestation or those manifestations will come about (perhaps including any *ceteris paribus* stipulations). So what distinguishes a *contingently* constantly manifested power from a *necessarily* constantly manifested power is that the former only manifests under certain stimulus conditions whereas the latter manifests under any – no internal[2]

---

[1] One might feel a bit leery applying the term 'constant'oto a disposition-manifestation that has any temporal restriction, but ordinary language is fairly permissive here. For instance, 'I have a constant headache' would be interpreted as involving a temporally restricted constancy. Scientific discourse is similarly permissive.

[2] That is, *internal to the relevant object*, another property or structure possessed by it. For some interesting work on internal finks, masks, and antidotes, see Choi (2005), Clarke (2008), Everett (2009), Handfield (2008), Molnar (2003, pp. 92–93), and Oderberg (2007, p. 135).

or external influence could block that manifestation, as long as the disposition remains in existence. This means that the necessity under consideration here is quite strong. A (mythical) fire hydrant with a necessarily constantly manifested power to spray water would have to be one that would be constantly spraying water not just in our world, and under any conditions in our world, but under any conditions in all possible worlds in which the hydrant existed *with that power*. Of course, there may be perfectly legitimate weaker senses of 'necessity' that could be employed here as well – but the really interesting ontological issues surrounding these dispositions are those involving the strongest form of necessity, and it is the strict sense that will be scrutinized here.

If the necessarily constantly manifested power is an *accidental* property of the hydrant, then there are some possible worlds in which the hydrant exists without the power. If, however, it is an *essential* property of the hydrant, then in all possible worlds in which the hydrant exists the power exists as well, and since the power is by stipulation necessarily constantly manifested, then in all possible worlds in which the hydrant exists it will be constantly spraying water. We thus have a further distinction, between accidentally versus essentially possessed necessarily constantly manifested dispositions.

Additional distinctions can be introduced at this stage. First, note that the spraying hydrant provides an example of a power that is manifested without necessarily having any impact on external objects. The hydrant's power to spray water is distinct from its power to make people wet. This is clear from the fact that the manifestation conditions of the two are different: the power to spray water is manifested whenever the hydrant sprays water, whereas the power to make people wet is manifested when the hydrant sprays water and when that water comes into contact with someone (under appropriate circumstances, etc.). One way to conceptualize this would be to say that there is a single *immediate* dispositional power here, the power to spray water, which, due to some further facts concerning the natures of water and of people, implies a further *mediate* power of the hydrant to make people wet. The hydrant has the power to produce something (a spray of water) which in turn is possessed of its own set of powers, one of which is to make people wet. An analogue in the micro realm would be an electron's ability to repel negatively charged particles. This is a mediate ability, resulting from an immediate power to produce and emit an electromagnetic field, or photons if one wants to think of it in quantum terms. The photons in turn carry the force that does the actual repelling.[3]

Some related divisions have been noted by Cartwright (2009) and Corry (2009). They constitute another threefold distinction, this time between:

(1)   The mere existence of a disposition
(2)   The exercise of a disposition
(3)   The effect or result of that exercise on some other entity

Returning to our hydrant example, we can divide the relevant facts as follows:

(1)   The mere existence of the hydrant's disposition to spray water
(2)   The exercise of that disposition in the actual spraying of water
(3)   The effect of that exercise on some other entity (someone being hit by the spray)

Or to use gravitational mass as an example, we might think of:

(1)   The mere existence of a particle's disposition to emit a gravitational field (or, in quantum terms, to emit gravitons)
(2)   The exercise of that disposition in actually emitting the field (which seems to be a constant exercise, as Cartwright (2007; 2009) observes)
(3)   The effect of that gravitational field on some other entity (the attraction that occurs when this field comes into contact with the gravitational field of another massive particle)

Both Cartwright and Corry stress the importance of the divide between items 2 and 3. A disposition can be exercised even if that exercise issues in no apparent impacts on external bodies. Thus, if the gravitational field that would normally move some massive body fails to actually move that body due to the presence of a countervailing electromagnetic force, what we have is not the lack of exercise of a power, but a fully exercised power

---

[3] Note that mediate dispositions are not equivalent to Molnar's (2003, p. 101) iterated powers. An iterated power is a power that an object has to acquire some other power. Thus, a power to do *x* is an iterated power when an object does not actually have the power to *x*, but has another power, *y*, which is the power to acquire the power to *x*. By contrast, an immediate power is a power to *x*, while a mediate power, *y*, is a further power that arises from the activity of *x*ing. It is not as if the electron has no power to repel negatively charged particles, and needs to acquire that power. Rather, it has the power to do so, but can only exercise it mediately, by first doing something else, namely producing a photon that in turn carries electromagnetic force.

which nevertheless fails to have its 'usual' effect. Corry (2009, p. 183) notes that the distinction has been largely neglected in recent literature, though he observes that Creary (1981) and Molnar (2003) draw attention to it, and I would add Persson (2010) to the list.[4]

They also emphasize a certain type of item 2, namely those that are *constant* activities. However, they differ somewhat in how they conceptualize these. Cartwright conceives them as constantly manifested powers (for which she adopts the particular term 'capacity,' seeing it as distinct from 'disposition'), whereas Corry prefers to use the terminology of constant *causal influences.*[5]

So, at this point we have encountered a threefold distinction between permanently unmanifested, variably manifested, and constantly manifested dispositions; a further distinction in the last of those three, between temporally restricted and temporally non-restricted constantly manifested dispositions; within the latter category, contingently and necessarily constantly manifested dispositions, and accidentally versus essentially possessed necessarily constantly manifested dispositions; a distinction between immediate and mediate dispositions; and an additional threefold distinction enumerated by Cartwright and Corry. Having laid out the conceptual groundwork, let's turn to some further questions specific to constantly manifested dispositions, and especially to necessarily constantly manifested dispositions.

---

[4] Since I mentioned in Section 8.1 that the topic under discussion has a long historical pedigree, it is also worth noting that the recently neglected distinction Corry is talking about here was commonly known in mediaeval philosophy. Consider for example the following passage from the thirteenth century Franciscan, Alexander of Hales (1924, p. 202):

> There is a potency in the sun, a potency to the act which is to light *[lucere]*, which activity is always carried out by the sun, being coeval with the sun of its essence. There follows from this a potency to the activity which is to illumine *[illuminare]* – which act indeed is carried over into another object by the sun: that very act, which is to illumine *[illuminare]*, is the act which the potency of the sun effects, while an act by nature, which is to light *[lucere]*, is the act by which it does this …

(From his *Summa Theologica*, I, Inq. I, Tract. IV, q. 1. My own translation.) This picture of the sun's activity was commonly adopted, and works like this: the sun, by its nature, has an inherent capacity to give off light ('to light' or *lucere*). It is constantly manifesting that power. Nevertheless, there is a real distinction between the potency to light and the activity of lighting, which is the potency's exercise. Now, the sun would carry out this activity even if there were no earth and no earth's atmosphere for the sun to illumine (*illuminare*). Yet, it so happens that the atmosphere is there, and the nature of the activity of lighting is such that it can have an external effect, namely the illumination of the atmosphere (given a further passive disposition of the atmosphere allowing it to receive light). So we have Cartwright and Corry's three items: the power, its exercise, and its effect on an external body.

[5] This shift of terminology is quite intentional on Corry's part. As we shall see below, he wishes to leave open the possibility of dropping item 1 from our ontology and sticking with items 2 and 3. Thus on his view, item 2 should not be conceptualized as an exercised *disposition*.

8.3   Necessarily Constantly Manifested Dispositions

Dispositionalists have a special interest in the dispositions of fundamental particles, as these are thought plausible candidates for being fundamental dispositions – dispositions not derived from or grounded in other properties. Ellis (2001, p. 47) writes: "p. 47) writes: Gravitational mass, for example, is a causal power: it is the power of an object to generate gravitational fields. Charge is a causal power: it is the power of a body to produce electromagnetic fields. The intrinsic angular momentum, or spin, of a particle is its power to contribute to the total angular momentum of a system."[6] The interesting thing about some of these dispositions is that they seem to be of the temporally non-restricted constantly manifested variety. So far as we can tell, a charged particle constantly emits an electromagnetic field. A massive particle constantly generates a gravitational field.[7] The fact that apparently constantly manifested dispositions are taken seriously in science speaks loudly in favour of the possibility of such dispositions. Further, there seems no inherent contradiction in the notion, and their possibility has not been challenged by anyone in the recent literature. As such, in what follows their possibility will be assumed.

Assume then for the sake of argument that there are such dispositions at the microlevel. Are they contingently or necessarily constantly manifested? First, it should be noted that this seems to be a question that can only be usefully asked of Cartwright and Corry's item 2. An item 3 manifestation requires some external object to be present as a recipient of the causal force of the item 2 constant activity, and so it will always be possible for that second entity to cease existing, thus ceasing the item 3 manifestation even while the item 2 exercise continues in being.[8] Bearing that

[6] These properties are commonly listed as examples of possible fundamental dispositions, and in Section 4.2 we saw Mumford (1998, pp. 229–230; 2006) employing them. Recall though the complication I noted there with respect to spin; the same point can be made here with respect to Ellis' characterization of that property.

[7] Or, put in relativistic terms, it constantly warps the spatial manifold. As noted previously, for most elementary particles it seems as if mass is not actually a fundamental property. It is now more common to see mass in electrons and most other particles as a non-fundamental property arising from interaction with a Higgs field. On this picture only the Higgs boson, the particle which mediates the Higgs field, would be inherently massive.

[8] A possible exception: if entity A is constantly affecting distinct entity B via a constantly manifested disposition to so affect B, but entity A also depends on entity B for its existence, then it is not the case that we could destroy entity B and have the power continue. General relativity might provide an example of this. On that theory, a massive body constantly exercises an impact on a distinct entity, the spatial manifold. It seems plausible to think that that body also depends on the spatial manifold for its existence, in the sense that it could not exist without existing in space. However, this case relies on the idea that mass depends for its existence not on space considered generically, but on relativistic space in particular (as mass does not warp Newtonian space, for instance). That would imply that no massive bodies could exist in universes where space was non-relativistic, which would be controversial.

in mind, we can ask questions of item 2, like: could a charged particle cease emitting an electromagnetic field and still be a charged particle? To some extent this is an empirical question. Perhaps an experiment could be devised, or conditions laid out theoretically, in which that would occur. But even if not, this might just be a contingent feature of other aspects of our physical universe. Perhaps, given the particular kinds instantiated in our world and the relevant background conditions, a charged particle must constantly emit an electromagnetic field, but in some other world with different background conditions the power need not always be exercised. A disposition would only be *necessarily* constantly manifested, in the strictest sense, if it were constantly manifested in all possible worlds in which it existed – if even God Himself could not stop the charged particle from emitting a field, short of destroying the dispositional property. It seems that we could not empirically verify the claim that there are any such particles in our world, though we might be able empirically to falsify the claim – again, by demonstrating experimentally that all the supposed constantly manifested powers can actually be blocked. (Recall though that it may still be the case that the object possessed of the necessarily constantly manifested power has it only *accidentally* rather than *essentially*, such that the object could lose the power while remaining in existence.)

If empirical means cannot verify the existence of necessarily constantly manifested powers, could the question of their possible existence be answered through the tools of metaphysics? I do not see how one could go about arguing that there *must be* such powers, which is the only sort of metaphysical argument that could show that there actually are any in our world.[9] Nevertheless, one might argue that such powers could serve some useful purposes in dispositionalist ontology. Notably, necessarily constantly manifested powers might evade some troubling antidispositionalist arguments. Consider two such arguments:

(1) One charge is that dispositions have a dubious existential status. Psillos (2006) brings this out nicely when he asks what exactly a disposition *does* when it is not being manifested. The unmanifested disposition has no categorical modes of being, so what does its existence *qua* property consist in?

(2) Moreover, their status as potencies to *future* manifestations can make them suspect.

---

[9] Of course, not being able to see how one might develop such an argument is not the same as seeing that one cannot develop such an argument.

Armstrong (1997, p. 79) writes:

> A disposition as conceived by a Dispositionalist is like a congealed hypothetical fact or state of affairs: 'If this object is suitably struck, then it is caused (or there is a certain objective probability of it being caused) to shatter.' It is, as it were, an inference ticket (as Ryle said), but one that exists in nature (as Ryle would hardly have allowed). That is all there is to a particular disposition. Consider, then, the critical case where the disposition is not mani-fested. *The object still has within itself, essentially, a reference to the manifestation that did not occur.* It points to a thing that does not exist. This must remind us of the *intentionality* of mental states and processes, the characteristic that Brentano held was the distinguishing mark of the mental, that is, their being directed upon objects or states of affairs that need not exist. But for physicalists such as myself it presents a *prima facie* problem. If the mental has intentionality, and if, as Brentano thought, it is also *ontologically irreducible*, then there is something here that would appear to falsify Physicalism … [Emphases in the original]

The first worry has no application here. It makes no sense to ask of a necessarily constantly manifested power what it does when it is not being manifested.[10] The second argument also lacks force. A necessarily constantly manifested disposition has no reference to a manifestation that does not occur, since the manifestation is always occurring. So if we could countenance such dispositions, we could defuse two important objections to dispositional realism, with respect to at least some dispositions.[11] If we could then find a way of showing that some necessarily constantly manifested dispositions could be essentially rather than accidentally possessed, we would have an answer to our question of whether there could be necessarily constantly active *objects*.

Still, the fact that necessarily constantly manifested dispositions would serve some useful purpose, from the dispositionalist's perspective, does not mean that they are real, or even possible. A number of thinkers have voiced suspicions on that score. Mumford (2006, p. 481) argues that "the possibility of unmanifested existence seems essential to being a dispositional property even though we can make sense of a disposition that is continuously manifested … Where a property is necessarily manifested, it is non-dispositional …" Kistler and Gnassounou (2007, p. 14)

---

[10] As we shall see momentarily, Psillos (2006, p. 141) would have an answer to this, namely that a necessarily constantly manifested disposition would not really be a disposition.

[11] An advantage that would not obtain for merely contingently constantly manifested powers. For with these, even if they are always manifested in our world, one can simply run the existential or intentionality objections with respect to their existence in some other possible world, and the objections will be just as effective (if they are effective at all, which is of course disputed).

concur: "However, by saying that force is always active or that power is always effective, one identifies power with its exercise and therefore makes non- sense of the distinction between power and exercise, which is necessary to give sense to the notion of power itself." Presumably they mean by a 'power that is always effective' a power which is so effective necessarily rather than contingently, as the identity would obviously not hold in the contingent case. Molnar (2003, p. 97) likewise questions whether a constantly manifested power can still be counted a power: "It is hard to understand the concept of a power that exists precisely when it manifests itself and for exactly as long as it manifests. Is such a power something genuine, a property in its own right? It seems to just be a reification of the causal relation that holds whenever the power is exercised." Psillos (2006, p. 141) for his part writes that

> it might well be problematic to talk about continuously manifested *powers*. It is arguable that when a property is necessarily continuously manifested, it is a non-power. For, the distinctive feature of powers is that they may be possessed, though not manifested. So the power ... should be such that it is *not* necessarily continuously manifested. In other words, it should be logically (or metaphysically) possible that it is not continuously manifested. [Emphases in original]

The common worry of three of these five authors is that the very nature of a disposition is such as to imply its possible non-manifestation. Unfortunately none of them expands on this idea, but one can develop it along the following lines.

Here we need to reflect on how a disposition is manifested. A disposition is, at root, a potential for a certain manifestation, a certain actualization of that disposition. Being a potency for actualization, it does not actualize itself. Consequently, when a disposition becomes manifest it must do so at least in part because the object to which it belongs receives a stimulus from something other than that very disposition; something outside of the disposition must trigger its actualization.[12] This is plausibly a metaphysically necessary fact, which one can make plausible by reference to examples, but which one cannot directly prove. For instance, my ability to learn Russian cannot give rise, in and of itself and with no external stimuli, to a knowledge of Russian; the ability of some spatial region to be occupied cannot entail the presence of an object there, etc.

---

[12] By 'outside' I just mean 'non-identical to the disposition.' One might claim that the trigger could be external to the disposition but still an internal property or structure of the object to which the disposition belongs. More on this shortly.

Any attempted justification of this principle will suffer from being less obvious than the principle itself. Just as you cannot get something from nothing, you cannot get something from the mere *potential for* something. And what actualizes a disposition? Something that is not itself an unmanifested disposition, lest we have a regress. So it will have to be made manifest by an object working via either a manifested disposition or (possibly, depending on one's ontology) a categorical property. Something genuinely distinct from the disposition must be involved in its actualization. Since these two are distinct, it cannot be the case that in all possible worlds in which the disposition is present, this external entity is present and doing the actualizing. Hence, there can be no necessarily constantly manifested dispositions.[13]

There are various ways one might object to such an argument. Most obviously, it might be thought that this method of ruling out necessarily constantly manifested dispositions carries too high a cost, in that it seems also to rule out an aspect of quantum indeterminacy. If every dispositional property requires an external trigger in order to be manifest, then the apparently spontaneous manifestations of particle decay appear to be disallowed. This would rankle at least some of the five authors whom we have seen objecting to necessarily constantly manifested powers, for Molnar (2003, p. 85) allows that there can be powers which spontaneously manifest, with no need of an outside trigger. (He uses beta-decay as a possible example.) And of course we saw spontaneously manifested

---

[13] The mediaeval scholastics agreed, thinking it always possible (if only by divine intervention) for a constantly manifested power to be blocked and yet for the power itself remain in existence, unmanifested. (Or rather they maintained this when the powers under discussion were *properties*; views on the status of *substantial* dispositions (i.e., prime matter) were more varied, with some holding that prime matter can only exist insofar as it is actualized, constantly, by substantial form. That point was briefly adverted to in the discussion of hylomorphism in Chapter 5. A dispositional property can stop manifesting while the underlying substance remains in existence, but in the case of a substantial disposition there is no such independent underlying substance to persist.) Recall our earlier quote from Alexander of Hales. He goes on later in the same passage to say of the sun's potency to light that 'in the sun this potency and act are not the same – as is evident from the obscurity, which was made during the death of our Lord, where the act and potency were separated ...' (1924, p. 202. From his *Summa Theologica*, I, Inq. I, Tract. IV, q. 1. My own translation.) Importantly, the potency he is talking about here is the potency to light (*lucere*), which is normally a constantly manifested potency. It corresponds to Cartwright and Corry's item 2. It is this manifestation which God directly blocks in the miracle, not the derivative item 3 manifestation, the illumination of the atmosphere. (Why does Hales affirm this? He doesn't tell us, but he probably does so in order to affirm the genuinely *miraculous* status of the sky's darkening at the crucifixion. A blocking of the item 3 manifestation, the illumination of the atmosphere, could have occurred by natural means, such as an eclipse, but not a blocking of the item 2 manifestation of lighting.) Though of course the scholastics also thought God could block an item 3 manifestation. See for instance Scotus' (1975, pp. 177–178) *Quodlibetal Questions*, 7.64–65.

powers playing an important role for Mumford in some of the discussion of perdurantism in Section 7.4.

Granted, if one allows spontaneously, causelessly manifesting dispositions into one's ontology, then there is in principle no way to rule out the idea that some such manifestations could occur constantly rather than intermittently.[14] But the same randomness that 'bestows' the spontaneous manifestation also rules out its being necessary. A constantly but randomly manifested power is by definition a *contingently* constantly manifested power. So even if one wants to weaken the rather robustly Aristotelian account of disposition-manifestation just given and allow for triggerless disposition-manifestations, one can still disallow necessarily constantly manifested dispositions. (Though for the record I remain sceptical of spontaneously manifesting powers.)

A related problem: if it were the case that every disposition needed an external stimulus, we might then wonder what to make of our scientific examples of constantly exercised dispositions. (Assuming for the sake of argument that an electron's constant emission of photons, or its constant warping of the spatial manifold, etc., are best thought of as disposition-manifestations rather than the other two options we will consider below, namely that they might instead be primitive activities, or activities grounded directly in kinds.) For instance, does an electron have an external trigger that constantly stimulates its field-generating activity? What would this trigger be? The second question is an empirical one, to be left up to the physicists to determine, while the answer to the first is simply 'yes,' if indeed charge is a dispositional property as opposed to a grounded or ungrounded activity. Even if one allows for spontaneous manifestations in theory, it is implausible to think of a charged particle's field-generation as a random, spontaneous activity which just happens to be constant.

Consider now a final objection, one that I take to be particularly powerful, but which will also be shown ultimately unsound: it was noted earlier that in order for a stimulus to count as external to a disposition, it is not necessary that the stimulus come from an object external to the object in which the disposition is instantiated. Perhaps then some property or structure within the same object could serve as a stimulus. Maybe one aspect of an object could serve as a necessarily constant stimulus for another aspect, a disposition, such that that disposition would be

---

[14] Of course, the manifestation that is particle decay could not occur as a constant manifestation, but one could conceive of other examples.

necessarily constantly manifested. In order for that to be the case, the sti-mulating aspect would have to be both genuinely distinct from the dis-position, and yet so closely interrelated with it that so long as one was in existence, the other would be as well.

This idea is only applicable at the level of fundamental objects – objects, that is, which have no proper parts that are themselves objects. A water molecule is an object that has proper parts that are themselves objects, and in fact objects belonging to distinct natural kinds, namely atoms of hydrogen and oxygen. One might argue that there is a sense in which the dispositions of one of these constituent atoms do not belong to a different object from those of another of the constituent atoms, since both atoms are really parts of one greater whole, the molecule, which is the real object here, in the fullest sense. The atoms, insofar as they are incorporated in the molecule, do not have sufficient independence of action so as to constitute substances on their own.[15] However, even on such a view, these atoms (or these structures that once were atoms) are nevertheless inherently capable of existing independently of one another, and they will do so if the molecule gets broken up. The same will apply for any such case of parts belonging to a larger whole. Because one part can always exist without the other (considered independently of the whole), the dispositions and categorical properties of one part will never be sufficiently strongly connected to the dispositions of another, in all possible worlds, to serve the needs of the present case.

So if this proposal is workable at all, it will only work for fundamental entities, which can have multiple properties but not multiple parts belonging to other natural kinds. Consider our options then. Could the constant stimulus itself be a dispositional property? If so, it too would need to be necessarily constantly manifested in order for the second dis-positional property to be necessarily constantly manifested. This leads to a regress. More importantly, the notion that one dispositional property, including a constantly manifested disposition, could act directly on another disposition (whether one belonging to the same object or a dif-ferent object) is likely mistaken, insofar as dispositions should probably not be viewed as themselves the literal subjects of causation, for reasons discussed in Section 5.5. Another option would be to suppose that an object could constantly stimulate one of its own dispositions by acting on itself, i.e. on the object rather than on one of its properties, in virtue

---

[15] For versions of such a view, see for instance Bobik (1998), Humphreys (1997; 1997a), Kronen (1994), Marmodoro (2013), and Toner (2008).

of some other property it has. That is, maybe the substance could, by virtue of some property, act directly on itself and in so doing indirectly stimulate one of its dispositions. Here the object's action on itself would have to be a necessary action, but what sort of property grounds a necessary action? If the grounding property supposed to be a disposition, we clearly have another regress. On the other hand, if it is supposed to be a categorical property (like a geometrical/structural property) it is not clear that the proposal would be welcomed by dispositionalists, committed as most of us are to the idea that categorical properties cannot by themselves (without dispositions) directly ground activities. Granted, these options may not be the only ones available to the advocate of this proposal, and I cannot claim to have been exhaustive in my refutations. However I do think any others will run into comparable problems: either some form of regress or reference to explanatory factors that will be unwelcome in a dispositionalist ontology.

To recap this section: we have looked at two reasons why dispositionalists might favour necessarily constantly manifested dispositions, given a positive argument for rejecting them, and have considered and refuted three objections to that argument. Consequently I believe our positive argument against the possibility of necessarily constantly manifested dispositions stands. (That being the case, we do not need to consider the further issue of whether such dispositions could be essentially possessed by some object, a further necessary component in answering this chapter's opening question.)

Even if such dispositions are ruled out, might a similar idea prove more promising? We have already seen Kistler and Gnassounou (2007) argue against necessarily constantly manifested dispositions by claiming that they collapse into their exercise, and it is natural to wonder whether primitive activities – doings of an object that are ungrounded by its dispositions, or its natural-kind essence, or anything else that might be intrinsic to the object – could be put into play here instead. This brings us to Corry's (2009) recent work, which I will review and critique. Then in Section 8.5 I will outline and defend a closely related alternative: activities grounded in natural-kind essences.

8.4   Primitive Activities

Recall Corry (2009) and Cartwright's (2009) distinction between (1) the mere existence of a disposition, (2) the exercise of a disposition, and (3) the effect or result of that exercise on some other entity. Corry's preferred terminology for item 2 is *causal influence*. This is because he thinks item 1 might be eliminable from our ontology in favour of items 2 and 3. He writes (2009, p. 180):

> Level (1) contains dispositional properties, including dispositions to pro-
> duce causal influ-ences. We should only posit level (1) as a distinct, irre-
> ducible ontological category if we think that these dispositions are
> irreducibly dispositional in the way that Ellis and Lierse describe.[16] But
> nothing in our discussion so far requires this. In particular, given the exis-
> tence of influences at level (2), one could choose to analyse the disposi-
> tions 'to have a causal influence of type X in circumstances C' in terms of
> a conditional just as Humeans do – the only difference being that the
> conditional will mention elements at levels (2) and (3) instead of just the
> Humean level (3). If we take this route, we can do without the kinds of
> thing that Cartwright, Ellis, and Lierse all seem to agree are necessary:
> irreducible causal powers, capacities and the like. Now I am not suggest-
> ing that we should take this route – I am personally rather fond of causal
> powers, and there may be other good reasons for endorsing them – my
> point is that nobody seems to have noticed the possibility.

So Corry is not setting himself up as a staunch defender of primitive causal influences unsupported by dispositions, or what I will refer to as *pri-*
mitive activities.[17] However, he does see them as potentially workable,
and a possible means for eliminating item 1. He does not say much by
way of justifying this further idea of elimination, beyond pointing to
some problems for the explanatory status of item 1 powers (2009,
pp. 170–172) and arguing that item 2 does not share those problems.
Still, there might be other ways of making a case for such elimination.
Machamer (2004, pp. 29–30) argues that activities are both conceptually
and ontologically prior to dispositions, but he does not argue for the
elimination of the latter by the former. Perhaps one could do so by
extending and expanding upon such a priority claim. But a more promising route would be to point out that by adopting Corry's proposal one
could employ all of the standard Humean and other categoricalist arguments against item 1, while avoiding some of the problems associated
with Humeanism, problems revolving around the related eliminations of
real causal relations and immanent necessary connections. For now primitive activities can supply those. Moreover, such activities are plausibly

---

[16] The reference is to Ellis and Lierse (1994).

[17] For purposes of clarity: for Corry, *causal influence* is a term of art with a precise meaning, but in
other contexts it will obviously mean something very different. I think *primitive activities* is less
liable to misunderstanding.

accessible to the senses; empiricist worries centre around item 1, not 2 and 3, so a traditional Humean argument would be cast aside. There would be no worries about physical intentionality or existential status. Indeed, primitive activities would escape most if not all of the traditional anti-dispositionalist arguments, even more effectively than would necessarily constantly manifested dispositions, while at the same time correcting some of the major ontological worries surrounding Humeanism.

In reply, it is first worth noting that, contra Corry's admittedly tentative suggestion, primitive activities *cannot* be used to eliminate dispositions. The reason is that (at least for a non-Humean realist about causation) you cannot have item 3 without item 1. While an electron is constantly emitting an electromagnetic field, it is not constantly being repelled by other negatively charged particles, nor is it constantly being attracted to positively charged particles (both item 3 manifestations). Rather, it can be in a state where it is in genuine potency to either item 3 activity, depending on what external inputs it receives. The non-Humean will still want a truthmaker for this openness to these possible future states of affairs, and item1 dispositions still fit the bill in a way that item 2 clearly cannot.

Leaving aside the elimination issue, we can ask: is this primitive activity supposed to be contingently engaged in by the object, or necessarily? Both options are unworkable, and thus primitive activities must be rejected. Consider the first option. Here the activity would be contingently present in some object, not being grounded in anything in that object per se; rather, it would simply be the case that there is nothing in the object inconsistent with the presence of the activity – nothing to prevent it – and then circumstances happen to come about resulting in the presence of that activity. The difficulty with such an idea is that it seems to reify the activity. The activity is seen as something which descends upon some hapless object. But this is wildly counter-intuitive. An activity is something an object *does*. There has to be a much tighter connection between what that object is and what activity it is engaged in.

The other option would be to say that the object necessarily engages in this primitive activity. (Indeed, if primitive activities are to give us the answer to our opening question, it must be that the activity is necessarily engaged in.) But once again, since the primitive activity is not in any way grounded in anything about that object, this seems as wildly counter-intuitive as the case of a contingent primitive activity – perhaps even more counter-intuitive, as on this option it must simply be posited that the activity is necessarily engaged in, without there being any further truthmaker for this supposed modal truth. What *about* the object makes it necessarily constantly engage in this activity? The present option posits that there is no answer to this question (otherwise the activity would not be basic), which seems implausible in the extreme.

From what we have seen in this section and in the preceding section, we can conclude that if necessarily constantly active objects are possible, they are not possible because of the possible existence of necessarily constantly manifested dispositions, nor are they possible because of the possible existence of primitive activities. Let us turn, then, to a third option.

8.5   Activity Directly Grounded in a Kind

Perhaps a necessary constant activity is something an object engages in by virtue of the *nature* of that object, the natural kind it belongs to – hence the 'necessary.' This option would avoid the problems just outlined for ungrounded, primitive activities, for now the activity has a ground, and we can therefore answer the question 'what about the object makes it necessarily constantly engage in this activity?' The answer is: the nature of the object. For instance, in the case of an up-quark's activity of constantly warping the spatio-temporal manifold (which characteristic of an up-quark we refer to by the term 'mass'), we could say that the activity is derived from the nature of this particle, the kind to which this individual object belongs. Consequently, as long as that particle exists as a member of that natural kind, it will of necessity engage in that activity.

This would require taking on board the robust natural-kind essentialism discussed in Chapter 6 and presupposed by several of the substance ontologies laid out in Chapter 5 (namely primitive substance theory and hylomorphism). For the natural-kind essence associated with an up-quark would have to be something 'over and above' its mass, spin, and other defining characteristics – including any constant activities. If it were not real and irreducible, if 'up-quark' were just a convenient label applied to the collection of those defining properties and/or activities, it could not literally function as a ground for those properties and/or activities. So, by adopting this ontology of natural kinds, one can entertain the possibility of necessarily constantly active objects, and we have an answer to the opening question of the chapter. For now we have a plausible ontology within which to situate necessarily constantly active objects. That, combined with the fact that such objects seem perfectly coherent, speaks strongly in favour of their possibility.[18]

An objection that might be raised at this point by my fellow dispositionalists is that there must still be a disposition lurking here somewhere, for we can ask of the up-quark, 'how is it able to engage in this constant activity?' And it might seem as if the answer to this question must refer to a disposition, since all abilities are or are grounded in powers. While I obviously have no wish to argue against the existence of fundamental dispositions, we should remain open to the idea that some common examples of dispositions are in fact activities grounded directly in the kind-essence of an object. However, that it no way threatens the irreducible reality of dispositions,[19] for a reason seen in the previous section in reply to Corry's suggested strategy for elimination in favour of primitive activities. For example, even if we re-conceive an electron's power to emit an electromagnetic field (or a stream of photons) as an activity directly grounded in the kind 'electron' rather than as a constantly manifested power, the electron's *passive* power to be impacted by the electromagnetic fields of other electrons is obviously not reducible either to a constantly manifested power or to an activity grounded in a kind.[20] A possible world containing a single electron and no other particles (except the photons it emits) would still give off an electromagnetic field, but it wouldn't be impacted by any other such fields. That passive power to be so affected is variably manifested depending on the contingent

---

[18] Regarding historical precedent, here some prominent mediaevals unfortunately stand opposed to the notion of activities being grounded directly in kinds rather than resulting from the triggering of dispositional properties, at least with respect to the activities of material objects. Aquinas for instance maintains that an activity can be rooted directly in an essence rather a distinct dispositional property, and that this will still constitute a power, in an extended sense. However, for reasons having to do with his particular understanding of divine simplicity he thinks this only holds for God. No finite entities will have an activity immediately and wholly grounded in their essences – their activities always occur via dispositional properties derived from the essence. In consequence he would reject my proposal. See his (1956, pp. 36–42) *Summa Contra Gentiles*, bk. 2, chs. 6–10; see also his (1920) *Summa Theologica*, Ia, q. 25, a. 1, and Ia, q. 54, a. 1–3. Alexander of Hales affirms likewise, in his (1928, pp. 158–160) *Summa Theologica*, II, Inq. 2, Tract. 3, Sect. 1, q. 1, and (1928, pp. 424–425), II, Inq. 4, Tract. I, Sect. 2, q. 1. However, not all prominent scholastics are in agreement on this point; notably, Suárez would support my view. See his (1994, pp. 91–98) *Metaphysical Disputations* 18. (My thanks to Jacob Tuttle for drawing my attention to the Suárez reference.)

[19] Contra the argument of Fisk (1973), for whom the reality of kinds (or rather, for him, the natures of individual substances) is a direct route to ridding ontology of fundamental powers, given that natures can themselves ground activities.

[20] Recall that we encountered the active power vs. passive power distinction in the previous chapter (Section 7.4), in the course of laying out Mumford's (2009) second argument for the incompatibility of dispositionalism and perdurantism.

availability of external stimuli, and cannot be reduced to any sort of constant activity. What this may indicate however is the need for dispositionalists to subject the fundamental properties of fundamental kinds to
further scrutiny; for instance perhaps from a metaphysical standpoint
'charge' is really a label for several distinct powers or powers + activities
grounded in kinds. Some such scrutiny has already taken place with
respect to mass (see for instance the brief discussions in Armstrong
(1999) and Bird (2007, pp. 211–212) concerning whether gravitational
mass and inertial mass refer to distinct properties), so this would just be
a matter of expanding existing research programs. So while the possibility
of there being some activities grounded directly in kinds may prompt
some uneasiness amongst dispositionalists (insofar as some may have
hoped that dispositionalism could have supplied a complete account of
all activities by itself, perhaps viewing all physical activities as disposition-
manifestations), the idea of such activities is nevertheless in no tension
with dispositionalism.

Moreover, a recognition of the possibility of some activities being
cashed out in terms of direct grounding by kind-essences rather than as
the manifestations of powers could provide novel support for robust
natural-kind essentialism (in a way), and by extension some indirect support for dispositonalism. Let's turn briefly to those possible implications.

8.6   Further Implications

I have used robust natural-kind essentialism to help establish the possibility of necessarily constantly active objects, but one might argue in the
opposite direction as well. Thus, one could observe that there is no evident incoherence in the notion of a necessarily constantly active object,
such that, *prima facie*, God at least could instantiate one. If one were to
find that line intuitively plausible by itself, even absent a worked-out
ontology of such objects (which I have tried to provide here, on the
assumption that most would demand such an ontology), one could then
ask what sort of object it would have to be in order to be necessarily constantly active. One could then run some of the arguments of the preceding sections to show that this possible object would have to be
instantiated as a member of a robust natural kind, rather than as an
object accidentally possessed of a necessarily constantly manifested power
or primitive activity (which latter options are unworkable, as we've seen).
Given that there seem not to be other good candidates for explicating
how a necessarily constantly active object might be instantiated, this

would then function as a new argument for this version of natural-kind essentialism:

Premise 1 If necessarily constantly active objects exist (or at least are possible), then robust natural-kind essentialism is true.

Premise 2 Necessarily constantly active objects exist (or at least are possible).

Conclusion Therefore robust natural-kind essentialism is true.

So the justification for premise 2 would be the prima facie coherence of such objects, and the justification for premise 1 would be the problems facing the alternative accounts of necessarily constantly active objects.

Moreover if the overall argument of Chapter 6 is correct, such that dispositionalism likely relies on robust natural-kind essentialism (or at least finds important support in robust natural-kind essentialism), then any argument for the truth of the latter contributes (if indirectly) to the defence of the former. That will hopefully serve to further alleviate the concerns of those who might worry that dispositionalism risks being undermined by admitting another basic source of activity into physical nature (i.e., a source other than the manifestation of powers).

8.7   Conclusion

To recap: after a brief introduction Section 8.1 to the historical and contemporary debate surrounding the possibility of necessarily active objects, we proceeded in Section 8.2 to examine crucial conceptual distinctions, especially those surrounding the various different modes of disposition-manifestation. Section 8.3 saw a sustained argument developed against admitting necessarily constantly manifested dispositions into our ontology. Then in Section 8.4 we looked at Corry's interesting alternative route to the possibility of a necessarily active object, namely that of entertaining primitive activities (activities that are neither the manifestations of dispositions nor grounded in other aspects of the object). It was argued that this approach is ultimately problematic, but the discussion still served as an effective lead-in to a more promising way of accommodating the possibility of necessarily constantly active objects, namely the strategy of grounding activities directly in kinds rather than in powers. That approach saw further development in Section 8.5, and two further implications were briefly laid out in Section 8.6 – namely the ways in which that argumentative strategy might be extended to provide novel support both for robust natural-kind essentialism and, indirectly, for dispositionalism.

CHAPTER 9

Dispositionalism and Emergentism

9.1 Introduction

Perhaps more than any of the other metaphysical debates engaged in this book, those surrounding the nature and existence of emergent realities (whether emergent properties, emergent substances, emergent systems, etc.) boast a high degree of complexity and foundational disagreement. A massive literature on emergence has arisen over the last twenty-five years, and at least some of the core issues at play also have long historical pedigrees. Nevertheless it is far from being the case that there is currently any settled definition of 'emergence' or 'emergentism,' and the most basic terms and concepts employed remain disputed and variably employed. While one might assert, and not without some justification, that comparable levels of disagreement are apparent in other areas of metaphysics, I would nevertheless venture to claim that the situation in the emergentism literature seems an extreme case.

I am hardly the first to make this sort of point, and Taylor (2015, pp. 653–654) draws attention to much the same complaint made by leading figures in that literature:

> There is a general consensus in contemporary philosophy that debates about emergence are confused and messy. Kim, for example, says *those discussing emergence, even face to face, more often than not talk past each other. Sometimes one gets the impression that the only thing the participants share is the word emergence.* O'Connor refers to emergence as *a notorious philosophical term of art*, while Chalmers adds *The term emergence often causes confusion in science and philosophy. Dialogue becomes even more difficult when we turn to scientific uses of the concept of emergence, which are often taken to be radically discontinuous with philosophical approaches.*[1]

---

[1] Her references are to Kim (2006), O'Connor (2006), and Chalmers (2006).

For another recent example consider Wilson (2015, p. 348), who, after summarizing a range of competing conceptions of emergence, writes:

> Though in general a thousand flowers may fruitfully bloom, this much diversity is unuseful for purposes of illuminating the structure of natural reality. Different accounts often disagree on whether an entity is emergent; and when they agree, there is often no clear basis for this agreement. Hence it is said that references to emergence 'seem to have no settled meaning' (Byrne 1994, p. 206), that accounts of emergence are 'not obviously reconcilable with one another (O'Connor 1994, p. 91) ...

I should note however that Taylor and Wilson each go on to suggest interesting strategies for cutting through the apparent confusion and unearthing underlying unities of approach in the literature.

I suspect that part of the reason for the hyper-contested nature of the emergentism debates has to do with the fact that they take place within multiple, very different areas, and that authors working in one stream do not always interact with authors working in another. Thus the emergentism debates seen in analytic metaphysics, philosophy of mind, philosophy of religion, general philosophy of science, and the philosophies of the special sciences (e.g., philosophy of chemistry, philosophy of biology, etc.), sometimes have a paradoxical tendency *both* towards unwitting overlap of content *and* towards the development of such specialized frameworks of discussion that explicit engagement is rendered difficult. This is exacerbated by the fact that those working in philosophy of chemistry (for instance) don't always attempt to keep track of potentially relevant developments in analytic metaphysics, or vice versa. On top of which, scientists across a range of disciplines also employ the language of emergence, differing both amongst themselves and from philosophers in how it is used.[2]

Still, I take it that one of the distinctive aims of the relatively new (or at least relatively newly labeled) sub-discipline that is the *metaphysics of science* is that of bridging such divides and bringing together the distinctive resources of analytic metaphysics and the philosophies of the general and special sciences – and, at least in this area, the philosophy of mind as well. So despite my frank intimidation in the face of the current state of the emergentism literature, in this chapter I will attempt to say something about the relationship between dispositionalism and emergentism.

---

[2] This point already came up in the Chalmers citation, and it is clearly reiterated by Tabaczek (2013, p. 382) who, writing mostly for an audience of scientists and theologians, states that the "pluralism of different realms of science and knowledge referring to the concept of EM [emergence] brings a pluralism of definitions and classifications of different types of emergent properties. Moreover, philosophical analyses and definitions of EM differ remarkably from the scientific ones."

My point of contact will be an important new work within the philosophy of mind, William Jaworski's *Structure and the Metaphysics of Mind: How Hylomorphism Solves the Mind-Body Problem* (OUP, 2016). Jaworski considers his hylomorphic theory a version of emergentism, though one quite different from past versions. For our present purposes its chief interest lies in its centrally employing not only dispositionalism but a specific version of dispositionalism we encountered in Chapter 5, namely *identity theory* dispositionalism.

The remainder of this chapter is divided as follows: in the next section I summarize some of the principal claims and lines of argument put forward by Jaworski, emphasizing along the way the role that dispositionalism plays in his account. Hopefully this section will succeed in conveying the interest and significance of his theory within the context of recent philosophy of mind, thereby motivating the concerns I take up in subsequent sections. In Section 9.3 I review some of the existing criticisms of identity theory dispositionalism, arguing that one of these, forcefully stated by Armstrong (2005), has not been satisfactorily answered. I do not claim that identity theory dispositionalism is unworkable, but I do suggest that its weaknesses (weaknesses not shared by the other three major dispositionalist views concerning the relationship between dispositional and categorical properties) should prompt defenders of Jaworski's theory to seek out alternative ways of formulating it. Then in Section 9.4 I suggest such an alternative, one relying on a notion discussed in earlier chapters: namely that dispositions may cross-cut ontological categories, such that there may be dispositions falling not only under the category of *property* (which of course receive the majority of attention in the dispositionalism literature), but also under the categories of *substance* and *relation*. If that last crosscutting is plausible, as several authors working in the ontic structural realism literature have maintained, then dispositional relations (specifically structural relations) can effectively replace the problematic identity theory dispositional properties that Jaworski's account currently employs. This switch avoids the problems facing identity theory dispositionalism without necessitating any major change in the rest of his emergentist theory of biological organisms and the mind.

9.2 Summary of Jaworski's Hylomorphic and Emergentist Account

Hylomorphism received some attention in Chapter 5; the label has mostly been used to denote a distinctive substance ontology in competition with the other three principal such theories (namely substratum theory, bundle theory, and primitive substance theory). Qua substance ontology, hylomorphism is the view that physical substances are compounds of two irreducible substantial principles, namely *substantial form* (a substance-universal/kind, e.g., 'electronhood') and *prime matter* (a power to take on/receive/bear/instantiate substantial form, in other words a power to become a member of a natural kind). Hylomorphism is thus similar in some ways to substratum theory (for instance in presenting us with an account of substance that involves a conjunction of multiple irreducible principles), and also similar to primitive substance theory (in its commitment to robust natural-kind essentialism). As a substance ontology, most contemporary advocates of hylomorphism are either self-identified scholastics (usually Thomists) or strongly influenced by the Scholastic tradition, including Bobik (1961; 1965; 1998), Brower (2014), Clarke (2001), Feser (2014), Goyette (2002), Madden (2013), Oderberg (2002; 2005; 2007), Pruss (2013), and Toner (2011). However, it was also noted in Chapter 5 that the term 'hylomorphism' has recently been applied to a set of related theories outside the substance ontology literature, theories attempting to resolve problems in such areas as the ontology of artifacts, the special composition question, puzzles of material constitution, and the philosophy of mind. Contributors to these discussions include Evnine (2016), Fine (1999), Johnston (2006), Koslicki (2008), and the focus of our current attention, Jaworski (2016). The versions of hylomorphism employed by these authors vary from one to the next in a number of respects, and they differ from traditional hylomorphism in that they are not seeking to provide a substance ontology.

One implication of this is that the notions of *form* they are working with must differ from that of traditional hylomorphism; form does not refer solely to a substance-universal/kind whose principal functional role it is to be instantiated in/borne by/manifested by prime matter. Jaworski (2016, p. 1) signals as much right from the outset:

> Hylomorphism claims that structure (or organization, form, arrangement, order, or configuration) is a basic ontological and explanatory principle. Some individuals, paradigmatically living things, consist of materials that are structured or organized in various ways. You and I are not mere quantities of physical materials; we are quantities of physical materials with a certain organization or structure. That structure is responsible for us being and persisting as humans, and it is responsible for us having the particular developmental, metabolic, reproductive perceptive, and cognitive capacities we have ... Hylomorphic structure carves out distinctive individuals

from the otherwise undifferentiated sea of matter and energy that is or will be described by our best physics, and it confers[3] on those individuals distinctive powers.

'Form' here clearly refers to something other than the formal substantial principle of traditional hylomorphism, and the 'matter' involved is not prime matter but rather materials, i.e., lower-level component objects that are being drawn together and structured.[4]

Jaworski later clarifies that the structures of central interest here (namely those obtaining in biology and neuroscience) are not merely static spatial relations between parts; while those do count as structures, the sort of structure he wants to focus on is *dynamic*, structure that consists in ordered patterns of interaction between parts – not only the physical components of what we take to be a single substance but also the ordered patterns of interaction with the external environment (2016, p. 15).[5]

To clarify further what Jaworski means by 'structure,' he provides a particularly vivid example (2016, p. 9): take a person and place him in a thoroughly sealed, hardy plastic bag. Then drop a multi-tonne weight on him. The person will be squashed, and so no person will remain in the bag. Yet all of the particles that had composed the person remain in the bag; not a single one broke through the seal during the squashing process. So all the parts remain, but the biological organism does not. The reason for this, intuitively, is that the biological organism consisted of a certain dynamic structuring of those parts, such that when that structure was irreversibly broken up the organism ceased to be. Structure

---

[3] As we'll soon see, he maintains that structures confer dispositional properties (specifically, tropes) by way of being identical with dispositional properties.

[4] Still, one ought not to over-state the split with traditional hylomorphism. One could argue that elements of Jaworski's larger account actually fit in well with some historical hylomorphic understandings of higher-level forms (e.g., forms of biological organisms), in particular Scotus' hylomorphism. I will not pursue that line of thought here.

[5] Jaworski provides multiple citations from philosophers of biology, biologists, and neuroscientists to show such a notion of dynamic structure at work in those literatures. For instance he quotes on page 14 from the philosopher of biology Michael Ruse (2001, p. 79):

> Order the molecules in one way and you get junk. Order the molecules in another way and you get William Shakespeare ... The order exists, it is not unreal, but it is not a thing in the way that a molecule is a thing. To think otherwise is to get oneself into that way of thinking which gives existence to such very nonuseful entities as ... *elans vitaux* ... The assembled and functioning DNA molecule is not a new substance. It is smaller substances (or substance parts), ordered ... And analogous comments apply to us humans.

And on page 15 he provides this from biologist J. Z. Young (1971, pp. 86–87): "The essence of a living thing is that it consists of atoms ... caught up into the living system and made part of it for a while. The living activity takes them up and organizes them in its characteristic way. The life of a man consists essentially in the activity he imposes upon that stuff."

determined the kind of object that had been there (a human being) and that object's distinctive causal capacities, and when that structure was destroyed the object was also destroyed, along with those distinctive capacities.

But why believe in the reality of structure as a basic, irreducible onto-logical and explanatory aspect of the physical world? Jaworski's principal justification lies in the ubiquity of structural concepts across the natural sciences, combined with a broadly Quinean naturalistic methodology according to which we should accept the reality of those entities refer-enced in our best scientific theories. As he puts it (2016, p. 19):

> If our best empirical descriptions, explanations, and methods posit entities of kind K, then that gives us good prima facie reason to think that Ks exist. Consider, then, empirical descriptions and explanations like those discussed earlier [his multiple citations of the use of structure within biol-ogy and neuroscience] ... If ontological naturalism is true, these descrip-tions and explanations give us good prima facie reason to think those structures exist.

Later in the book Jaworski provides still further detail on the precise nature of structure, distinguishing between *individual-making structures* and *activity-making structures*, where the former structures serve to make individuals the sort of individuals they are and the latter make activities the sort of activities they are. Both sorts of structure play a role in his ultimate account of the mind and its relation to the body, and both are classified as properties, more specifically as *tropes* (in accordance with his preferred view of universals, trope nominalism).[6] Still, the structured individual is a real and emergent *object*, emergent because it has novel causal powers that are distinct from and irreducible to the powers of the individual objects that are its proper parts. Jaworski's hylomorphism thus involves a two fold emergentism: it affirms the reality of emergent sub-stances (the individual constituted by the individual-making-structure) and emergent properties (the novel causal powers associated with that structure). As he puts it (2016, pp. 104–105):

> The idea that structured individuals are emergent is perhaps the most surprising element of the hylomorphic theory I defend ... [W]hat it is for a structured individual to be is for there to be an individual that

---

[6] Throughout the preceding chapters I have kept to a sharp distinction between properties on the one hand and relations on the other, as representing two fundamentally distinct ontological cate-gories. By contrast Jaworski uses 'property' (and by extension 'trope') in a broad sense as inclusive of both monadic properties and relations (2016, p. 27). I'll have more to say on this shortly.

configures its parts a certain way. For example, what it is for a human organism to be is for there to be an individual that configures its parts human-wise. The human-wise relation among a human's parts is necessary for it to exist, and it is also sufficient since the existence of a structured whole is both necessitated by and supervenient upon the conditions of their parts … A human organism cannot exist unless its parts are spatially arranged human-wise, and necessarily if some physical materials come to be spatially arranged human-wise, a human organism will come to exist (or perhaps an exact replica of a human organism will come to exist if being a human requires having come into existence as the result of some type of evolutionary history). But on the hylomorphic view I defend, these claims needn't be taken to amount to a statement of a human's real essence.

That real essence is the structure, specifically the individual-making-structure, which though supervening on the parts and their spatial arrangement remains distinct from them: again, structure (and especially *dynamic* structure) is here viewed as a basic, irreducible ontological and explanatory principle.[7] Think of the squashing example: after the squashing all the material parts are still there. And post-squashing, even if those parts were to be spatially re-arranged such that an outwardly human-like appearance were restored (imagine some advanced mortician robot could accomplish this for the benefit of the grieving family), what would then be present would not be a human being but a human corpse. Why? Because the dynamic structure, the individual-making structure that had functioned actively to configure those parts not only at a time but over time, remains absent.

Jaworski's hylomorphism affirms also the irreducible reality of activity-making structures. These need to be posited because the activities of an individual implicate not just the individual as a whole as causal agent, but in a subsidiary fashion also the individual's proper parts. In order for a biological organism or other structured individual to act (if indeed there are any such individuals outside of biology – Jaworski remains neutral on this[8]), a whole array of that individual's proper parts must manifest their own individual causal powers, and manifest them in a coordinated fashion, which coordination is supplied by the emergent

[7] Later Jaworski (2016, chs. 9 and 10) argues at length that supervenience and necessitation (in the relevant, carefully clarified senses) are not explanatory relations, such that the individual-making-structure remains emergent and a basic explanatory principle on its own accord, despite its supervening on and being necessitated by its arranged parts.
[8] See his discussion of allegedly emergent chemical kinds (ibid., pp. 107–108).

whole of which they are a part (i.e., the structured individual). As he puts it (2016, p. 157):

> When I throw a baseball, swim, or play a musical instrument, I manifest my power to structure the way my biofunctional parts manifest their powers. My parts needn't manifest their powers in this way. It is possible for my neurons to fire or my muscles to contract in ways to that do not compose an activity of throwing a baseball ... But when I succeed in throwing ... I succeed in imposing a structure on the way my parts manifest their powers ...

Not all of this structuring is conscious of course; the metabolic processes taking place within a human being are not under her direct deliberate control in the way that throwing a baseball is. Still, both are activities of the biological organism being coordinated by the whole that is that biological organism. That goes for purely psychological activities as much as it does for unconscious metabolic activities. If this fact seems to undermine the standard hard and fast distinction between the physical and the mental, that is all to the good: Jaworski maintains that "within a hylomorphic framework, the mental-physical distinction is an artifact of our descriptive and explanatory interests" (2016, p. 177). That claim is buttressed by the fact that our psychological activities seem necessarily to be embodied, that so far as scientific inquiry can ascertain human consciousness relies on a well-functioning brain, contrary to the apparent commitments of substance dualists and the more traditional, scholastic hylomorphists (2016, pp. 162–170).

Given his conception of structure as a basic ontological and explanatory principle, it is understandable that Jaworski combines his hylomorphism with identity theory dispositionalism, according to which every irreducible property plays multiple explanatory roles, both roles we associate with prima facie categorical properties (like geometrical structure) and roles we associate with dispositional properties (2016, pp. 53–54):

> The identity theory of powers claims that each property is essentially dispositional ... Each property essentially empowers its individual possessor to interact with other individuals in various kinds of ways. A diamond's hardness empowers the diamond to do a variety of things – to scratch glass, for instance ... But the diamond's hardness plays other roles that we describe in different terms. We say, for instance, that the diamond has a tetrahedral arrangement of carbon atoms. According to the identity theory of powers, these descriptions are of numerically one and the same property. The diamond's hardness = the diamond's power to scratch glass = the diamond's having a tetrahedral arrangement of carbons atoms. These descriptions simply bring out different theoretical roles that the one property plays.

As we saw in Chapter 5, identity theory is a prominent account of the relationship between dispositional and categorical properties, whose advocates include Heil (2003; 2005; 2012), Martin (1997), Martin and Heil (1999), Ingthorsson (2013), Jacobs (2011), Schroer (2010), and Strawson (2008).[9]

Certainly it seems a good theory for Jaworski to adopt, given that he wants to present structure (a prima facie categorical property) as *inherently* explanatory of natural phenomena. The structure of a structured individual, like a human being, both supervenes upon its proper parts and functions as the dynamic organizer of those same parts, such that the organism as a whole boasts novel causal powers, *powers that are in fact identical to the structure of that structured individual* in accordance with identity theory dispositionalism. Given his view of structure as inherently explanatory, it would have been awkward to think of structure as of itself inert and as requiring the intervention of external, governing laws of nature to provide for its explanatory relevance, as a nomological necessitarian might have suggested. It would also have been awkward to think of structure as of itself inert and requiring pairing with a distinct dispositional property to have at least indirect explanatory relevance, as a mixed view dispositionalist might have suggested. Pan-dispositionalism likewise seems a bad option for Jaworski's purposes, since its advocates often treat prima facie structural properties as reducible to (or eliminable in favour of) powers. Something similar can be said with respect to neutral monism, on which neither dispositional nor categorical properties are really fundamental. And Jaworski rightly takes time to present objections against both nomological necessitarianism and these alternative forms of dispositionalism (except neutral monism[10]), devoting part of the fourth chapter and the whole of the fifth chapter of his book to that task.

---

[9] Recall that the other three main dispositionalist accounts of this relationship are: **(a) the mixed view**, on which dispositions and categorical properties are really distinct from each other, and both among the fundamental properties found in nature. Advocates include Cross (2005), Ellis (2001; 2002; 2009), Molnar (2003), and Oderberg (2007); **(b) pan-dispositionalism** (sometimes referred to as **dispositional monism**), is a view on which all irreducible natural properties are dispositions. What we think are 'categorical properties' aare either unreal or are actually powers. See Bauer (2013), Bird (2007), Bostock (2008), Coleman (2010), Mumford and Anjum (2011), and Shoemaker (1980); and **(c) neutral monism** is the view that the really fundamental natural kind of property is neither dispositional nor categorical, but of such a nature that it can nevertheless be properly described using dispositional or categorical predicates. See Bartels (2013) and Mumford (1998, ch. 8).

[10] 'Neutral monism' also denotes a theory within the philosophy of mind, and Jaworski does discuss it (2016, pp. 325–327), but it is not the same thing as the neutral monism at issue in the dispositionalism literature.

Jaworski goes on to distinguish hylomorphism from existing versions of emergentism within the philosophy of mind literature (2016, pp. 272–276). He takes these standard emergentisms to be centrally committed to two distinctive claims: (a) mental properties are generated by physical properties, and (b) mental properties can themselves generate physical effects. One of the core objections against such emergentisms is that there seems no intelligible way to explain how physical properties can manage to generate mental properties. How do neuron-firings (really just particles attracting and repelling particles) manage to produce con- sciousness? A common emergentist line of reply is to fall back on primi- tive psychophysical laws, laws governing the relationship between mental and physical and which are just as fundamental as the laws of physics. And a common counter-reply is to demand some intelligible account just how there could be such laws, insofar as many find it implausible to claim that their existence could be brute. Arguably emergentists have not succeeded in answering this, or at least they have not succeeded in doing so from within a framework that preserves metaphysical naturalism, which is generally taken to be among the desiderata of any contemporary theory of consciousness. (The apparent clash with naturalism is a particu- lar problem for panpsychist emergentism.) Another core objection against standard emergentism is the problem of downward causation, of plausibly explaining how mental properties can possibly affect the physi- cal realm without either violating naturalism or committing to an implausible causal overdetermination (whereby the motions of particles are causally explained both by the laws of physics *and* by the emergent laws of psychophysics).

Jaworski maintains that his hylomorphism avoids these central worries that have plagued past versions of emergentism. With respect to problem (a) he writes (2016, pp. 277–278):

> [H]ylomrophism denies that emergent properties are generated or pro- duced by lower-level processes or states. According to hylomorphists, higher-level phenomena are ways in which lower-level occurrences are structured, and structures in general are not generated or produced by the things they structure … [B]rains do not generate or produce thoughts, feelings, perceptions, and actions. The latter are instead co-ordinated man- ifestations of the powers of brains (along with other organic subsystems and surrounding materials). The powers to think, feel, perceive, and act are embodied in muscular contractions, neural firings, and other physiolo- gical occurrences, but they are not generated or produced by those occur- rences, for on the hylomorphic view, structured things are not in general

causal byproducts of the lower-level things they structure. Requesting an explanation of how lower-level occurrences generate higher level phenomena thus misunderstands the hylomorphic notion of structure. It assumes, contrary to hylomorphism, that structure is not a basic principle, but is instead something that is derived from lower-level materials ... Moreover, the very fact that the problem of emergence arises for opponents, but not for hylomorphists, weighs in favour of taking hylomorphic structure as a primitive.

In addition, problem (b) dissolves in a way that it doesn't on past emergentisms (2016, pp. 280–285). Those emergentisms have typically assumed a univocal account of causation, according to which there is only one kind of cause, and that's the mechanistic-style efficient causation commonly associated (rightly or wrongly) with the core causal notion employed within physics. But while that is certainly one legitimate type of causation, it is not the only type; for example rationalization, as a kind of mental act, is also a legitimate form of causation, but it's not the same type as that referenced within physics and the two should not be seen as being in competition for explaining the same phenomena.

> Explanations that appeal to reasons and explanations that appeal to physiological mechanism pick out causal factors of different sorts: they answer requests for different kinds of information, just as explanations that appeal to roadway grading and explanations that appeal to blood-alcohol levels provide different kinds of information about car crashes. There is thus no threat of actions being overdetermined by reasons and physiological triggers. (2016, p. 281)[11]

While he observes that others within the philosophy of mind (for instance Burge (2007)) have given this sort of answer to the causal overdetermination worry, Jaworski maintains that his hylomorphism can supply a more convincing version of the reply because it can situate it within a background metaphysics that better justifies such explanatory pluralism. The relevant bit of that background metaphysics here is his account of irreducible activity-making structures. Explanations that reference rationalizations and explanations that reference physiological

---

[11] It's worth emphasizing that as Jaworski construes it, an appeal to explanatory pluralism does not involve any essential appeal to subjectivity or mere arbitrary choice on the part of the theorizer. With respect to picking out explanatory factors to focus on,

> which factors we select is doubtless a function of our subjective interests. But making a selection among objective causal factors does not make them or their contributions to the effect any less objective: it does not turn them into subjective, internal, or mind-dependent occurrences ... [E]xplanations in general map onto causes, and different kinds of explanations map onto different kinds of causes ... (2016, pp. 291–929)

triggering mechanisms are not really seeking to explain the same things. The former pertain to the mental activities of a person, while the latter are dealing with the material parts whose appropriate coordination helps to constitute those mental activities, in the sense that they function as a supervenience base for them. Once activity-making structures are accepted as basic ontological and explanatory factors in nature, one can discern that the conscious action of a person is not the same as the lower-level physiological processes involved in that action, precisely because those lower-level processes have been *configured* by the person's action. "Since hylomorphists are committed to the existence of activity-making structures, they deny that actions are identical to the physiological occurrences that compose them" (2016, p. 283).

Jaworski's overarching aim is to supply an account of the mind-body relation compatible with *metaphysical naturalism* without also affirming *physicalism* (the latter understood here as the claim that all natural phenomena can be exhaustively described and explained by the resources of either present or completed physics, such that the special sciences are subject to intertheoretic reduction). Provided that structure, as Jaworski defines it, is an ontologically and explanatorily basic reality, the autonomy of at least some special sciences (most importantly biology) is preserved and mental phenomena can be addressed in naturalistic but non-reductionist terms.

A great deal more could be said by way of explicating Jaworski's theory and reviewing the replies he gives to a wide assortment of possible objections, but hopefully the preceding will suffice to provide a basic understanding of his hylomorphism and of the important role dispositionalism plays within it. In the next section I will lay out a possible criticism arising from his use of identity theory dispositionalism.

9.3   Hylomorphism and Identity Theory Dispositionalism

As we've seen, Jaworski pairs his account of the mind with identity theory dispositionalism, and has good reason for doing so, insofar as his core notion of structure as a basic explanatory aspect of the world seems to combine much less readily with the other three major accounts of the relationship between dispositional and categorical properties (and still less with nomological necessitarianism). However, as one might expect identity theory has faced criticisms, which Jaworski discusses. I would like to focus on one of those criticisms in particular, levelled forcefully by Armstrong. He considers the notion that categorical properties could be literally identical with dispositional properties to be radically mistaken. He first describes the view and then states his opposition (2005, p. 315):

> There are not two 'things' here but just one: quality and power are the very same thing somewhat differently identified. A scholastic philosopher might put it by saying that here only a 'distinction of reason' involved. Models suggested have bee[*sic*] the duck-rabbit and Necker's cube. This identity ... is not to be thought of as an identity with a direction, as in a reductive identity such as 'lightning is an electrical discharge'. Rather, I suppose, it may be compared to 'the morning star is the evening star' where no direction is evident. There are not two planets, just one. There is not a quality and an associated power, there is just the one entity.[12] I confess that I find this totally incredible. If anything is a category mistake, it is a category mistake to identify a quality – a categorical property – and a power, essentially something that points to a certain effect. They are just different, that's all. An identity here seems like identifying a raven with a writing desk.

Here Armstrong equates 'quality' and 'categorical property,' but whether one is thinking of *geometrical/structural* properties (like the irreducible shape of an extended simple) or of allegedly *irreducible physical qualitative* properties (of the sort entertained by advocates of colour primitivism) or of *quiddities* (properties consisting of nothing more than bare self-identity and distinction from other properties, which play an important role in Armstrong's own ontology of laws), Armstrong's observation appears cogent: such properties, if they exist, are just not dispositions. Dispositions are defined by their inherent causal import, their identities involving one or more stimulus conditions and manifestation conditions and assorted ceteris paribus clauses. 'Squareness' is just not definable in this way, nor is 'greenness' (if it or anything akin to it exists as a fundamental qualitative property), nor is a quiddity.

Jaworski (2016, pp. 79–80) supplies several responses to Armstrong's point. First Jaworski claims that this is basically an 'incredulous stare' move, and that in this case it is not particularly compelling because the intuition motivating it is not widespread. Second, Armstrong's contention that identity theorists are making a category mistake simply begs the question against the identity theorist; basically Armstrong is saying that categorical and dispositional properties can't be identical, identity

---

[12] Armstrong's description certainly reflects the earlier formulations of both Martin and Heil; for instance, Martin and Heil (1999, pp. 46–47) wrote: "Dispositionality and qualitativity are built into each property; indeed they *are* the property ... A property just *is* a certain dispositionality that just *is* a certain qualitativity."

theorists are saying they can be, and all other things beings equal we simply have a stalemate, such that Armstrong has made no real progress
against identity theory. Third, whatever intuition Armstrong is appealing
to here is probably influenced by his own commitment to categoricalism,
which Jaworski maintains is ultimately implausible. Fourth, Jaworski
points out that there is a certain irony in Armstrong's pushing this particular criticism, given Armstrong's (1968) own earlier advocacy of identity
theory within the philosophy of mind, according to which mental states
and physical states are identical. Surely the incredulous stare move can
be made just as forcefully against that theory of mind (how can conscious
awareness literally be identical to a series of neurone firings?) if not
more forcefully.

In response, I'll first note that I for one share Armstrong's intuition
here, finding it very odd indeed to think that a shape (for instance) could
literally be numerically identical to a power. I have no way of assessing
whether or not this intuition is widespread (or even how to understand
'widespread' in this context – could we test this out in undergraduate
metaphysics classes, polling our students after a thorough and balanced
introduction to dispositionalism?), but in my own case I have long found
Armstrong's point rather persuasive. Whether or not the identity theorist
is making a category mistake is, in my view, a question of lesser importance; that a mistake is being made is of more significance than is the
diagnosis of precisely what sort of mistake is being made. I cannot assess
to what extent Armstrong's categoricalism is influencing his stance, but I
am no categoricalist and I share his intuition in this case. And I simply
accept that one who finds Armstrong's present criticism persuasive
should probably be similarly moved against mind-brain identity theory
(at least in its token-identity version), but since I don't find that theory
of mind at all plausible the tu quoque move Jaworski makes against
Armstrong needn't move me.[13]

I doubt this makes for a decisive case against identity theory dispositionalism – for those who do not share Armstrong's initial motivating
intuition, it certainly won't. Still, for those who *do* share it, his argument
provides some reason to explore whether Jaworski's hylomorphic emergentist theory of the mental might be plausibly formulated on some
other version of dispositionalism, insofar as commitment to that theory

---

[13] All that having been said, I should clarify: while I personally find identity theory dispositionalism
problematic (I incline towards the mixed view), that personal view on this intra-dispositionalist
debate does not impact the arguments I've made in previous chapters. So far as I can tell, those
arguments are neutral between the four (except of course where I've specifically noted otherwise).

can be construed as a problem for it. To state that problem a bit more formally:

Premise 1 If Jaworski's hylomorphism (as currently formulated) is true, then identity theory dispositionalism is true.
Premise 2 But identity theory dispositionalism is probably not true.
Conclusion Therefore Jaworski's hylomorphism (as currently formulated) is probably not true.

But can one substitute an alternative version of dispositionalism without disrupting Jaworski's larger theory? It might seem as if the prospects for such an alternative are dim – after all, we've already reviewed the reasons why the other three major dispositionalist views concerning the relationship between categorical and dispositional properties are problematic candidates for Jaworski's hylomorphism (as is nomological necessitarian categoricalism). Still, I think there is at least one alternative available here, which I will explore briefly in the next section.

9.4   Appealing to Cross-Cutting Dispositions

Armstrong formulates his objection in terms of properties. We simply discern that a quality is a different sort of property than is a power. And I think at least part of the intuitive force of this objection comes from the fact that he takes us to be discerning an irreducible distinction between two *properties*, two realities belonging to one and the same ontological category. Think of this in terms of traditional classification by way of genus and specific difference: here the genus is a broad ontological category, *property*, which apparently breaks down into such differentiae as power and quality and shape, etc. These are distinct species of one and the same genus, differing from each other precisely as differentiae of that genus. Considered from this traditional perspective, to think of a power and a shape as identical would be akin to thinking of red and green as identical; the latter two properties are species of the genus *colour* (itself a species of *quality* which is a species of *property*) and clearly non-identical.[14]

---

[14] To avoid any confusion: recall that Armstrong uses 'quality' as a synonym for 'categorical property', whereas in this book I have been taking 'quality' to indicate physical qualities (like colour or sound or texture) and 'categorical property' to mean 'non-dispositional property.' (Of course the identity theory dispositionalist must find another way of formulating the dispositional/categorical distinction, and I have no wish to rule out identity theory by definitional fiat, so for present purposes I will bracket my preferred understanding of 'categorical property.')

However, this is not to say that our commonsensical categorical divisions are always reflective of fundamental reality as it really is; as we saw earlier in Chapters 4 and 5, it is debated whether any prima facie geometrical/structural properties are actually and irreducibly the intrinsic properties of objects, or whether instead what we think of as 'shape' (for instance) refers to an ordered set of relations obtaining between distinct objects. In other words, what initially seemed a sort of property might turn out to be something belonging to an entirely distinct ontological category, *relation*. Similarly, it might be that what we initially thought of as being one sort of property might turn out to be another sort; unless one is a colour primitivist, one will likely cash out the reality of *colours* not in terms of irreducible physical qualitative properties but rather in terms of dispositions (as *capacities* of objects to reflect light in certain ways or to appear in certain ways) and/or as subjective perceptual qualia of organisms possessed of working visual systems. Counter-intuitive as such re-identifications may seem, provided they have sufficient theoretical justification (say, in the affirmation of atomism version 1 in the case of the re-identification of shape,[15] or in the reasoned rejection of colour primitivism) they may come to be accepted.

That we engage in such re-identifications might initially be taken to lend support to identity theory dispositionalism; after all, if those other prima facie surprising re-identifications are widely accepted, why not allow for the identification of powers and categorical properties? Note however a key difference between these three cases. The proponent of atomism version 1 (who also rejects emergentism and the irreducible reality of macro-level objects) is claiming that shape is real, it's just that it belongs to a different ontological category – it's not a property but a relation. Similarly, in the case of colour, it is granted that colour is real but it is denied that its reality consists in being an irreducible physical *quality* – rather, the reality of colour consists in powers and/or mental qualia. By contrast, the identity theory dispositionalist is saying that there is a genuine sense in which dispositional and categorical properties are both real and both properties – it's just that they are not *distinct* realities, but one and the same reality. Every property is necessarily both dispositional and categorical in nature. This sort of re-identification is clearly very different, insofar as one is claiming that two known realities are indeed

---

[15] Though note that atomism version 1 does not by itself entail that no objects have shape as an intrinsic property; that depends on whether there are emergent objects, such that a macro-level object could have shape as an irreducible intrinsic property even though none of its component atoms did.

real but identical rather than distinct, rather than reducing one of those realities to something else or switching the categorical allegiance of that reality. Again, trying to identify powers with categorical properties while claiming that both are genuinely real is more akin to identifying redness and greenness while claiming that both are genuinely real. It is decidedly unlike identifying greenness with a power + subjective mental state.

All of that simply serves to clarify part of what may be underlying Armstrong's intuition (and mine); it does not necessarily strengthen that intuition. However it does suggest a way of re-working Jaworski's hylomorphism in such a way as to avoid reliance on identity theory dispositionalism: namely, rather than identifying the *structure* adverted to in Jaworski's hylomorphism with a power (or set of powers) all the while taking them both to be properties, instead re-locate the *structure* of hylomorphism to the distinct ontological category of *relation*, and then argue that this specific sort of relation is dispositional.

Recall that the notion of dispositions cross-cutting ontological categories (such that there can be dispositional *properties* as well as *substantial* dispositions and dispositional *relations*) was raised in Chapters 3 and 5. In the former chapter it was observed that some advocates of ontic structural realism (like French (2006) and Esfeld (2009)) propose that fundamental relations are of themselves causally significant, such that we can rightly count them as dispositions. For dispositionalists who are open to the idea that dispositions cross-cut ontological categories, such a proposal needn't be seen as threatening to dispositionalism; far from it, if anything it broadens the range of application and appeal of the theory. Then in Chapter 5 we saw how two of the four major competing substance ontologies are committed to there being substantial principles (prime matter and substrata, respectively) that are of themselves causally significant, such that they too can rightly be counted as dispositions. Now, if such cross-cutting is viewed as a plausible option, and in particular if its application within the OSR literature is viewed as workable, then Jaworski's hylomorphism can be re-formulated accordingly. Moreover such a re-formulation, involving only the re-categorization of the core notion of structure, need have no major impacts on the remainder of his theory. The ontology of biological organisms and minds that arises out of Jaworski's hylomorphic metaphysics does not require that structure be viewed specifically as a property, but merely that it be viewed as a basic ontological and explanatory reality.

This suggestion also carries the interesting implication that Jaworski's hylomorphism may not be so far removed from OSR as he supposes

(2016, pp. 8 and 22). In fact, one might argue that his theory could be seen as a sort of adaptation and modification of the metaphysics of OSR for application to the macro-realm of organisms and minds. By way of supporting this interpretation, one might draw attention to interesting parallels between Jaworski's theory and the *conservative reductionism* developed by Esfeld and Sachse (2011). The latter is a form of moderate OSR that is in some respects closely akin to Jaworski's background ontology. There are still notable differences (for instance the fact that Jaworski formulates his view as a version of emergentism whereas Esfeld and Sachse formulate their account as a non-eliminativist reductionism), but also important similarities. These include a shared emphasis on the causal/explanatory import of structure, the use of trope nominalism, and a thoroughly developed application of the basic principles of the ontology to the macro realm.

What I am proposing then is that Jaworski drop identity theory dispo-sitionalism and instead run with the idea (arising out of the OSR litera-ture) that there are dispositional relations, and identify his core notion of structure as just such a dispositional relation, though in this case an emergent one obtaining at the macro-level of nature. On the one hand this may seem a considerable modification of Jaworski's hylomorphism, insofar as he has devoted a good deal of attention (the fourth and fifth chapters of his book) to the explication and defence of identity theory dispositionalism and its place within his theory. On the other hand it may seem a relatively minor modification, insofar as it has no substantive implications for how the rest of that theory is developed, defended, and applied to the philosophy of mind. I think in fact it is a minor change within the context of Jaworski's larger theory, though still an important one insofar as it carries the advantage of avoiding existing criticisms levelled against identity theory dispositionalism, most significantly the one provided by Armstrong (2005).

On that last note: one might criticize my suggested re-formulation by arguing that little real progress has been made against Armstrong's objec-tion. After all, if one's intuitions are scandalized by the attempted identi-fication of a dispositional property and a categorical property, are one's intuitions likely to be any less shocked by the identification of a disposi-tional property with a relation?

However such a criticism is misplaced, since I am not identifying a dispositional property with a relation (that would be incoherent – properties are not relations), but rather affirming the reality (or at least the metaphysical possibility) of a certain sort of cross-cutting disposition, namely a *dispositional relation*. I submit that this proposal is simply not as counter-intuitive as the identity-theorist's; just as some properties have identity conditions involving stimulus and manifestation conditions and CP clauses, some relations might also have such identity conditions. Not only does it not seem as counter-intuitive as the purported identification of a dispositional property with a categorical property, there are also independent theoretical (and even empirical) reasons for taking dispositional relations seriously – or at least that has been argued in the OSR literature.

I have said that this suggested re-formulation need not be seen as making a major change to Jaworski's overall theory. One might in fact argue that it needn't be seen as constituting a change in the content of the theory at all, but only in its presentation. For it was noted above that while I have in this book made a sharp distinction between the ontological categories of property and relation (which sharp distinction has been the norm in metaphysics historically and which remains important in the OSR literature especially), Jaworski uses 'property' neutrally between monadic properties and relations. Moreover so far as I can tell he does not specify whether he views his core notion of structure as a monadic property (presumably of the emergent individual or emergent activity) or as a relation. So perhaps my 're-formulation' can be viewed simply as an explicit choosing of the latter option, and as pointing out an advantage of making that choice explicit: it allows one to drop the theory's use of identity theory dispositionalism, which becomes redundant once one takes on board the notion of a dispositional relation. On the other hand, Jaworski's very use of identity theory dispositionalism may indicate that he had been thinking of structure as a property (i.e., a monadic property), insofar as that is how the proponents of the theory he chiefly references (Martin and Heil) think of it. In fact Heil in particular makes a sharp distinction between properties and relations and would not use 'property' to refer to the latter, since Heil has argued (2012, ch. 7) that while there are fundamental properties, fundamental relations do not exist.[16]

So unfortunately I think my suggestion does still involve a change to Jaworski's hylomorphism. However, I suspect it is one he might welcome (at least for the benefit of those who have difficulty with identity theory dispositionalism), and in fact he states explicitly that portions of the specific background metaphysics he has paired with his hylomorphism

---

[16] See Esfeld (2016) for a critique of Heil from the perspective of OSR.

might be changed even while leaving the larger theory intact in its essentials (2016, p. 5): "I do not claim that the metaphysics I defend is the only one capable of supporting a hylomorphic theory. I do not even claim that it is the best. I claim only that it provides a workable basis for understanding hylomorphism and its implications for the philosophy of mind."

9.5   Conclusion

To recap: after a brief introduction, I proceeded to provide a concise summary of some of the core claims and arguments of Jaworski's novel hylomorphic theory of organisms and of the mind Section 9.2, including coverage of the prominent role accorded identity theory dispositionalism. In Section 9.3 I reviewed one of Armstrong's (2005) criticisms of identity theory and Jaworski's replies to that criticism, then relayed my own partly idiosyncratic, intuition-based reasons for dissenting from those replies. The lingering (though of course not universally shared) worries surrounding identity theory dispositionalism provided motivation for exploring whether Jaworski's hylomorphism might be paired effectively with an alternative version of dispositionalism, and in Section 9.4 I laid out my suggested alternative: *dispositional relations* of the sort championed by some advocates of OSR.

CHAPTER 10

Conclusion

The primary purpose of this book has been to explore the connections between dispositionalism and a variety of other debates in metaphysics, focusing on those debates that are also of interest to philosophers of science. Consequently the project as a whole can be viewed as falling within the *metaphysics of science*. Along the way we have seen that some of those connections seem to favour dispositionalism (depending on one's background commitments anyway), such that novel arguments for dispositionalism have been provided along the way; or, alternatively, one might read those arguments as providing novel reasons as to why categoricalists need to add or drop certain items from their own ontologies. Either way, hopefully both dispositionalists and categoricalists have gotten something out of the discussion.

While I view the project as on the whole pro-dispositionalist, I expect that some proposals may prove unpopular among my fellow dispositionalists: for instance my claim in Chapter 2 that dispositionalism implies nomic realism; my claim in Chapters 6 and 8 that dispositionalism supports robust natural-kind essentialism; or my claim in Chapter 8 that there may be natural activities that do not consist in the manifestation of powers. I hope these can be viewed as properly intramural disagreements. Dispositionalism has historically been a big-tent theory, and it remains so today. Many metaphysical systems have adopted it while diverging on specific points concerning the details of dispositionalism, and diverging on the details of those larger systems. Nevertheless, while intramural many of these disputes retain considerable importance. Now that dispositionalism has once again achieved major status within the philosophical world, and dispositionalists can focus on more than just defending the irreducible reality of causal powers, I trust that considerable progress will be made on these issues in the coming years.

As a reader I often find it helpful to be given a short re-cap of the major claims made in a work, and so I will conclude this book in the

same way, briefly highlighting principal findings and lines of reasoning
chapter-by-chapter, beginning with Chapter 2.

In that chapter I argued that rather than there being a conflict
between dispositionalism and a robust realism concerning the laws
of nature, the former position actually implies the latter. Though a
first version of this argument appeared in my (Dumsday 2013), so
far the view has failed to gain many converts. In fact my sole ally
in advocating for this tight link between powers and laws (which
I have labeled 'nomic dispositionalism') is Tugby (2016), though
his (very interesting) argument for our shared conclusion works
quite differently from my own. The overarching argument of
Chapter 2 was formalized as follows:

> **Premise 1** At least some dispositions have CP clauses incorporating
> uninstantiated universals (which CP clauses help to delimit the
> range of manifestations of those dispositions).
>
> **Premise 2** If at least some dispositions have CP clauses incorporating
> uninstantiated universals (which CP clauses help to delimit the
> range of manifestations of those dispositions), then laws of nature
> exist.
>
> **Conclusion** Therefore laws of nature exist.

The justification for P1 was that this a relatively uncontroversial commitment of dispositionalism; powers generally (always?) have ceteris
paribus (CP) clauses as part of their identity conditions, among which
are some clauses that involve uninstantiated universals (whether
uninstantiated determinates of instantiated determinables, or alien
properties). The justification of P2 was that CP clauses incorporating
uninstantiated universals meet commonly accepted criteria for lawhood, on the assumption that lawhood involves governance. Two
objections were then explicated and addressed. In the course of replying to the first objection, various options for developing the relevant
ontology of uninstantiated-universals-bound-up-with-CP-clauses-of-
instantiated-powers were laid out, insofar as this is an area that has
received little attention in the recent literature.

Chapter 3 explored the links between dispositionalism and OSR.
After introducing structural realism, I distinguished between epistemic
versus ontic structural realism and then laid out a taxonomy of seven
existing versions of the latter. I proceeded to argue that two pressing
objections against OSR served to motivate a new version, and that the
nomic realism advocated in Chapter 2 provided a ready route to just

such a new version. The overarching argument of Chapter 3 was formalized simply:

Premise 1 If nomic dispositionalism is true, then a novel version of Moderate OSR is true.
Premise 2 Nomic dispositionalism is true.
Conclusion Therefore, a novel version of Moderate OSR is true.

The new version of moderate OSR was one in which the identity conditions of objects are irreducibly bound up with abstract structures/relations, by way of the uninstantiated universals figuring in the CP clauses of objects' powers. The central content of this version was laid out as:

Moderate OSR Version #4 At the level of fundamental physics (the unobservable realm), relations exist and so do objects. The latter have an intrinsic identity defined partly in terms of the possession of intrinsic properties. These intrinsic properties include one or more dispositions, the identity conditions of which place them in essential relation to a vast structure of uninstantiated abstracta. As such, the identity of objects is not wholly reducible to their structural role, yet they cannot exist independently of structure and their identity is essentially bound up with it.

I then showed how this new version could handily defuse the two objections against OSR laid out earlier in the chapter.

In Chapter 4 I introduced the ongoing debate over fundamental material composition, and proceeded to argue that two of the four major positions in that debate support dispositionalism; specifically, atomism version 1 led to a probabilistic argument in favour of dispositionalism, while the theory of extended simples entailed it. The first argument:

Premise 1 If atomism version 1 is true, then dispositionalism is probably true.
Premise 2 Atomism version 1 is true.
Conclusion Therefore, dispositionalism is probably true.

P2 was assumed by hypothesis, while P1 was supported by a sort of argument-from-elimination: after examining the major options, it turned out that the only sort of intrinsic property that could plausibly be attributed to an unextended point particle was a dispositional property.

The argument to dispositionalism from the theory of extended simples was lengthier; the overarching argument was provided as:

> **Premise 1** If MaxCon extended simples exist, then there is a real and irreducible distinction between objects and stuff.
>
> **Premise 2** If there is a real and irreducible distinction between objects and stuff, then dispositionalism is true.
>
> **Conclusion** Therefore, if MaxCon extended simples exist, then dispositionalism is true.

P1 was supported by way of laying out in detail the background ontology and internal logic of Markosian's (1998; 2004; 2015) important MaxCon account of extended simples. There it was seen that the real distinction between objects and stuff plays a vital role in the theory (a fact which is perhaps unsurprising given historical precedents – e.g., advocates of scholastic hylomorphism believed in extended simples and likewise in something at least closely akin to the object vs. stuff distinction). The justification for P2 involved another argument, formalized thusly:

> **Premise 1** If categoricalism is true (and dispositionalism false), then there are no irreducible intrinsic dispositional properties.
>
> **Premise 2** But stuff (as understood in Markosian's theory of MaxCon simples) is possessed of at least one irreducible intrinsic dispositional property: the capacity to take on new shapes.
>
> **Conclusion** Therefore categoricalism is false (and dispositionalism true).

P1 of this argument simply followed from the standard definitions of dispositionalism and categoricalism, so more time was spent on justifying P2. The argument was that the nature and explanatory role of stuff demands that it possesses the determinable categorical property 'shape' as an essential property without also possessing any specific determinate of that determinable as an essential property. That aspect of stuff in turn was seen to imply the possession of a distinct, irreducible power, namely the power to take on new determinates of that essential determinable.

While others (notably Mumford (2006)) had previously drawn out the support connection between atomism version 1 and dispositionalism, my development of the argument made some new moves; and the argument for the entailment relation between the theory of extended simples and dispositionalism was wholly novel. The upshot of this chapter was that two of the four major theories of material composition support dispositionalism; for categoricalist readers the corresponding takeaway was that they should pair categoricalism either with atomism version 2 or the theory of gunk – and given the likely unworkability of the former theory, they should probably go for gunk. This connection between categoricalism and the theory of gunk has not been previously noted (though as a matter of fact some categoricalists have shown a fondness for gunk, and gunkers for categoricalism).

The overarching argument of Chapter 5 was concisely summarized:

Premise 1 If any one of the four main substance ontologies is true, then dispositionalism is probably true.
Premise 2 At least one of the four main substance ontologies is true.
Conclusion Therefore dispositionalism is probably true.

P2 was assumed as an hypothesis, while P1 was supported by a distinct argument for each of the four main substance ontologies (substratum theory, bundle theory, primitive substance theory, and hylomorphism). I won't lay out all of these supporting arguments here. The upshot of the chapter was that for proponents of one or another of these four theories, there is powerful new reason to favour dispositionalism over categoricalism. Conversely, the takeaway for categoricalists was that they should either (A) develop a fifth sort of substance ontology compatible with the rejection of dispositionalism, or (B) reject substances from their ontology altogether, perhaps by availing themselves of one of the versions of radical OSR canvassed in Chapter 3.

Chapter 6 sought to develop a new connection between dispositionalism and a robust form of natural-kind essentialism by showing that advocates of the former theory can sidestep an important objection by committing to the latter. So:

Premise 1 If dispositionalism is true, then it is probably the case that robust natural-kind essentialism is true.
Premise 2 Dispositionalism is true.
Conclusion Therefore, it is probably the case that robust natural-kind essentialism is true.

P2 was granted for the sake of argument, so the emphasis was on P1. It was justified by laying out in detail an important objection against dispositionalism formulated by Lange (2004; 2009) and Whittle (2009), according to which irreducible powers can and should be dropped in favour of primitive subjunctive facts. It was seen that pairing dispositionalism with robust natural-kind essentialism provided an escape route from this worry, insofar as the grounding of powers in kinds (kinds which also ground categorical properties) blocked the proposed elimination.

In Chapter 7 three interrelated topic areas pertaining to the metaphysics of spacetime were discussed: the debate between proponents of spacetime substantivalism versus relationism; the prospects for backwards time travel; and perdurantism. With respect to the first area, it was argued that insofar as substantivalism and relationism are typically formulated in such a way as to be realist about the category 'substance,' both end up supporting dispositionalism. Why? Because it was seen in Chapter 5 that any kind of substance realism supports dispositionalism. This served to draw out a heretofore unnoticed link between the metaphysics of spacetime and dispositionalism. With respect to the second, I summarized and critiqued an interesting new argument from Koons and Pickavance (2015) to the effect that the truth of dispositionalism would rule out the possibility of backwards time travel. With respect to the third area, I laid out Mumford's (2009) arguments for the incompatibility of dispositionalism with perdurantism, critiqued them, and suggested several new strategies for rendering the two views compatible (if perhaps uncomfortably so).

The central focus of Chapter 8 was on the old question of the possibility of necessarily constantly active objects. After developing the relevant background ontology in some detail, laying out a variety of relevant distinctions, I went on to argue that such objects are indeed possible provided that the sort of robust natural-kind essentialism discussed in Chapter 6 is true. Moreover I argued that this fact could provide at least indirect support for dispositionalism.

Finally, in the 9th chapter I explored Jaworski's (2016) new theory of hylomorphism. On his account of biological organisms and minds, *structures* (conceived as irreducible properties with both categorical and dispositional identity conditions, in line with identity theory dispositionalism) function as basic explanatory principles in nature. He maintains that conceiving structure in this manner allows for a new understanding of emergentism, one that solves key questions in the philosophy of mind without falling prey to the crippling objections that have been levelled against past formulations of emergentism. I laid out an objection against Jaworski's account, based on its use of identity theory dispositionalism, and attempted to address his counter-replies. I then put forward an alternative dispositionalist ontology of structure (one closely aligned with suggestions that have arisen in the OSR literature), and showed how this alternative would allow Jaworski's model to keep all its central tenets while sidestepping the worry about identity theory dispositionalism.

Works Cited

Ainsworth, Peter (2010) "What is Ontic Structural Realism?" *Studies in History and Philosophy of Modern Physics*, 41, pp. 50–57.

Alexander of Hales (1924) *Summa Theologica*, Part I (Quaracchi: Collegii s. Bonaventurae).

(1928) *Summa Theologica*, Part II (Quaracchi: Collegii s. Bonaventurae).

Allen, Keith (2011) "Revelation and the Nature of Colour", *Dialectica*, 65, pp. 153–176.

(2015) "Colour Physicalism, Naive Realism, and the Argument from Structure", *Minds & Machines*, 25, pp. 193–212.

Aquinas (1920) *Summa Theologica*. Translated by the Fathers of the English Dominican Province. Accessed online via www.newadvent.org

(1956) *Summa Contra Gentiles: On the Truth of the Catholic Faith, Book 2: Creation*, translated by James F. Anderson (New York, NY: Image Books)

Armstrong, David (1978) *Nominalism and Realism: Universals and Scientific Realism*, Volume 1 (Cambridge: Cambridge University Press).

(1980) "Identity Through Time", in: *Time and Cause: Essays in Honor of Richard Taylor*, ed. Peter van Inwagen (Dordrecht: Reidel), pp. 67–78.

(1983) *What is a Law of Nature?* (Cambridge: Cambridge University Press).

(1989) *Universals: An Opinionated Introduction* (Boulder, CO: Westview Press).

(1997) *A World of States of Affairs* (Cambridge: Cambridge University Press).

(1999) "The Causal Theory of Properties: Properties According to Shoemaker, Ellis, and Others", *Philosophical Topics*, 26, pp. 25–37.

(2005) "Four Disputes about Properties", *Synthese*, 144, pp. 309–320.

Arntzenius, Frank (2006) "Time Travel: Double Your Fun", *Philosophy Compass*, 1, pp. 599–616.

Ayers, Michael (1991) "Substance: Prolegomena to a Realist Theory of Identity", *Journal of Philosophy*, 88, pp. 69–90.

Baker, David (2005) "Spacetime Substantivalism and Einstein's Cosmological Constant", *Philosophy of Science*, 72, pp. 1299–1311.

(2016) "Does String Theory Posit Extended Simples?" *Philosophers' Imprint*, 16, pp. 1–15.

Balashov, Yuri (2000) "Relativity and Persistence", *Philosophy of Science*, 67 (supplement), pp. S549–S562.

(2002) "What is a Law of Nature? The Broken-Symmetry Story", *Southern Journal of Philosophy*, 40, pp. 459–475.

Barker, Stephen (2013) "The Emperor's New Metaphysics of Powers", *Mind*, 122, pp. 605–653.

Bartels, Andreas (2013) "Why Metrical Properties are not Powers", *Synthese*, 190, pp. 2001–2013.

Bauer, William (2013) "Dispositional Essentialism and the Nature of Powerful Properties", *Disputatio*, 5, pp. 1–19.

Beebee, Helen (2000) "The Non-Governing Conception of Laws of Nature", *Philosophy and Phenomenological Research*, 3, pp. 571–595.

(2011) "Necessary Connections and the Problem of Induction", *Noûs*, 45, pp. 504–527.

Belot, Gordon (1999) "Rehabilitating Relationalism", *International Studies in the Philosophy of Science*, 13, pp. 35–52.

Benovsky, Jiri (2009) "Presentism and Persistence", *Pacific Philosophical Quarterly*, 90, pp. 291–309.

Bettoni, Efrem (1961) *Duns Scotus: The Basic Principles of His Philosophy*, translated by Bernardine Bonansea (Washington, DC: Catholic University of America Press).

Bigelow, John, Ellis, Brian, and Lierse, Caroline (1992) "The World as One of a Kind: Natural Necessity and the Laws of Nature", *British Journal for the Philosophy of Science*, 43, pp. 371–388.

Bird, Alexander (2005) "The Ultimate Argument Against Armstrong's Contingent Necessitation View of Laws", *Analysis*, 65, pp. 147–155.

(2006) "Potency and Modality", *Synthese*, 149: 491–508.

(2007) *Nature's Metaphysics: Laws and Properties* (Oxford: Oxford University Press).

(2012) "Are Any Kinds Ontologically Fundamental?", in: *Contemporary Aristotelian Metaphysics*, ed. Tuomas Tahko (Cambridge: Cambridge University Press), pp. 94–104.

Bird, Alexander, Ellis, Brian, Mumford, Stephen, and Psillos, Stathis (2006) "Looking for Laws", *Metascience*, 15, pp. 437–469.

Black, Robert (2000) "Against Quidditism", *Australasian Journal of Philosophy*, 78, pp. 87–104.

Bobik, Joseph (1961) "St. Thomas on the Individuation of Bodily Substances", in: *Readings in the Philosophy of Nature*, ed. Henry Koren (Westminster, MD: The Newman Press), pp. 327–340.

(1965) *Aquinas on Being and Essence: A Translation and Interpretation* (Notre Dame, IN: University of Notre Dame Press).

(1998) *Aquinas on Matter and Form and the Elements: A Translation and Interpretation of the De Principiis Naturae and the De Mixtione Elementorum of St. Thomas Aquinas* (Notre Dame, IN: University of Notre Dame Press).

Borghini, Andrea, and Williams, Neil (2008) "A Dispositional Theory of Possibility", *dialectica*, 62, pp. 21–41.

Bostock, Simon (2003) "Are All Possible Laws Actual Laws?" *Australasian Journal of Philosophy*, 81, pp. 517–533.

(2008) "A Defence of Pan-Dispositionalism", *Metaphysica*, 9, pp. 139–157.

Braddon-Mitchell, David, and Miller, Kristie (2006) "The Physics of Extended Simples", *Analysis*, 66, pp. 222–226.

Briceno, Sebastian, and Mumford, Stephen (2016) "Relations All the Way Down? Against Ontic Structural Realism", in: *The Metaphysics of Relations*, eds. Anna Marmodoro and David Yates (Oxford: Oxford University Press), pp. 198–217.

Broackes, Justin (2006) "Substance", *Proceedings of the Aristotelian Society*, 106, pp. 131–166.

Broad, C. D. (1923) *Scientific Thought* (London: Routledge & Kegan Paul).

(1925) *The Mind and Its Place in Nature* (London: Routledge & Kegan Paul).

Brogaard, Berit (2000) "Presentist Four-Dimensionalism", *Monist*, 83, pp. 341–356.

Brower, Jeffrey (2014) *Aquinas's Ontology of the Material World: Change, Hylomorphism, and Material Objects* (Oxford: Oxford University Press).

Burge, Tyler (2007) *Foundations of Mind* (Oxford: Oxford University Press).

Byrne, Alex (1994) *The Emergent Mind* (Doctoral Dissertation, Princeton University).

Byrne, Alex, and Hilbert, David (2007) "Color Primitivism", *Erkenntnis*, 66, pp. 73–105.

Campbell, Keith (1990) *Abstract Particulars* (Oxford: Blackwell).

Cartwright, Nancy (1989) *Nature's Capacities and Their Measurement* (Oxford: Oxford University Press).

(2004) "No God, No Laws", in: *God and the Laws of Nature*, eds. Stefano Moriggi and Elio Sindoni (Milan: Angelicum Mondo X), pp. 183–190.

(2007) "What Makes a Capacity a Disposition?", in: *Dispositions and Causal Powers*, eds. Max Kistler and Bruno Gnassounou (Aldershot: Ashgate), pp. 195–205.

(2009) "Causal Laws, Policy Predictions, and the Need for Genuine Powers", in: *Dispositions and Causes*, ed. Toby Handfield (Oxford: Oxford University Press), pp. 127–157.

Chakravartty, Anjan (2003) "The Structuralist Conception of Objects", *Philosophy of Science*, 70, pp. 867–878.

(2007) *A Metaphysics for Scientific Realism: Knowing the Unobservable* (Cambridge: Cambridge University Press).

(2012) "Ontological Priority: The Conceptual Basis of Non-eliminative, Ontic Structural Realism", in: *Structural Realism: Structure, Object, and Causality*, eds. Elaine Landry and Dean Rickles (Dordrecht: Springer), pp. 187–206.

Chalmers, David (2006) "Strong and Weak Emergence", in: *The Re-Emergence of Emergence*, eds. Paul Davies and Philip Clayton (Oxford: Oxford University Press).

Choi, Sungho (2005) "Do Categorical Ascriptions Entail Counterfactual Conditionals?" *Philosophical Quarterly*, 55, pp. 495–503.

Christensen, Jonas (2014) "Determinable Properties and Overdetermination of Causal Powers", *Philosophia: Philosophical Quarterly of Israel*, 42, pp. 695–711.

Clarke, Randolph (2008) "Intrinsic Finks", *Philosophical Quarterly*, 58, pp. 512–518.

Clarke, William, and Norris, S. J. (2001) *The One and the Many: A Contemporary Thomistic Metaphysics* (Notre Dame, IN: University of Notre Dame Press).

Cameron, Ross (2016) "On Characterizing the Presentism/Eternalism and Actualism/Possibilism Debates", *Analytic Philosophy*, 57, pp. 110–140.

Coleman, Mary (2010) "Could there Be a Power World?" *American Philosophical Quarterly*, 47, pp. 161–170.

Connolly, Niall (2015) "Yes: Bare Particulars!" *Philosophical Studies*, 172, pp. 1355–1370.

Corry, Richard (2009) "How is Scientific Analysis Possible?", in: *Dispositions and Causes*, ed. Toby Handfield (Oxford: Oxford University Press), pp. 158–188.

Cowling, Sam (2014) "Instantiation as Location", *Philosophical Studies*, 167, pp. 667–682.

(2017) *Abstract Entities* (New York, NY: Routledge).

Creary, L. G. (1981) "Causal Explanation and the Reality of Natural Component Forces", *Pacific Philosophical Quarterly*, 62, pp. 148–157.

Crisp, Thomas (2003) "Presentism", in: *The Oxford Handbook of Metaphysics*, eds. Michael Loux and Dean Zimmerman (Oxford: Oxford University Press), pp. 211–245.

Cross, Richard (1998) *The Physics of Duns Scotus: The Scientific Context of a Theological Vision* (Oxford: Oxford University Press).

Cross, Troy (2005) "What is a Disposition?" *Synthese*, 144, pp. 321–341.

Daniels, Paul (2012) "Back to the Present: Defending Presentist Time Travel", *Disputatio*, 4, pp. 469–484.

Deasy, Daniel (2015) "The Moving Spotlight Theory", *Philosophical Studies*, 172, pp. 2073–2089.

Demarest, Heather (2017) "Powerful Properties, Powerless Laws", in: *Causal Powers*, ed. Jonathan Jacobs (Oxford: Oxford University Press), pp. 38–54.

Denby, David (1999) "Determinable Nominalism", *Philosophical Studies*, 102, pp. 297–327.

(2007) "A Note on Analysing Substancehood", *Australasian Journal of Philosophy*, 85, pp. 473–484.

Denkel, Arda (1996) *Object and Property* (Cambridge: Cambridge University Press).

(1997) "On the Compresence of Tropes", *Philosophy and Phenomenological Research*, 57, pp. 599–606.

Dieks, Dennis (2001) "Space–Time Relationism in Newtonian and Relativistic Physics", *International Studies in the Philosophy of Science*, 15, pp. 5–17.

(2001a) "Space and Time in Particle and Field Physics", *Studies in History and Philosophy of Modern Physics*, 32, pp. 217–241.

Dipert, Randall (1997) "The Mathematical Structure of the World: The World as Graph", *Journal of Philosophy*, 94, pp. 329–358.

Donnelly, Maureen (2011) "Endurantist and Perdurantist Accounts of Persistence", *Philosophical Studies*, 154, pp. 27–51.

Dorato, Mauro (2008) "Is Structural Spacetime Realism Relationism in Disguise? The Supererogatory Nature of the Substantivalism/Realism Debate", in: *The Ontology of Spacetime II*, ed. Dennis Dieks (Amsterdam: Elsevier), pp. 17–37.

Dretske, Fred (1977) "Laws of Nature", *Philosophy of Science*, 44, pp. 248–268.

Du Maurier, Daphne (1969) *The House on the Strand* (London: Victor Gollancz).

Dumsday, Travis (2011) "Have the Laws of Nature Been Eliminated?", in: *Reading the Cosmos: Nature, Science and Wisdom*, ed. Giuseppe Butera (Washington, DC: Catholic University of America Press/American Maritain Association), pp. 111–128.

(2012) "An Argument for Hylomorphism or Theism (But Not Both)", *Proceedings of the American Catholic Philosophical Association*, 86, pp. 245–254.

(2012a) "Dispositions, Primitive Activities, and Essentially Active Objects", *Pacific Philosophical Quarterly*, 93, pp. 43–64.

(2013) "Laws of Nature Don't *Have* Ceteris Paribus Clauses, They *Are* Ceteris Paribus Clauses", *Ratio*, 26, pp. 134–147.

(2013a) "Using Natural-Kind Essentialism to Defend Dispositionalism", *Erkenntnis*, 78, pp. 869–880.

(2014) "Nominalist Dispositionalism and a Cosmological Argument", *Philosophia Christi*, 16, pp. 423–432.

(2015) "Atoms vs. Extended Simples: Towards a Dispositionalist Reconciliation", *Philosophia: Philosophical Quarterly of Israel*, 43, pp. 1023–1033.

(2016) "Dispositionalism and Moral Nonnaturalism", *Journal of Value Inquiry*, 50, pp. 97–110.

(2016a) "Lowe's Unorthodox Dispositionalism", *Res Philosophica*, 93, pp. 79–101.

(2016b) "Natural-Kind Essentialism, Substance Ontology, and the Unity Problem: Two Dispositionalist Solutions", *Dialectica*, 70, pp. 609–626.

(2017) "MaxCon Extended Simples and the Dispositionalist Ontology of Laws", *Synthese*, 194, pp. 1627–1641.

Elder, Crawford (1994) "Laws, Natures, and Contingent Necessities", *Philosophy and Phenomenological Research*, 54, pp. 649–667.

(1996) "Realism and Determinable Properties", *Philosophy and Phenomenological Research*, 56, pp. 149–159.

(2004) *Real Natures and Familiar Objects* (Cambridge, MA: MIT Press).

(2007) "Realism and the Problem of Infimae Species", *American Philosophical Quarterly* 44, pp. 111–127.

Ellis, Brian (2001) *Scientific Essentialism* (Cambridge: Cambridge University Press).

(2002) *The Philosophy of Nature: A Guide to the New Essentialism* (Montreal & Kingston: McGill-Queen's University Press).

(2009) *The Metaphysics of Scientific Realism* (Montreal & Kingston: McGill-Queen's University Press).

Ellis, Brian, and Lierse, Caroline (1994) "Dispositional Essentialism", *Australasian Journal of Philosophy*, 72, pp. 27–45.

Esfeld, Michael (2009) "The Modal Nature of Structures in Ontic Structural Realism", *International Studies in the Philosophy of Science*, 23, pp. 179–194.

(2016) "The Reality of Relations: The Case from Quantum Physics", in: *The Metaphysics of Relations*, eds. Anna Marmodoro and David Yates (Oxford: Oxford University Press), pp. 218–234.

Esfeld, Michael, and Lam, Vincent (2008) "Moderate Structural Realism About Space-Time", *Synthese*, 160, pp. 27–46.

(2011) "Ontic Structural Realism as a Metaphysics of Objects", in: *Scientific Structuralism*, eds. Alisa Bokulich and Peter Bokulich (Dordrecht: Springer), pp. 143–159.

Esfeld, Michael, and Sachse, Christian (2011) *Conservative Reductionism* (New York, NY: Routledge).

Everett, Anthony (2009) "Intrinsic Finks, Masks, and Mimics", *Erkenntnis*, 71, pp. 191–203.

Evnine, Simon (2016) *Making Objects and Events: A Hylomorphic Theory of Artifacts, Actions, and Organisms* (Oxford: Oxford University Press).

Fales, Evan (1982) "Generic Universals", *Australasian Journal of Philosophy*, 60, pp. 29–39.

(1990) *Causation and Universals* (New York, NY: Routledge).

(1993) "Are Causal Laws Contingent?", in: *Ontology, Causality, and Mind: Essays in Honour of D.M. Armstrong*, eds. John Bacon, Keith Campbell, and Lloyd Reinhardt (Cambridge: Cambridge University Press), pp. 121–151.

Feser, Edward (2014) *Scholastic Metaphysics: A Contemporary Introduction* (Heusenstamm: Editiones Scholasticae).

(2015) *Neo-Scholastic Essays* (South Bend, IN: St. Augustine's Press).

Fine, Kit (1994) "Essence and Modality", *Philosophical Perspectives*, 8, pp. 1–16.

(1999) "Things and their Parts", *Midwest Studies in Philosophy*, 23, pp. 61–74.

Fisk, Milton (1973) *Nature and Necessity: An Essay in Physical Ontology* (Bloomington, IN: Indiana University Press).

Floridi, Luciano (2011) *The Philosophy of Information* (Oxford: Oxford University Press).

Forrest, Peter (2004) "Grit or Gunk: Implications of the Banach-Tarski Paradox", *Monist*, 87, pp. 351–370.

Foster, John (2004) *The Divine Lawmaker: Lectures on Induction, Laws of Nature, and the Existence of God* (Oxford: Oxford University Press).

Franklin, James (1986) "Are Dispositions Reducible to Categorical Properties?" *Philosophical Quarterly*, 36, pp. 62–64.

(2015) "Uninstantiated Properties and Semi-Platonist Aristotelianism", *Review of Metaphysics*, 69, pp. 25–45.

French, Steven (2006) "Structure as a Weapon of the Realist", *Proceedings of the Aristotelian Society*, 106, pp. 167–185.

(2010) "The Interdependence of Structure, Objects, and Dependence", *Synthese*, 175, pp. 89–109.

French, Steven, and Ladyman, James (2011) "In Defence of Ontic Structural Realism", in: *Scientific Structuralism*, eds. Alisa Bokulich and Peter Bokulich (Dordrecht: Springer), pp. 25–42.

French, Steven, and Redhead, Michael (1988) "Quantum Physics and the Identity of Indiscernibles", *British Journal for the Philosophy of Science*, 39, pp. 233–246.

Frigg, Roman, and Votsis, Ioannis (2011) "Everything You Ever Wanted to Know About Structural Realism but Were Afraid to Ask", *European Journal for Philosophy of Science*, 1, pp. 227–276.

Funkhouser, Eric (2006) "The Determinable-Determinate Relation", *Noûs*, 40, pp. 548–569.

(2014) *The Logical Structure of Kinds* (Oxford: Oxford University Press).

Gert, Joshua (2008) "What Colors Could Not Be: An Argument for Color Primitivism", *Journal of Philosophy*, 105, pp. 128–155.

Gibermam, Daniel (2012) "Against Zero-Dimensional Material Objects (and Other Bare Particulars)", *Philosophical Studies*, 160, pp. 305–321.

(2014) "Tropes in Space", *Philosophical Studies*, 167, pp. 453–472.

Gibson, Ian, and Pooley, Oliver (2006) "Relativistic Persistence", *Philosophical Perspectives*, 20, pp. 157–198.

Gilmore, Cody, Costa, Damiano, and Calosi, Claudio (2016) "Relativity and Three Four-Dimensionalisms", *Philosophy Compass*, 11, pp. 102–120.

Goddu, G. C. (2003) "Time Travel and Changing the Past: (Or How to Kill Yourself and Live to Tell the Tale)", *Ratio*, 16, pp. 16–32.

Goyette, John (2002) "Substantial Form and the Recovery of an Aristotelian Natural Science", *Thomist*, 66, pp. 519–533.

Greaves, Hilary (2011) "In Search of (Spacetime) Structuralism", *Philosophical Perspectives*, 25, pp. 189–204.

Grey, William (1999) "Troubles With Time Travel", *Philosophy*, 74, pp. 55–70.

Groff, Ruth, and Greco, John (eds.) (2013) *Powers and Capacities in Philosophy: The New Aristotelianism* (New York, NY: Routledge).

Hales, Steven, and Johnson, Timothy (2003) "Endurantism, Perdurantism, and Special Relativity", *Philosophical Quarterly*, 53, pp. 524–539.

Hall, Thomas (2014) "In Defense of the Compossibility of Presentism and Time Travel", *Logos & Episteme*, 5, pp. 141–159.

Handfield, Toby (2005) "Armstrong and the Modal Inversion of Dispositions", *Philosophical Quarterly*, 55, pp. 452–461.

(2005a) "Lange on essentialism, counterfactuals, and explanation", *Australasian Journal of Philosophy*, 83, pp. 81–85.

(2008) "Unfinkable Dispositions", *Synthese*, 160, pp. 297–308.

Harré, Rom, and Madden, E. H. (1975) *Causal Powers: A Theory of Natural Necessity* (Oxford: Blackwell).

Haslanger, Sally (2003) "Persistence Through Time", in: *The Oxford Handbook of Metaphysics*, eds. Michael Loux and Dean Zimmerman (Oxford: Oxford University Press), pp. 315–354.

Hawley, Katherine (2001) *How Things Persist* (Oxford: Oxford University Press).

Hawley, Katherine, and Bird, Alexander (2011) "What Are Natural Kinds?" *Philosophical Perspectives* 25, pp. 205–221.

Heil, John (2003) *From an Ontological Point of View* (Oxford: Oxford University Press).

(2005) "Dispositions", *Synthese*, 144, pp. 343–356.

(2012) *The Universe As We Find It* (Oxford: Oxford University Press).

(2017) "Real Modalities", in: *Causal Powers*, ed. Jonathan Jacobs (Oxford: Oxford University Press), pp. 90–104.

Heller, Mark (1990) *The Ontology of Physical Objects: Four-Dimensional Hunks of Matter* (Cambridge: Cambridge University Press)

Hoefer, Carl (1996) "The Metaphysics of Space–Time Substantivalism", *Journal of Philosophy*, 93, pp. 5–27.

(1998) "Absolute Versus Relational Space-Time: For Better or Worse, the Debate Goes On", *British Journal for the Philosophy of Science*, 49, pp. 451–467.

Hoffman, Joshua (2012) "Neo-Aristotelianism and Substance", in: *Contemporary Aristotelian Metaphysics*, ed. Tuomas Tahko (Cambridge: Cambridge University Press), pp. 140–155.

Hoffman, Joshua, and Rosenkrantz, Gary (2003) "Platonistic Theories of Universals", in: *The Oxford Handbook of Metaphysics*, eds. Michael Loux andDean Zimmerman (Oxford: Oxford University Press), pp. 46–74.

Holden, Thomas (2004) *The Architecture of Matter: Galileo to Kant* (Oxford: Oxford University Press).

Hudson, Hud (2014) *The Fall and Hypertime* (Oxford: Oxford University Press).

Huggett, Nick (2006) "The Regularity Account of Relational Spacetime", *Mind*, 115, pp. 41–73.

Hughes, Christopher, and Adams, Robert (1992) "Miracles, Laws of Nature and Causation", *Proceedings of the Aristotelian Society Supplementary Volume*, 66, pp. 179–224.

Humphreys, P. (1997) "How Properties Emerge", *Philosophy of Science*, 64, pp. 1–17.

(1997a) "Emergence, Not Supervenience", *Philosophy of Science*, 64 (supplement), pp. S337–S345.

Huntelmann, Rafael, and Hattler, Johannes (eds.) (2014) *New Scholasticism Meets Analytic Philosophy* (Heusenstamm: Editiones Scholasticae).

Ingthorsson, R. D. (2013) "Properties: Qualities, Powers, or Both?" *Dialectica*, 67, pp. 55–80.

Isaacs, A. (ed.) (2000) *Oxford Dictionary of Physics*, 4th edition (Oxford: Oxford University Press).

Jacobs, Jonathan (2010) "A Powers Theory of Modality: Or, How I Learned to Stop Worrying and Reject Possible Worlds", *Philosophical Studies*, 151, pp. 227–248.

(2011) "Powerful Qualities, Not Pure Powers", *Monist*, 94, pp. 81–102.

Jaeger, Andrew (2014) "Back to the Primitive: From Substantial Capacities to Prime Matter", *American Catholic Philosophical Quarterly*, 88, pp. 381–395.

Jaeger, Lydia (1999) *Croire et connaître: Einstein, Polanyi et les lois de la nature* (Paris: Institut Biblique de Nogent).

Jantzen, Benjamin (2011) "No Two Entities Without Identity", *Synthese*, 181, pp. 433–450.

Jaworski, William (2016) *Structure and the Metaphysics of Mind: How Hylomorphism Solves the Mind–Body Problem* (Oxford: Oxford University Press).

Johansson, Ingvar (2000) "Determinables as Universals", *Monist*, 83, pp. 101–121.

Johnston, Mark (2006) "Hylomorphism", *Journal of Philosophy*, 103, pp. 652–698.

Kantorovich, Aharon (2003) "The Priority of Internal Symmetries in Particle Physics", *Studies in History and Philosophy of Modern Physics*, 34, pp. 651–675.

(2009) "Ontic Structuralism and the Symmetries of Particle Physics", *Journal for General Philosophy of Science*, 40, pp. 73–84.

Katzav, Joel (2005) "On What Powers Cannot Do", *Dialectica*, 59, pp. 331–345.

Kedar, Yael, and Hon, Giora (2017) "'Natures' and 'Laws': The Making of the Concept of Law of Nature Robert Grosseteste (1168–1253) and Roger Bacon (1214/1220–1292)", *Studies in History and Philosophy of Science*, 61, pp. 21–31.

Keinänen, Markku (2011) "Tropes – The Basic Constituents of Powerful Particulars?" *Dialectica*, 65, pp. 419–450.

Keller, Simon, and Nelson, Michael (2001) "Presentists Should Believe in Time Travel", *Australasian Journal of Philosophy*, 79, pp. 333–345.

Khalidi, Muhammad Ali (2011) "The Pitfalls of Microphysical Realism", *Philosophy of Science*, 78, pp. 1156–1164.

Kim, Jaegwon (2006) "Emergence: Core Ideas and Issues", *Synthese*, 151, pp. 547–559.

Kistler, Max (2012) "Powerful Properties and the Causal Basis of Dispositions", in: *Properties, Powers, and Structures: Issues in the Metaphysics of Realism*, eds. Alexander Bird, Brian Ellis, and Howard Sankey (New York, NY: Routledge), pp. 119–137.

Koons, Robert, and Pickavance, Timothy (2015) *Metaphysics: The Fundamentals* (Oxford: Wiley-Blackwell).

Koslicki, Kathrin (2008) *The Structure of Objects* (Oxford: Oxford University Press).

Kronen, John (1994) "The Substantial Unity of Material Substances According to John Poinsot", *Thomist* 58, pp. 599–615.

Kuhlmann, Meinard (2012) "Quantum Field Theory", *The Stanford Encyclopedia of Philosophy* (Summer 2015 edition), Edward N. Zalta (ed.), https://plato.stanford.edu/archives/sum2015/entries/quantum-field-theory/

Kutach, Douglas (2003) "Time Travel and Consistency Constraints", *Philosophy of Science*, 70, pp. 1098–1113.

LaBossiere, Michael (1994) "Substances and Substrata", *Australasian Journal of Philosophy*, 72, pp. 360–370.

Ladyman, James (1998) "What is Structural Realism?" *Studies in History and Philosophy of Science*, 29, pp. 409–424.

(2016) "Structural Realism", *The Stanford Encyclopedia of Philosophy* (Winter 2016 edition), Edward N. Zalta (ed.), https://plato.stanford.edu/archives/win2016/entries/structural-realism/

(2016a) "The Foundations of Structuralism and the Metaphysics of Relations", in: *The Metaphysics of Relations*, eds. Anna Marmodoro and David Yates (Oxford: Oxford University Press), pp. 177–197.

Ladyman, James, and Ross, Don (with David Spurrett and John Collier) (2007) *Every Thing Must Go: Metaphysics Naturalized* (Oxford: Oxford University Press).

Lam, Vincent (2014) "Entities Without Intrinsic Physical Identity", *Erkenntnis*, 79, pp. 1157–1171.

Lam, Vincent, and Wuthrich, Christian (2015) "No Categorial Support for Radical Ontic Structural Realism", *British Journal for the Philosophy of Science*, 66, pp. 605–634.

Lange, Marc (2004) "A Note on Scientific Essentialism, Laws of Nature, and Counterfactual Conditionals", *Australasian Journal of Philosophy*, 82, pp. 227–241.

(2006) "Farewell to Laws of Nature?" *Studies in History and Philosophy of Science*, 37, pp. 361–369.

(2009) "Why Do the Laws Explain Why?", in: *Dispositions and Causes*, ed. Toby Handfield (Oxford: Oxford University Press), pp. 286–321.

(2009a) *Laws and Lawmakers: Science, Metaphysics, and the Laws of Nature* (Oxford: Oxford University Press).

Latham, Noa (2011) "Are Fundamental Laws Necessary or Contingent?", in: *Carving Nature at its Joints: Natural Kinds in Metaphysics and Science*, eds. Joseph K. Campbell, Michael O'Rourke, and Matthew Slater (Cambridge, MA: MIT Press), pp. 97–112.

Laudan, Larry (1981) "A Confutation of Convergent Realism", *Philosophy of Science*, 48, pp. 19–49.

Laudisa, Federico (2015) "Laws Are Not Descriptions", *International Studies in the Philosophy of Science*, 29, pp. 251–270.

Le Bihan, Baptiste (2016) "Super-Relationism: Combining Eliminativism About Objects and Relationism About Spacetime", *Philosophical Studies*, 173, pp. 2151–2172.

Lehoux, Daryn (2006) "Laws of Nature and Natural Laws", *Studies in History and Philosophy of Science*, 37, pp. 527–549.

Legg, Cathy (1999) "Real Laws in Peirce's 'Pragmaticism' (Or: How Scholastic Realism Met the Scientific Method)", in: *Causation and the Laws of Nature*, ed. Howard Sankey (Dordrecht: Kluwer), pp. 125–142.

Lewis, David (1976) "The Paradoxes of Time Travel", *American Philosophical Quarterly*, 13, pp. 145–152.

(1983) "Survival and Identity", in: *Philosophical Papers Volume I* (Oxford: Oxford University Press).

(1986) *On the Plurality of Worlds* (Oxford: Blackwell).

(2009) "Ramseyan Humility", in *Conceptual Analysis and Philosophical Naturalism*, eds. David Braddon-Mitchell and Robert Nola (Cambridge, MA: MIT Press), pp. 203–222.

Lewis, Peter (2006) "GRW: A Case Study in Quantum Ontology", *Philosophy Compass*, 1, pp. 224–244.

Loux, Michael (1974) "Kinds and the Dilemma of Individuation", *Review of Metaphysics*, 27, pp. 773–784.

(1978) *Substance and Attribute: A Study in Ontology* (Dordrecht: Reidel).

(2002) *Metaphysics: A Contemporary Introduction*, 2nd edition (New York, NY: Routledge).

(2006) "Aristotle's Constituent Ontology", in: *Oxford Studies in Metaphysics Volume II*, ed. Dean Zimmerman (Oxford: Oxford University Press), pp. 207–250.

Lowe, E. J. (1994) "Primitive Substances", *Philosophy and Phenomenological Research*, 54, pp. 531–552.

(1995) "The Metaphysics of Abstract Objects", *Journal of Philosophy*, 92, pp. 509–524.

(1998) "Form Without Matter", *Ratio*, 11, pp. 214–234.

(2000) "Locke, Martin, and Substance", *Philosophical Quarterly*, 50, pp. 499–514.

(2001) "Dispositions and Laws", *Metaphysica*, 2, pp. 5–23.

(2005) "Vagueness and Endurance", *Analysis*, 65, pp. 104–112.

(2006) *The Four-Category Ontology: A Metaphysical Foundation for Natural Science* (Oxford: Oxford University Press).

(2012) "A Neo-Aristotelian Substance Ontology: Neither Relational Nor Constituent", in: *Contemporary Aristotelian Metaphysics*, ed. Tuomas Tahko (Cambridge: Cambridge University Press), pp. 229–248.

(2013) "Neo-Aristotelian Metaphysics: A Brief Exposition and Defense", in: *Aristotle on Method and Metaphysics*, ed. Edward Feser (New York, NY: Palgrave Macmillan), pp. 196–205.

Macdonald, Cynthia (2005) *Varieties of Things: Foundations of Contemporary Metaphysics* (Oxford: Blackwell).

Machamer, Peter (2004) "Activities and Causation: The Metaphysics and Epistemology of Mechanisms", *International Studies in the Philosophy of Science*, 18, pp. 27–39.

Mackie, J. L. (1977) "Dispositions, Grounds and Causes", *Synthese*, 34, pp. 361–369.

Madden, James (2013) *Mind, Matter, and Nature: A Thomistic Proposal for the Philosophy of Mind* (Washington, DC: Catholic University of America Press).

Markosian, Ned (1998) "Simples", *Australasian Journal of Philosophy*, 76, pp. 213–226.

(2004) "Simples, Stuff, and Simple People", *Monist*, 87, pp. 405–428.

(2015) "The Right Stuff", *Australasian Journal of Philosophy*, 93, pp. 665–687.

Marmodoro, Anna (2013) "Aristotelian Hylomorphism Without Reconditioning", *Philosophical Inquiry*, 36, pp. 5–22.

Martin, C. B. (1980) "Substance Substantiated", *Australasian Journal of Philosophy*, 58, pp. 3–10.

(1997) "On the Need for Properties: The Road to Pythagoreanism and Back", *Synthese*, 112, pp. 193–231.

Martin, C. B., and Heil, John (1999) "The Ontological Turn", *Midwest Studies in Philosophy*, 23, pp. 34–60.

Maudlin, Timothy (1993) "Buckets of Water and Waves of Space: Why Spacetime is Probably a Substance", *Philosophy of Science*, 60, pp. 183–203.

(2007) *The Metaphysics Within Physics* (Oxford: Oxford University Press).

McCall, Storrs (1994) *A Model of the Universe* (Oxford: Oxford University Press).

McDaniel, Kris (2007) "Extended Simples", *Philosophical Studies*, 133, pp. 131–141.

(2009) "Extended Simples and Qualitative Heterogeneity", *Philosophical Quarterly*, 59, pp. 325–331.

(2010) "A Return to the Analogy of Being", *Philosophy and Phenomenological Research*, 81, pp. 688–717.

(2010a) "Being and Almost Nothingness", *Noûs*, 44, pp. 628–649.

(2013) "Degrees of Being", *Philosophers' Imprint*, 13, pp. 1–19.

McKenzie, Kerry (2014) "Priority and Particle Physics: Ontic Structural Realism as a Fundamentality Thesis", *British Journal for the Philosophy of Science*, 65, pp. 353–380.

Merricks, Trenton (1995) "On the Incompatibility of Enduring and Perduring Entities", *Mind*, 104, pp. 523–531.

Miller, Elizabeth (2015) "Humean Scientific Explanation", *Philosophical Studies*, 172, pp. 1311–1332.

Miller, Kristie (2009) "Ought a Four-Dimensionalist to Believe in Temporal Parts?" *Canadian Journal of Philosophy*, 39, pp. 619–646.

Molnar, George (2003) *Powers: A Study in Metaphysics*, ed. Stephen Mumford (Oxford: Oxford University Press).

Moreland, J. P. (1998) "Theories of Individuation: A Reconsideration of Bare Particulars", *Pacific Philosophical Quarterly*, 79, pp. 251–263.

(2000) "Naturalism and the Ontological Status of Properties", in: *Naturalism: A Critical Analysis*, eds. William Lane Craig and J. P. Moreland (New York, NY: Routledge), pp. 67–109.

(2001) *Universals* (Montreal & Kingston: McGill-Queen's University Press).

(2013) "Exemplification and Constituent Realism: A Clarification and Defense", *Axiomathes*, 23, pp. 247–259.

Moreland, J. P., and Pickavance, Timothy (2003) "Bare Particulars and Individuation: A Reply to Mertz", *Australasian Journal of Philosophy*, 81, pp. 1–13.

Morganti, Matteo (2004) "On the Preferability of Epistemic Structural Realism", *Synthese*, 142, pp. 81–107.

(2011) "Is There a Compelling Argument for Ontic Structural Realism?" *Philosophy of Science*, 78, pp. 1165–1176.

(2011a) "Substrata and Properties: From Bare Particulars to Supersubstantivalism?" *Metaphysica*, 12, pp. 183–195.

Mumford, Stephen (1998) *Dispositions* (Oxford: Oxford University Press).

(2004) *Laws in Nature* (New York, NY: Routledge).

(2006) "The Ungrounded Argument", *Synthese*, 149, pp. 471–489.

(2007) "Powers, Dispositions, Properties: Or a Causal Realist Manifesto", in: *Revitalizing Causality: Realism About Causality in Philosophy and Social Science*, ed. Ruth Groff (New York, NY: Routledge), pp. 139–151.

(2009) "Powers and Persistence", in: *Unity and Time in Metaphysics*, eds. Ludger Honnefelder, Edmund Runggaldier, and Benedikt Schlick (Berlin: De Gruyter), pp. 223–236.

Mumford, Stephen, and Anjum, Rani Lill (2011) *Getting Causes from Powers* (Oxford: Oxford University Press).

Mumford, Stephen, Anjum, Rani Lill, and Lie, Svein Anders Noer (2013) "Dispositions and Ethics", in: *Powers and Capacities in Philosophy: The New Aristotelianism*, eds. Ruth Groff and John Greco (New York, NY: Routledge), pp. 231–247.

Nagasawa, Yujin (2012) "Infinite Decomposability and the Mind-Body Problem", *American Philosophical Quarterly*, 49, pp. 357–367.

Nerlich, Graham (2003) "Space-Time Substantivalism", in: *The Oxford Handbook of Metaphysics*, eds. Michael Loux and Dean Zimmerman (Oxford: Oxford University Press), pp. 281–314.

Newman, Andrew (2013) "On the Constitution of Solid Objects Out of Atoms", *Monist*, 96, pp. 149–171.

Ney, Alyssa (2010) "Are There Fundamental Intrinsic Properties?", in: *New Waves in Metaphysics*, ed. Allan Hazlett (New York, NY: Palgrave Macmillan), pp. 219–239.

Novak, Lukas, Novotny, Daniel, Sousedik, Prokop, and Svoboda, David (eds.) (2013) *Metaphysics: Aristotelian, Scholastic, Analytic* (Heusenstamm: Ontos Verlag).

Novotny, Daniel, and Novak, Lukas (eds.) (2014) *Neo-Aristotelian Perspectives in Metaphysics* (London: Routledge).

Oakes, M. Gregory (2004) "Perdurance and Causal Realism", *Erkenntnis*, 60, pp. 205–227.

O'Conaill, Donnchadh (2014) "Ontic Structural Realism and Concrete Objects", *Philosophical Quarterly*, 64, pp. 284–300.

O'Connor, Timothy (1994) "Emergent Properties", *American Philosophical Quarterly*, 31, pp. 91–104.

(2006) "Emergent Properties", in: *Stanford Encyclopedia of Philosophy*, Edward, N. Zalta (ed.) https://plato.stanford.edu/archives/win2006/entries/properties-emergent/

Oderberg, David (1996) "Coincidence Under a Sortal", *Philosophical Review*, 105, pp. 145–171.

(2002) "Hylomorphism and Individuation", in: *Mind, Metaphysics, and Value in the Thomistic and Analytic Traditions*, ed. John Haldane (Notre Dame, IN: University of Notre Dame Press), pp. 125–142.

(2004) "Temporal Parts and the Possibility of Change", *Philosophy and Phenomenological Research*, 69, pp. 686–708.

(2005) "Hylemorphic Dualism", *Social Philosophy & Policy*, pp. 70–99.

(2007) *Real Essentialism* (New York, NY: Routledge).

(2011) "Essence and Properties", *Erkenntnis*, 75, pp. 85–111.

Okasha, Samir (2002) *Philosophy of Science: A Very Short Introduction* (Oxford: Oxford University Press).

O'Leary-Hawthorne, John, and Cover, Jan (1998) "A World of Universals", *Philosophical Studies*, 91, pp. 205–219.

Paoletti, Michele (2016) "Who's Afraid of Non-Existent Manifestations?", in: *Metaphysics and Scientific Realism: Essays in Honour of David Malet Armstrong*, ed. Francesco Calemi (Berlin: De Gruyter), pp. 193–206.

(2016a) "How Powers Emerge from Relations", *Axiomathes*, 26, pp. 187–204.

Parsons, Josh (2000) "Must a Four Dimensionalist Believe in Temporal Parts?" *Monist*, 83, pp. 399–418.

Pashby, Thomas (2013) "Do Quantum Objects Have Temporal Parts?" *Philosophy of Science*, 80, pp. 1137–1147.

Pasnau, Robert (2011) *Metaphysical Themes: 1274–1671* (Oxford: Oxford University Press).

Paterson, Craig, and Pugh, Matthew (eds.) (2006) *Analytical Thomism: Traditions in Dialogue* (Aldershot: Ashgate).

Paul, Laurie (2002) "Logical Parts", *Noûs*, 36, pp. 578–596.

Pawl, Timothy (2017) "Nine Problems (And Even More Solutions) for Powers Accounts of Possibility", in: *Causal Powers*, ed. Jonathan Jacobs (Oxford: Oxford University Press), pp. 105–124.

Persson, Johannes (2010) "Activity-Based Accounts of Mechanism and the Threat of Polygenic Effects", *Erkenntnis*, 72, pp. 135–149.

Peterson, John (1996) "Law and Thomistic Exemplarism", *Thomist*, 60, pp. 81–108.

Pickavance, T. (2009) "In Defence of 'Partially Clad' Bare Particulars", *Australasian Journal of Philosophy*, 87, pp. 155–158.

(2014) "Bare Particulars and Exemplification", *American Philosophical Quarterly*, 51, pp. 95–108.

Psillos, Stathis (1999) *Scientific Realism: How Science Tracks Truth* (New York, NY: Routledge).

(2006) "What Do Powers Do When They Are Not Manifested?" *Philosophy and Phenomenological Research*, 72, pp. 137–156.

(2009) *Knowing the Structure of Nature: Essays on Realism and Explanation* (New York, NY: Palgrave Macmillan).

Poincaré, Henri (1905) *Science and Hypothesis*, reprint edition from 1952 (New York, NY: Dover).

Pooley, Oliver (2013) "Substantivalist and Relationalist Approaches to Spacetime", in: *The Oxford Handbook of Philosophy of Physics*, ed. Robert Batterman (Oxford: Oxford University Press), pp. 522–586.

Pruss, Alexander (2011) *Actuality, Possibility, and Worlds* (London: Continuum).

(2013) "Aristotelian Forms and Laws of Nature", *Analiza i Egzystencja*, 24, pp. 115–132.

Quine, W. V. O. (1966) *The Ways of Paradox and Other Essays* (Cambridge, MA: Harvard University Press).

(1974) *Roots of Reference* (La Salle, IL: Open Court).

Rea, Michael (2003) "Four-Dimensionalism", in: *The Oxford Handbook of Metaphysics*, eds. Michael Loux and Dean Zimmerman (Oxford: Oxford University Press), pp. 246–280.

Reck, Erich, and Price, Michael (2000) "Structures and Structuralism in Contemporary Philosophy of Mathematics", *Synthese*, 125, pp. 341–383.

Robb, David (2005) "Qualitative Unity and the Bundle Theory", *Monist*, 88, pp. 466–492.

Ruby, Jane (1986) "The Origins of Scientific 'Law'", *Journal of the History of Ideas*, 47, pp. 341–359.

Ruse, Michael (2001) *Can a Darwinian Be a Christian? The Relationship Between Science and Religion* (Cambridge: Cambridge University Press).

Russell, Bertrand (1915/1951) "The Ultimate Constituents of Matter", in: *Mysticism and Logic* (New Jersey: Barnes and Noble), pp. 94–107.

Schaffer, Jonathan (2003) "Is There a Fundamental Level?" *Noûs*, 37, pp. 498–517.

Schneider, Susan (2007) "What is the Significance of the Intuition that Laws of Nature Govern?" *Australasian Journal of Philosophy*, 85, pp. 307–324.

Schnieder, Benjamin (2006) "A Certain Kind of Trinity: Dependence, Substance, Explanation", *Philosophical Studies*, 129, pp. 393–419.

Schrenk, Markus (2017) *Metaphysics of Science: A Systematic and Historical Introduction* (New York, NY: Routledge).

Schroer, Robert (2010) "Is There More Than One Categorical Property?" *Philosophical Quarterly*, 60, pp. 831–850.

Schumm, Bruce (2004) *Deep Down Things: The Breathtaking Beauty of Particle Physics* (Baltimore, MD: The Johns Hopkins University Press).

Scotus (1975) *God and Creatures: The Quodlibetal Questions*, translated by Felix Alluntis and Allan Wolter (Princeton, NJ: Princeton University Press).

Shiver, Anthony (2014) "Mereological Bundle Theory and the Identity of Indiscernibles", *Synthese*, 191, pp. 901–913.

Shoemaker, Sydney (1980) "Causality and Properties", in: *Time and Cause*, ed. Peter van Inwagen (Dordrecht: Reidel); reprinted in (1999) *Metaphysics: An Anthology*, eds. Jaegwon Kim and Ernest Sosa (Oxford: Blackwell), pp. 253–268.

(1998) "Causal and metaphysical necessity", *Pacific Philosophical Quarterly*, 79, pp. 59–77.

Sider, Theodore (1993) "Van Inwagen and the Possibility of Gunk", *Analysis*, 53, pp. 285–289.

(2001) *Four-Dimensionalism: An Ontology of Persistence and Time* (Oxford: Oxford University Press).

(2006) "Bare Particulars", *Philosophical Perspectives*, 20, pp. 387–397.

Simons, Peter (1994) "Particulars in Particular Clothing: Three Trope Theories of Substance", *Philosophy and Phenomenological Research*, 54, pp. 553–575.

(2004) "Extended Simples: A Third Way Between Atoms and Gunk", *Monist*, 87, pp. 371–384.

Skow, Bradford (2007) "Are Shapes Intrinsic?" *Philosophical Studies*, 133, pp. 111–130.

Smart, Benjamin (2013) "Is the Humean Defeated by Induction?" *Philosophical Studies*, 162, pp. 319–332.

Smart, J. J. C. (2008) "The Tenseless Theory of Time", in: *Contemporary Debates in Metaphysics*, eds. Ted Sider, John Hawthorne, and Dean Zimmerman (London: Blackwell), pp. 226–238.

Stachel, John (2006) "Structure, Individuality, and Quantum Gravity", in: *Structural Foundations of Quantum Gravity*, eds. Dean Rickles, Steven French, and Juha Saatsi (Oxford: Oxford University Press), pp. 53–82.

Stanford, P. Kyle (2006) *Exceeding Our Grasp: Science, History, and the Problem of Unconceived Alternatives* (Oxford: Oxford University Press).

Strawson, Galen (2008) "The Identity of the Categorical and the Dispositional", *Analysis*, 68, pp. 271–282.

Suárez, Francisco (1994) *Metaphysical Disputations 17, 18, and 10*, translated by Alfred Freddoso (New Haven, CT: Yale University Press).

Suárez, Mauricio (2007) "Quantum Propensities", *Studies in History and Philosophy of Modern Physics*, 38, pp. 418–438.

Swoyer, Chris (1982) "The Nature of Natural Laws", *Australasian Journal of Philosophy*, 60, pp. 203–223.

Tabaczek, Mariusz (2013) "The Metaphysics of Downward Causation: Rediscovering the Formal Cause", *Zygon: Journal of Religion and Science*, 48, pp. 380–404.

Taylor, Elanor (2015) "An Explication of Emergence", *Philosophical Studies*, 172, pp. 653–669.

Tegmark, Max (2007) "The Mathematical Universe", *Foundations of Physics*, 38, pp. 101–150.

Thompson, I. J. (1988) "Real Dispositions in the Physical World", *British Journal for the Philosophy of Science*, 39, pp. 67–79.

Toner, Patrick (2008) "Emergent Substance", *Philosophical Studies*, 141, pp. 281–297.

(2010) "On Substance", *American Catholic Philosophical Quarterly*, 84, pp. 25–48.

(2011) "Hylemorphic Animalism", *Philosophical Studies*, 155, pp. 65–81.

(2012) "On Aristotelianism and Structure as Parts", *Ratio*, 31, pp. 148–161.

Tooley, Michael (1977) "The Nature of Laws", *Canadian Journal of Philosophy*, 74, pp. 667–698.

Tugby, Matthew (2013) "Platonic Dispositionalism", *Mind*, 122, pp. 451–4800.

(2016) "Universals, Laws, and Governance", *Philosophical Studies*, 173, pp. 1147–1163.

Tweedale, Martin (1984) "Armstrong on Determinable and Substantival Universals", in: *D. M. Armstrong*, ed. R. J. Bogdan (Dordrecht: Reidel), pp. 171–189.

Vallicella, William (2000) "Three Conceptions of States of Affairs", *Noûs*, 34, pp. 237–259.

Van Fraassen, Bas (1980) *The Scientific Image* (Oxford: Oxford University Press).

Van Inwagen, Peter (1981) "The Doctrine of Arbitrary Undetached Parts", *Pacific Philosophical Quarterly*, 62, pp. 123–137.

(2011) "Relational Vs. Constituent Ontologies", *Philosophical Perspectives*, 25, pp. 389–405.

(2016) "In Defense of Transcendent Universals", in: *Metaphysics and Scientific Realism: Essays in Honour of David Malet Armstrong*, ed. Francesco Calemi (Berlin: De Gruyter), pp. 51–70.

Vetter, Barbara (2013) "Multi-Track Dispositions", *Philosophical Quarterly*, 63, pp. 330–352.

(2015) *Potentiality: From Dispositions to Modality* (Oxford: Oxford University Press).

Wahlberg, Tobias Hannsson (2009) "4-D Objects and Disposition Ascriptions", *Philosophical Papers*, 38, pp. 35–72.

(2017) "Meso-Level Objects, Powers, and Simultaneous Causation", *Metaphysica*, 18, pp. 107–125.

Wasserman, Ryan (2016) "Theories of Persistence", *Philosophical Studies*, 173, pp. 243–250.

Watkins, Eric (2016) "The Rise and Fall of Laws of Nature", in: *Rethinking Order: After the Laws of Nature*, eds. Nancy Cartwright and Keith Ward (London: Bloomsbury), pp. 7–24.

Whittle, Ann (2009) "Causal Nominalism", in: *Dispositions and Causes*, ed. Toby Handfield (Oxford: Oxford University Press), pp. 242–285.

(2016) "A Defense of Substance Causation", *Journal of the American Philosophical Association*, 2, pp. 1–20.

Wiggins, David (2001) *Sameness and Substance Renewed* (Cambridge: Cambridge University Press).

Wildman, Nathan (2015) "Load Bare-ing Particulars", *Philosophical Studies*, 172, pp. 1419–1434.

Williams, Neil (2011) "Putting Powers Back on Multi-Track", *Philosophia: Philosophical Quarterly of Israel*, 39, pp. 581–595.

(2017) "Powerful Perdurance: Linking Parts with Powers", in: *Causal Powers*, ed. Jonathan Jacobs (Oxford: Oxford University Press), pp. 139–164.

(Forthcoming) *The Powers Metaphysic* (Oxford: Oxford University Press).

Wilson, Jessica (2011) "Non-Reductive Realization and the Powers-Based Subset Strategy", *Monist*, 94, pp. 121–154.

(2012) "Fundamental Determinables", *Philosophers' Imprint*, 12, pp. 1–17.

(2013) "A Determinable-Based Account of Metaphysical Indeterminacy", *Inquiry*, 56, pp. 359–385.

(2015) "Metaphysical Emergence: Weak and Strong", in: *Metaphysics in Contemporary Physics: Poznan Studies in the Philosophy of the Sciences and the Humanities*, Vol. 104, eds. Tomasz Bigaj and Christian Wuthrich (Amsterdam: Brill), pp. 345–402.

Wolterstorff, Nicholas (1970) "Bergmann's Constituent Ontology", *Noûs*, 4, pp. 109–134.

(1991) "Divine Simplicity", *Philosophical Perspectives*, 5, pp. 531–552.

Woodward, James (1992) "Realism About Laws", *Erkenntnis*, 36, pp. 181–218.

Worrall, John (1989) "Structural Realism: The Best of Both Worlds?" *Dialectica*, 43, pp. 99–124.

Young, J. Z. (1971) *An Introduction to the Study of Man* (Oxford: Oxford University Press).

Yudell, Zanja (2011) "Structuralism and the New Way of Worlds: A Sellarsian Argument for Necessitarianism About Laws", *Philosophy of Science*, 78, pp. 678–695.

Zimmerman, Dean (1996) "Indivisible Parts and Extended Objects: Some Philosophical Episodes from Topology's Prehistory", *Monist*, 79, pp. 148–181.

(1996a) "Could Extended Objects be Made Out of Simple Parts? An Argument for 'Atomless Gunk'" *Philosophy and Phenomenological Research*, 51, pp. 1–29.

Index

Lightning Source UK Ltd.
Milton Keynes UK
UKHW020115020421
381349UK00021B/688